THE AUTOBIOGRAPHY OF
Andrew Carnegie

Andrew Carnegie

THE AUTOBIOGRAPHY OF
Andrew Carnegie

WITH AN INTRODUCTION BY VARTAN GREGORIAN
President, Carnegie Corporation of New York

PUBLICAFFAIRS
New York

Copyright © 2011 Introduction by Vartan Gregorian.

Published in the United States in 2011 by PublicAffairs™,
a Member of the Perseus Books Group

For information, address PublicAffairs,
250 West 57th Street, Suite 1321, New York, NY 10107.

PublicAffairs books are available at special discounts for bulk purchases in the U.S. by corporations, institutions, and other organizations. For more information, please contact the Special Markets Department at the Perseus Books Group, 2300 Chestnut Street, Suite 200, Philadelphia, PA 19103, call (800) 810-4145, ext. 5000, or e-mail special.markets@perseusbooks.com.

Book Design by RE:CREATIVE

Library of Congress Control Number: 2011925072
ISBN 978-1-61039-080-4 (HC)
ISBN 978-1-61039-082-8 (PB)
ISBN 978-1-61039-081-1 (EB)

First Edition

10 9 8 7 6 5 4 3 2 1

INTRODUCTION

A ndrew Carnegie begins his autobiography by telling a story about a similar work written by a friend of his, Judge Mellon of Pittsburgh, the steel town where Mr. Carnegie made his great fortune. In praising the judge for the fact that his book "contains one essential feature of value — it reveals the man. . . without any intention of attracting public notice, being designed only for his family," Andrew Carnegie reveals much about himself. He was what I think of as an "insider-outsider," a man at ease with his comfortable position in society but still able to regard it with the perspective of a working man, both grateful for and humbled by his own achievements. I think this dichotomy is evident when one examines the many photos that exist of a smiling, jovial Andrew Carnegie, who seems to be enjoying the limelight that shone upon him as one of the richest men in the world but was also thoughtful enough not to fool himself about how he had attained his station in life. He had earned his wealth and position by hard work and though he ended his life surrounded by the trappings of a rich gentleman, he never forgot his hardscrabble beginnings. One of the great delights of reading this autobiography is to enjoy, along with Andrew Carnegie, what he calls the "whirligig of time" and events that made up his remarkable journey from living in poverty to more or less inventing the modern field of philanthropy.

That is not to say there weren't great disappointments in his life, because there were. As his wife, Louise, notes in her introduction to this volume, "His heart was broken" by the onset of World War I. That conflict dashed his hopes and personal efforts to advance the cause of international peace. Still, Louise tells us, Andrew Carnegie remained, "Always patient, considerate, cheerful, grateful for any little pleasure or service, never thinking of himself, but always of the dawning of the better day, his spirit ever shone brighter and brighter until 'he was not, for God took him.'"

It is very touching to read her introduction to her husband's autobiography, which was first published posthumously in 1920. This is one of the few instances I know of in which a wife has written the introduction to her spouse's autobiography. But then, Louise was a remarkable woman who not only loved but supported her husband in all his endeavors, including his philanthropy. We know this because Louise Whitfield, soon to be Mrs. Carnegie, signed an unusual and endearing prenuptial agreement in which the steel magnate and his intended bride declared their intentions to devote the bulk of his wealth to the public good, precluding any future arguments about the disposition of what amounted to a great fortune. The document was signed on April 22, 1887, the same day that the Carnegies were married. Among the statements it includes is this unmistakable declaration: *"Andrew Carnegie desires and intends to devote the bulk purposes and said Louise Whitfield sympathizes and agrees with him in said desire..."*

Loving portraits of Louise Carnegie and Margaret Carnegie (later Margaret Carnegie Miller), the Carnegies' only child, are included in this volume. Other photographs show the happy family at one of Mr. and Mrs. Carnegie's favorite places in the world, their Skibo Castle home in Scotland. As I noted earlier, there are many additional photographs of Mr. Carnegie that show him as a happy husband, doting father, joyous benefactor, even a contented golfer and proud owner of a fine looking col-

lie. Contrast those images with some of the dour coun-
tenances of his contemporaries whose photos are also
found in this book and it is difficult not to conclude that
here was a man who knew he had lived an unexpectedly rewarding life but didn't want to make more of a fuss
about it than he felt was warranted. In fact, to conclude
the story Andrew Carnegie tells about Judge Mellon, it is
illuminating to read Mr. Carnegie's own words. "In like
manner," he writes, "I intend to tell my story, not as one
posturing before the public, but as in the midst of my own
people and friends, tried and true, to whom I can speak
with the utmost freedom, feeling that even trifling incidents may not be wholly destitute of interest for them."

The events of Andrew Carnegie's life are hardly "destitute of interest" for any of us, but particularly those
who have been involved in the work of the more than
twenty-two institutions and organizations he founded
in his lifetime that are dedicated to achieving goals that
include advancing teaching and education, promoting
international peace and ethical leadership, enriching
knowledge about science and technology, preserving
and sharing the cultural heritage of our nation and others, and, through the numerous Hero Funds he created
in the U.S. and abroad, recognizing what is extraordinary
in "everyday" men and women. The work of these groups
continues today, though one can imagine that even these
entities could hardly contain Andrew Carnegie's vision,
which was always centered on improving the human
condition. Perhaps his ideals can be best expressed in
the simple yet profound mission he gave to Carnegie
Corporation of New York, the philanthropic foundation
he created in 1911, which was to support "the advancement and diffusion of knowledge and understanding."
Mr. Carnegie, who felt he had a moral imperative to give

away his wealth, had one ultimate goal, which has been realized many, many times over — it was for the money that he'd amassed during his lifetime to be used, as he put it, "to do real and permanent good in this world." Fond of saying that he who dies rich, dies disgraced, he eventually gave away $350 million, an almost unimaginable fortune in an era when there was no income tax and hence no tax incentives for philanthropy.

He wanted his fortune to be invested in creating real, long-term impact on people's lives. Toward that end, he thought about every detail of how his goals would be accomplished and decided that one important element of the dissemination of his wealth would be for the work of the institutions he created to go on in perpetuity. In the case of Carnegie Corporation of New York, for example, he was very specific about that point. In his November 10, 1911, Letter of Gift to the Corporation, providing the first part of its endowment, he wrote (using the shortened spelling form he was fond of), "My desire is that the work which I [hav] been carrying on, or similar beneficial work, shall continue during this and future generations."

In addition, with astonishing prescience and even modesty, he understood that the pressing issues of his day might be overshadowed by other problems as times changed. Hence, he did something almost unprecedented: in essence, he told the future stewards of his wealth, men and women who would be born after he was gone, that he trusted them. With hope and optimism, he literally entrusted the future to those who would carry on his philanthropy. In the aforementioned Letter of Gift, he said, "Conditions upon the [erth] inevitably change; hence, no wise man will bind Trustees forever to certain paths, causes or institutions. I disclaim any intention of doing so. On the contrary, I [giv] my trustees full authority to change policy or causes hitherto aided, from time to time, when this, in their opinion, has become necessary or desirable. They shall best conform to my wishes by using their own judgment..."

Truly, he was a unique individual — and today, when the term "unique" is overused, it is important to stress how exceptional an individual Mr. Carnegie really was. In that connection, it is remarkable to think about the impact that this one person has had. Andrew Carnegie came to the United States as a poor boy, an immigrant from Scotland who first found work in a cotton mill but eventually became a great steel baron and then one of the most important philanthropists the world has ever known. In addition to the many organizations he created and personal benefactions he was responsible for, perhaps his crowning glory — and his first major, sustained philanthropic effort — was the creation of more than 2,500 public libraries in the United States and abroad. As he notes in this autobiography, "It was from my own early experience that I decided there was no use to which money could be applied so productive of good to boys and girls who have good within them and ability and ambition to develop it, as the founding of a public library in a community which is willing to support it as a municipal institution."

As dramatic as Carnegie's story is, it is certainly not without precedent. After all, he found his footing and made his fortune in the land that had been described by Alexis de Tocqueville as the embodiment of "individualism," a term he coined in his seminal 1835 work, *Democracy in America*, which recounted his travels through the U.S. That was Tocqueville's way of describing the self-reliant character of Americans, who reveled in their freedom from paternalism and aristocratic rule.

In Mr. Carnegie's time, the same as today, individuals with the will and the persistence to nurture and build on their ideas have shown that time and time again they can not only move the proverbial mountain but also whole societies, as well.

In that regard, the reissuance of this autobiography of Andrew Carnegie in the year that we celebrate Carnegie Corporation's Centennial has led me to reflect not only on Andrew Carnegie's impact on society but, in a general sense, on the role of the individual in history. Naturally, this has been the subject of debate and discussion throughout recorded history. Conservatives, liberals, radicals, and those all along the spectrum[1] have offered their verdicts. But it should be noted that while political theorists, scholars, and leaders may diverge on many issues, what they all have in common is an acknowledgment that human will, individuality, and creativity cannot be devalued. The political philosophies of even the most autocratic governments have been first articulated and then defended by individuals. Individuals carry the banners of despots as they march in support of their regimes. But it is also individuals who raise the flag of freedom and revolt in opposition to those who would impose repressive diktats on the populace. Our founding fathers are examples of such extraordinary individuals. We all remember, for example, how boldly John Hancock signed the Declaration of Independence. A committee did not put their names to that remarkable document. Individuals did.

For Americans, the concept of the individual and his or her centrality to the very nature of the social and political compacts that define our national life has been the driv-

---

[1] See, for example, the works of Isaiah Berlin, Benjamin Constant, David Hume, Russell Kirk, John Locke, John Stuart Mill, C.B. MacPherson, Montesquieu, Georgi Plekhanov, Ayn Rand, Jean-Jacques Rousseau, *et al.*

ing issue at the heart of our society. What we often think of as "rugged individualism" is ingrained in the foundational conversation about the ideals and principles of our nation that began before the American Revolution and continues today. Nevertheless, within this context, questions arise that relate to individual rights, self-reliance, the relationship and tensions between private and public good, local autonomy and national sovereignty, states' rights and federal power, even to what extent an individual perceives himself or herself to be part of the connective tissue of a nation represented by the term "citizen." One also may find that the ambiguities inherent in honoring the rights and dignity of the individual are not only difficult to reconcile but also extraordinarily challenging. For example, Americans in particular must confront the reality that "Individualism, the first language in which [they] tend to think about their lives, values independence and self-reliance about all else... [yet] American cultural traditions define personality, achievement and the purpose of human life in ways that leave the individual suspended in glorious, but terrifying isolation."[1]

One thing is clear: for America's founding fathers, individual rights were paramount. Thomas Jefferson gave powerful expression to this notion, linking the ideals of the eighteenth-century European Enlightenment and the light of democracy and freedom that he helped to bring forth in stating the powerful truths about equality and unalienable rights that the Declaration of Independence proclaims as self-evident. "The equal rights of man, and the happiness of every individual," Jefferson wrote some years after American independence had

---

[1] *Habits of the Heart: Individualism and Commitment in American Life* by Robert N. Bellah, Richard Madsen, William M. Sullivan, Ann Swidler, and Steven M. Tipton (University of California Press, 1985, 1996, 2008).

been achieved, "are now acknowledged to be the only legitimate objects of government." Nearly two hundred years later, scholar Yehoshua Arieli captured the essence of Jefferson's ideas in *Individualism and Nationalism in American Ideology*[1] when he described the foundation of American society and the democracy it cherished as the "consent of free individuals to be united together in a higher community which comprise[s] their common ideals and interests."

I believe I can say with reasonable certainty that the notion of free individuals working together toward a higher common good is one that Andrew Carnegie would have celebrated. Though he was influenced by Social Darwinism, a set of late nineteenth-century ideologies that primarily focused on "the survival of the fittest" as an organizing principle of society, he came to very different conclusions about how these ideas played out in real life. He believed that in the ranks of the disadvantaged, one might find what he called "the epoch-makers"[2] because those who triumphed over adversity had to be possessed of extraordinary will and indomitable spirit. A true idealist, he believed in the maxim that a rising tide lifts all boats, and hence, his "epoch-makers" and others like them were obligated to make every effort to advance society and improve conditions for all men, women, and children.

Andrew Carnegie, of course, was also a capitalist, and as such, he welcomed Adam Smith's arguments in favor of free market economies in *The Wealth of Nations*.[3]

---

[1] *Individualism and Nationalism in American Ideology* by Yehoshua Arieli (Penguin Books 1964).

[2] *The Gospel of Wealth and Other Timely Essays* by Andrew Carnegie (The Century Company 1901).

[3] *An Inquiry into the Nature and Causes of the Wealth of Nations*, 1776.

But he was also aware that despite being most famously known as the father of modern capitalism, Smith was a moral philosopher. Adam Smith wrote with conviction about the importance of the connections between individual aspirations and the enlightened evolution of society. In fact, he based his economic theories upon his view of human nature, which he described in his first book, *The Theory of Moral Sentiments*, published in 1759. There, he theorized that man is driven by passionate self-interests, but moderates them with his intellect and innate sympathy for others. In this book, Smith first made the statement that when people are left to follow their self-interests they are "led by an invisible hand, without knowing it, without intending it, to advance the interest of the society."

Andrew Carnegie must also have been influenced by Samuel Smiles and his book, *Self Help*,[1] which was well known in Carnegie's day. In my estimation, this volume is a neglected classic that incisively analyzes the importance of self-reliance and self-motivation. "Even the best institutions can give a man no active help. Perhaps the most they can do is to leave him free to develop himself and improve his individual condition," wrote Smiles, who also authored profiles of self-made men. His overall theme was that life is not just a preordained journey but allows individuals to change direction along the way—sometimes knowingly, and sometimes due to circumstances. This idea — that the journey is more important than the destination — is also conveyed in a famous poem called *Ithaca*, by C.P. Cavafy, who wrote, "When you set out for distant Ithaca... fervently wish that your journey may be long."

[1] *Self-Help; with Illustrations of Character and Conduct,* by Samuel Smiles, 1859.

In all these observations, ideas, and philosophies, one finds the theme of convergence. Like strands in a great skein of time and events, even opposing ideologies oftentimes knit themselves together to create new ideas, new movements, new social orders, even new nations. Yet at the heart of this ferment is always the individual. Different governing regimes, political systems, and social orders, even those at polar opposites, must all cope with the reality that the will of human beings — their yearning to be free, to express themselves, to gain knowledge, and to use it — may be bent, but it is never bowed for very long. Time and circumstances may differ, but human creativity lives on. It cannot be obliterated from the record of civilization. It cannot be denied.

It is interesting to consider how time and events almost always converge around individuals. Perhaps this seems especially true now, when we are living in an era that has seen, and continues to see, revolutions, proto-revolutions, and all manner of political and social upheavals taking place around the world. Often, those motivated to action in these situations are individuals who become the actualization of political theory or social-cultural ideas that form the impetus for change. Many are also the epitome of Smiles' self-motivated individuals who have made education, achievement, professional success, and intellectual pursuits the hallmark of their lives. In Crane Brinton's seminal work, *The Anatomy of Revolution*,[1] in which he analyzes four major historical revolutions — the English, American, French, and Russian — he notes this phenomenon of "a mixture of gentlemen of good breeding, of self-educated careerists, and of humble men inspired by a fury

---

[1] *The Anatomy of Revolution*, by Crane Brinton (Vintage Books 1952).

as yet divine." Specifically, he was describing the leaders of the English revolution, but they had much in common with their rebellious counterparts on the American continent. For example, Brinton tells us that of the fifty-six signers of the Declaration of Independence, "thirty-three held college degrees in an age when few ever went to college; only about four had little or no formal education." And they had aspirations, which through their own efforts — and in the service of a great ideal — they fulfilled. As the *Middlesex Journal* of April 6, 1776, declaimed of the leaders of the American Revolution, "From shopkeepers, tradesmen and attorneys they are become statesmen and legislators. . ." The *Journal*, a British paper, meant to be condescending, but with history's hindsight, one can imagine that Jefferson and his compatriots would have been pleased by this assessment.

Having said all this, I must stress that there have always been, and will always be, countless individuals whose work and ideas have moved humanity forward but whose identities few will ever know. Still, history does sometimes converge around an individual whose name becomes synonymous with eras, events, discoveries, and social or political movements. This, I would suggest, is the case with the man I began this introduction with: Andrew Carnegie. Making his intentions clear in his dictum, "There is nothing inherently valuable in mere money. . . unless it is to be administered as a sacred trust for the good of others," he used his wealth in a way that profoundly affected the field of philanthropy. In fact, in the modern age, along with John D. Rockefeller, Mr. Carnegie can be viewed as one of the founders of what we now call "strategic philanthropy," meaning, grantmaking intended as an investment that will bring about lasting, long-term results. This is a great change from earlier times, when people who were economically secure were often moved to help others, but more in the line of charitable works. This brings to mind an important distinction between charity and philanthropy that has eroded over time, but should be noted because it highlights the different concerns that donors may have. Charity, which is derived from the Latin word *caritas,* meaning dear, has a long religious history; for Jews, Christians, and Muslims, for example, it has meant giving immediate relief to human suffering without passing judgment on those who suffer — and, it should be mentioned, usually without getting directly involved with them. Philanthropy has a more secular history and comes from the Greek word *philanthropos,* meaning love of mankind. The Greek meaning carried over to English and, for the longest time, philanthropy referred only to a caring disposition toward one's fellow man. Now the word is used to describe generosity that promotes human progress in any field.

Andrew Carnegie was the architect of his own giving, which he meant to endure in perpetuity. His intention was not to glorify himself or his name in future generations but for his wealth to act as a perpetual motion machine, being constantly reinvested in order to serve the ultimate purpose of doing good. To achieve that end, Andrew Carnegie had a vision that he accompanied with action. He did not speculate; he researched and acted upon his convictions and his vision of America as a vibrant democracy that needed education to become stronger, required an educated citizenry to maintain its strength and ensure its progress, and would thrive in a global community where international peace was a common value among nations.

Andrew Carnegie's philanthropy embodied his belief that while society is always going to be confronted by challenges, individuals can lead the way in meeting those challenges and in doing so, continue the work of improving the human condition that one generation passes on to the next. In that regard, I imagine he would have appreciated the question asked by Fathali M. Moghaddam in his book, *The Specialized Society: The Plight of the Individual in an Age of Individualism*[1]: "What kind of being do we humans want to become? Our most precious quality is *becoming*. . . The human being "partly is," but "wholly hopes to be."[2]

What Andrew Carnegie hoped to be, he became: an individual, as he wrote in this volume, "who feels there is not a human being to whom he does not wish happiness, long life, and deserved success, not one in whose path he would cast an obstacle nor to whom he would not do a service if in his power." Andrew Carnegie dedicated himself wholeheartedly to the service of his fellow men and women. His philanthropy was his gift to the future, his everlasting investment in the belief that education is our greatest tool, that peace is our most sacred goal, and that the betterment of humanity is the shared aspiration of us all.

VARTAN GREGORIAN
President, Carnegie Corporation of New York

---

[1] *The Specialized Society: The Plight of the Individual in an Age of Individualism,* by Fathali M. Moghaddam (Praeger Publishers 1997).
[2] Robert Browning, "A Death in the Desert."

PREFACE

A FTER retiring from active business my husband yielded to the earnest solicitations of friends, both here and in Great Britain, and began to jot down from time to time recollections of his early days. He soon found, however, that instead of the leisure he expected, his life was more occupied with affairs than ever before, and the writing of these memoirs was reserved for his play-time in Scotland. For a few weeks each summer we retired to our little bungalow on the moors at Aultnagar to enjoy the simple life, and it was there that Mr. Carnegie did most of his writing. He delighted in going back to those early times, and as he wrote he lived them all over again. He was thus engaged in July, 1914, when the war clouds began to gather, and when the fateful news of the 4th of August reached us, we immediately left our retreat in the hills and returned to Skibo to be more in touch with the situation.

These memoirs ended at that time. Henceforth he was never able to interest himself in private affairs. Many times he made the attempt to continue writing, but found it useless. Until then he had lived the life of a man in middle life — and a young one at that — golfing, fishing, swimming each day, sometimes doing all three in one day. Optimist as he always was and tried to be, even in the face of the failure of his hopes, the world disaster was too much. His heart was broken. A severe attack of influenza followed by two serious attacks of pneumonia precipitated old age upon him.

It was said of a contemporary who passed away a few months before Mr. Carnegie that "he never could have borne the burden of old age." Perhaps the most inspiring part of Mr. Carnegie's life, to those who were privileged to know it intimately, was the way he bore his "burden of old age." Always patient, considerate, cheerful, grateful for any little pleasure or service, never thinking of himself, but always of the dawning of a better day, his spirit ever shone brighter and brighter until "he was not, for God took him."

Written with his own hand on the fly-leaf of his manuscript are these words: "It is probable that material for a small volume might be collected from these memoirs which the public would care to read, and that a private and larger volume might please my relatives and friends. Much I have written from time to time may, I think, wisely be omitted. Whoever arranges these notes should be careful not to burden the public with too much. A man with a heart as well as a head should be chosen."

Who, then, could so well fill this description as our friend Professor John C. Van Dyke? When the manuscript was shown to him, he remarked, without having read Mr. Carnegie's notation, "It would be a labor of love to prepare this for publication." Here, then, the choice was mutual, and the manner in which he has performed this "labor" proves the wisdom of the choice—a choice made and carried out in the name of a rare and beautiful friendship.

LOUISE WHITFIELD CARNEGIE

New York
April 16, 1920

EDITOR'S NOTE

THE story of a man's life, especially when it is told by the man himself, should not be interrupted by the hecklings of an editor. He should be allowed to tell the tale in his own way, and enthusiasm, even extravagance in recitation should be received as a part of the story. The quality of the man may underlie exuberance of spirit, as truth may be found in apparent exaggeration. Therefore, in preparing these chapters for publication the editor has done little more than arrange the material chronologically and sequentially so that the narrative might run on unbrokenly to the end. Some footnotes by way of explanation, some illustrations that offer sight — help to the text, have been added; but the narrative is the thing.

This is neither the time nor the place to characterize or eulogize the maker of "this strange eventful history," but perhaps it is worth while to recognize that the history really was eventful. And strange. Nothing stranger ever came out of the *Arabian Nights* than the story of this poor Scotch boy who came to America and step by step, through many trials and triumphs, became the great steel master, built up a colossal industry, amassed an enormous fortune, and then deliberately and systematically gave away the whole of it for the enlightenment and betterment of mankind. Not only that. He established a gospel of wealth that can be neither ignored nor forgotten, and set a pace in distribution that succeeding millionaires have followed as a precedent. In the course of his career he became a nation-builder, a leader in thought, a writer, a speaker, the friend of workmen, schoolmen, and statesmen, the associate of both the lowly and the lofty. But these were merely interesting happenings in his life as compared with his great inspirations — his distribution of wealth, his passion for world peace, and his love for mankind.

Perhaps we are too near this history to see it in proper proportions, but in the time to come it should gain in perspective and in interest. The generations hereafter may realize the wonder of it more fully than we of to-day. Happily it is preserved to us, and that, too, in Mr. Carnegie's own words and in his own buoyant style. It is a very memorable record — a record perhaps the like of which we shall not look upon again.

JOHN C. VAN DYKE

New York
 August, 1920

CONTENTS

CONTENTS

THE AUTOBIOGRAPHY OF
Andrew Carnegie

Andrew Carnegie

CHAPTER I

Parents and Childhood

IF the story of any man's life, truly told, must be interesting, as some sage avers, those of my relatives and immediate friends who have insisted upon having an account of mine may not be unduly disappointed with this result. I may console myself with the assurance that such a story must interest at least a certain number of people who have known me, and that knowledge will encourage me to proceed.

A book of this kind, written years ago by my friend, Judge Mellon, of Pittsburgh, gave me so much pleasure that I am inclined to agree with the wise one whose opinion I have given above; for, certainly, the story which the Judge told has proved a source of infinite satisfaction to his friends, and must continue to influence succeeding generations of his family to live life well. And not only this; to some beyond his immediate circle it holds rank with their favorite authors. The book contains one essential feature of value — it reveals the man. It was written without any intention of attracting public notice, being designed only for his family. In like manner I intend to tell my story, not as one posturing — before the public, but as in the midst of my own people and friends, tried and true, to whom I can speak with the utmost freedom, feeling that even trifling incidents may not be wholly destitute of interest for them.

To begin, then, I was born in Dunfermline, in the attic of the small one-story house, corner of Moodie Street and Priory Lane, on the 25th of November, 1835, and, as the saying is, "of poor but honest parents, of good kith and kin." Dunfermline had long been noted as the center of the damask trade in Scotland.[1] My father, William Carnegie, was a damask weaver, the son of Andrew Carnegie after whom I was named.

My Grandfather Carnegie was well known throughout the district for his wit and humor, his genial nature and irrepressible spirits. He was head of the lively ones of his day, and known far and near as the chief of their joyous club — "Patiemuir College." Upon my return to Dunfermline, after an absence of fourteen years, I remember being approached by an old man who had been told that I was the grandson of the "Professor," my grandfather's title among his cronies. He was the very picture of palsied eld:

"His nose and chin they threatened ither."

As he tottered across the room toward me and laid his trembling hand upon my head he said: "And ye are the grandson o' Andra Carnegie! Eh, mon, I ha'e seen the day when your grandfaither and I could ha'e hallooed ony reasonable man, oot o' his jidgment."

Several other old people of Dunfermline told me stories of my grandfather. Here is one of them:

One Hogmanay night[2] an old wifey, quite a character

---

[1] The Eighteenth-Century Carnegies lived at the picturesque hamlet of Patiemuir, two miles south of Dunfermline. The growing importance of the linen industry in Dunfermline finally led the Carnegies to move to that town.

[2] The 31st of December.

in the village, being surprised by a disguised face suddenly thrust in at the window, looked up and after a moment's pause exclaimed, "Oh, it's jist that daft callant Andra Carnegie." She was right; my grandfather at seventy-five was out frightening his old lady friends, disguised like other frolicking youngsters.

I think my optimistic nature, my ability to shed trouble and to laugh through life, making "all my ducks swans," as friends say I do, must have been inherited from this delightful old masquerading grandfather whose name I am proud to bear.[1] A sunny disposition is worth more than fortune. Young people should know that it can be cultivated; that the mind like the body can be moved from the shade into sunshine. Let us move it then. Laugh trouble away if possible, and one usually can if he be anything of a philosopher, provided that self-reproach comes not from his own wrongdoing. That always remains. There is no washing out of these "damned spots." The judge within sits in the supreme court and can never be cheated. Hence the grand rule of life which Burns gives:

> "Thine own reproach alone do fear."

This motto adopted early in life has been more to me than all the sermons I ever heard, and I have heard not a few, although I may admit resemblance to my old friend Baillie Walker in my mature years. He was asked by his doctor about his sleep and replied that it was far

---

[1] "There is no sign that Andrew, though he prospered in his wooing, was specially successful in acquisition of worldly gear. Otherwise, however, he became an outstanding character not only in the village, but in the adjoining city and district. A 'brainy' man who read and thought for himself he became associated with the radical weavers of Dunfermline, who in Patiemuir formed a meeting-place which they named a college (Andrew was the 'Professor' of it)." (*Andrew Carnegie: His Dunfermline Ties and Benedictions*, by J. B. Mackie, F. J. I.)

from satisfactory, he was very wakeful, adding with a twinkle in his eye: "But I get a bit fine doze i' the kirk noo and then."

On my mother's side the grandfather was even more marked, for my grandfather Thomas Morrison was a friend of William Cobbett, a contributor to his "Register," and in constant correspondence with him. Even as I write, in Dunfermline old men who knew Grandfather Morrison speak of him as one of the finest orators and ablest men they have known. He was publisher of "The Precursor," a small edition it might be said of Cobbett's "Register," and thought to have been the first radical paper in Scotland. I have read some of his writings, and in view of the importance now given to technical education, I think the most remarkable of them is a pamphlet which he published seventy-odd years ago entitled "Headication versus Hand-ication." It insists upon the importance of the latter in a manner that would reflect credit upon the strongest advocate of technical education to-day. It ends with these words, "I thank God that in my youth I learned to make and mend shoes." Cobbett published it in the "Register" in 1833, remarking editorially, "One of the most valuable communications ever published in the 'Register' upon the subject, is that of our esteemed friend and correspondent in Scotland, Thomas Morrison, which appears in this issue." So it seems I come by my scribbling propensities by inheritance — from both sides, for the Carnegies were also readers and thinkers.

My Grandfather Morrison was a born orator, a keen politician, and the head of the advanced wing of the radical party in the district — a position which his son, my Uncle Bailie Morrison, occupied as his successor. More than one well-known Scotsman in America has called upon me, to shake hands with "the grandson of Thomas Morrison." Mr. Farmer, president of the Cleveland and Pittsburgh Railroad Company, once said to me, "I owe all that I have of learning and culture to the influence of your grandfather"; and Ebenezer Henderson, author of the remarkable history of Dunfermline, stated that he largely owed his advancement in life to the fortunate fact that while a boy he entered my grandfather's service.

I have not passed so far through life without receiving some compliments, but I think nothing of a complimentary character has ever pleased me so much as this from a writer in a Glasgow newspaper, who had been a listener to a speech on Home Rule in America which I delivered in Saint Andrew's Hall. The correspondent wrote that much was then being said in Scotland with regard to myself and family and especially my grandfather Thomas Morrison, and he went on to say, "Judge my surprise when I found in the grandson on the platform, in manner, gesture and appearance, a perfect *facsimile* of the Thomas Morrison of old."

My surprising likeness to my grandfather, whom I do not remember to have ever seen, cannot be doubted, because I remember well upon my first return to Dunfermline in my twenty-seventh year, while sitting upon a sofa with my Uncle Bailie Morrison, that his big black eyes filled with tears. He could not speak and rushed out of the room overcome. Returning after a time he explained that something in me now and then flashed before him his father, who would instantly vanish but come back at intervals. Some gesture it was, but what precisely he could not make out. My mother continually noticed in me some of my grandfather's peculiarities. The doctrine of inherited tendencies is proved every day and hour, but how subtle is the law which transmits gesture, something as it were beyond the material body. I was deeply impressed.

My Grandfather Morrison married Miss Hodge, of Edinburgh, a lady in education, manners, and position, who died while the family was still young. At this time he was in good circumstances, a leather merchant conducting the tanning business in Dunfermline; but the peace after the Battle of Waterloo involved him in ruin, as it did thousands; so that while my Uncle Bailie, the eldest son, had been brought up in what might be termed luxury, for he had a pony to ride, the younger members of the family encountered other and harder days.

The second daughter, Margaret, was my mother, about whom I cannot trust myself to speak at length. She inherited from her mother the dignity, refinement, and air of the cultivated lady. Perhaps some day I may be able to tell the world something of this heroine, but I doubt it. I feel her to be sacred to myself and not for others to know. None could ever really know her — I alone did that. After my father's early death she was all my own. The dedication of my first book[1] tells the story. It was: "To my favorite Heroine My Mother."

Fortunate in my ancestors I was supremely so in my birthplace. Where one is born is very important, for different surroundings and traditions appeal to and stimulate different latent tendencies in the child. Ruskin truly observes that every bright boy in Edinburgh is influenced by the sight of the Castle. So is the child of Dunfermline, by its noble Abbey, the Westminster of Scotland, founded early in the eleventh century (1070) by Malcolm Canmore and his Queen Margaret, Scotland's patron saint. The ruins of the great monastery

[1] *An American Four-in-Hand in Great Britain.* New York, 1888.

and of the Palace where kings were born still stand, and there, too, is Pittencrieff Glen, embracing Queen Margaret's shrine and the ruins of King Malcolm's Tower, with which the old ballad of "Sir Patrick Spens" begins:

> "The King sits in Dunfermline *tower*,[1]
> Drinking the bluid red wine."

The tomb of The Bruce is in the center of the Abbey, Saint Margaret's tomb is near, and many of the "royal folk" lie sleeping close around. Fortunate, indeed, the child who first sees the light in that romantic town, which occupies high ground three miles north of the Firth of Forth, overlooking the sea, with Edinburgh in sight to the south, and to the north the peaks of the Ochils clearly in view. All is still redolent of the mighty past when Dunfermline was both nationally and religiously the capital of Scotland.

The child privileged to develop amid such surroundings absorbs poetry and romance with the air he breathes, assimilates history and tradition as he gazes around. These become to him his real world in childhood — the ideal is the ever-present real. The actual has yet to come when, later in life, he is launched into the workaday world of stern reality. Even then, and till his last day, the early impressions remain, sometimes for short seasons disappearing perchance, but only apparently driven away or suppressed. They are always rising and coming again to the front to exert their influence, to elevate his thought and color his life. No bright child of Dunfermline can escape the influence of the Abbey, Palace, and Glen. These touch him and set fire to the latent spark within, making him something

[1] *The Percy Reliques* and *The Oxford Book of Ballads* give "town" instead of "tower"; but Mr. Carnegie insisted that it should be "tower."

different and beyond what, less happily born, he would
have become. Under these inspiring conditions my parents had also been born, and hence came, I doubt not,
the potency of the romantic and poetic strain which
pervaded both.

As my father succeeded in the weaving business we
removed from Moodie Street to a much more com-
modious house in Reid's Park. My father's four or five
looms occupied the lower story; we resided in the
upper, which was reached, after a fashion common in
the older Scottish houses, by outside stairs from the
pavement. It is here that my earliest recollections begin,
and, strangely enough, the first trace of memory takes
me back to a day when I saw a small map of America.
It was upon rollers and about two feet square. Upon
this my father, mother, Uncle William, and Aunt
Aitken were looking for Pittsburgh and pointing out
Lake Erie and Niagara. Soon after my uncle and Aunt
Aitken sailed for the land of promise.

At this time I remember my cousin-brother, George
Lauder ("Dod"), and myself were deeply impressed
with the great danger overhanging us because a law-
less flag was secreted in the garret. It had been painted
to be carried, and I believe was carried by my father,
or uncle, or some other good radical of our family, in a
procession during the Corn Law agitation. There had
been riots in the town and a troop of cavalry was quar-
tered in the Guildhall. My grandfathers and uncles on
both sides, and my father, had been foremost in addressing meetings, and the whole family circle was in
a ferment.

I remember as if it were yesterday being awakened
during the night by a tap at the back window by men
who had come to inform my parents that my uncle,

Bailie Morrison, had been thrown into jail because he had dared to hold a meeting which had been forbidden. The sheriff with the aid of the soldiers had arrested him a few miles from the town where the meeting had been held, and brought him into the town during the night, followed by an immense throng of people.[1]

Serious trouble was feared, for the populace threatened to rescue him, and, as we learned afterwards, he had been induced by the provost of the town to step forward to a window overlooking the High Street and beg the people to retire. This he did, saying: "If there be a friend of the good cause here to-night, let him fold his arms." They did so. And then, after a pause, he said, "Now depart in peace!"[2] My uncle, like all our family, was a moral-force man and strong for obedience to law, but radical to the core and an intense admirer of the American Republic.

One may imagine when all this was going on in public how bitter were the words that passed from one to the other in private. The denunciations of monarchical and aristocratic government, of privilege in all its forms, the

[1] At the opening of the Lauder Technical School in October, 1880, nearly half a century after the disquieting scenes of 1842, Mr. Carnegie thus recalled the shock which was given to his boy mind: "One of my earliest recollections is that of being wakened in the darkness to be told that my Uncle Morrison was in jail. Well, it is one of the proudest boasts I can make to-day to be able to say that I had an uncle who was in jail. But, ladies and gentlemen, my uncle went to jail to vindicate the rights of public assembly." (Mackie.)

[2] "The Crown agents wisely let the proceedings lapse. . . . Mr. Morrison was given a gratifying assurance of the appreciation of his fellow citizens by his election to the Council and his elevation to the Magisterial Bench, followed shortly after by his appointment to the office of Burgh Chamberlain. The patriotic reformer whom the criminal authorities endeavored to convict as a law-breaker became by the choice of his fellow citizens a Magistrate, and was further given a certificate for trustworthiness and integrity." (Mackie.)

grandeur of the republican system, the superiority of America, a land peopled by our own race, a home for free-men in which every citizen's privilege was every man's right — these were the exciting themes upon which I was nurtured. As a child I could have slain king, duke, or lord, and considered their deaths a service to the state and hence an heroic act.

Such is the influence of childhood's earliest associations that it was long before I could trust myself to speak respectfully of any privileged class or person who had not distinguished himself in some good way and there-fore earned the right to public respect. There was still the sneer behind for mere pedigree — "he is nothing, has done nothing, only an accident, a fraud strutting in bor-rowed plumes; all he has to his account is the accident of birth; the most fruitful part of his family, as with the potato, lies underground." I wondered that intelligent men could live where another human being was born to a privilege which was not also their birthright. I was never tired of quoting the only words which gave proper vent to my indignation:

> "There was a Brutus once that would have brooked
> Th' eternal devil to keep his state in Rome
> As easily as a king."

But then kings were kings, not mere shadows. All this was inherited, of course. I only echoed what I heard at home.

Dunfermline has long been renowned as perhaps the most radical town in the Kingdom, although I know Paisley has claims. This is all the more creditable to the cause of radicalism because in the days of which I speak the population of Dunfermline was in large part composed of men who were small manufacturers, each owning his own loom or looms. They were not tied down to regular hours, their labors being piece work. They got webs from the larger manufacturers and the weaving was done at home.

These were times of intense political excitement, and there were frequently seen throughout the entire town, for a short time after the midday meal, small groups of men with their aprons girt about them discussing affairs of state. The names of Hume, Cobden, and Bright were upon everyone's tongue. I was often attracted, small as I was, to these circles and was an earnest listener to the conversation, which was wholly one-sided. The generally accepted conclusion was that there must be a change. Clubs were formed among the townsfolk, and the London newspapers were subscribed for. The leading editorials were read every evening to the people, strangely enough, from one of the pulpits of the town. My uncle, Bailie Morrison, was often the reader, and, as the articles were commented upon by him and others after being read, the meetings were quite exciting.

These political meetings were of frequent occurrence, and, as might be expected, I was as deeply interested as any of the family and attended many. One of my uncles or my father was generally to be heard. I remember one evening my father addressed a large outdoor meeting in the Pends. I had wedged my way in under the legs of the hearers, and at one cheer louder than all the rest I could not restrain my enthusiasm. Looking up to the man under whose legs I had found protection I informed him that was my father speaking. He lifted me on his shoulder and kept me there.

To another meeting I was taken by my father to hear John Bright, who spoke in favor of J. B. Smith as the Liberal candidate for the Stirling Burghs. I made the criticism at home that Mr. Bright did not speak correctly, as he said "men" when he meant "maan." He did not give the broad *a* we were accustomed to in Scotland. It is not to be wondered at that, nursed amid such surroundings, I developed into a violent young Republican whose motto was "death to privilege." At that time I did not know what privilege meant, but my father did.

One of my Uncle Lauder's best stories was about this same J. B. Smith, the friend of John Bright, who was standing for Parliament in Dunfermline. Uncle was a member of his Committee and all went well until it was proclaimed that Smith was a "Unitawrian." The district was placarded with the enquiry: Would you vote for a "Unitawrian"? It was serious. The Chairman of Smith's Committee in the village of Cairney Hill, a blacksmith, was reported as having declared he never would. Uncle drove over to remonstrate with him. They met in the village tavern over a gill:

"Man, I canna vote for a Unitawrian," said the Chairman.

"But," said my uncle, "Maitland [the opposing candidate] is a Trinitawrian."

"Damn; that's waur," was the response.

And the blacksmith voted right. Smith won by a small majority.

The change from hand-loom to steam-loom weaving was disastrous to our family. My father did not recognize the impending revolution, and was struggling under the old system. His looms sank greatly in value, and it became necessary for that power which never failed in any emergency — my mother — to step forward and endeavor to repair the family fortune. She opened a small shop in Moodie Street and contributed to the revenues which, though slender, nevertheless at

that time sufficed to keep us in comfort and "respectable."

I remember that shortly after this I began to learn
what poverty meant. Dreadful days came when my father
took the last of his webs to the great manufacturer, and
I saw my mother anxiously awaiting his return to know
whether a new web was to be obtained or that a period
of idleness was upon us. It was burnt into my heart then
that my father, though neither "abject, mean, nor vile," as
Burns has it, had nevertheless to

> "Beg a brother of the earth
> To give him leave to toil."

And then and there came the resolve that I would cure
that when I got to be a man. We were not, however, reduced to anything like poverty compared with many of
our neighbors. I do not know to what lengths of privation
my mother would not have gone that she might see her
two boys wearing large white collars, and trimly dressed.

In an incautious moment my parents had promised that I should never be sent to school until I asked
leave to go. This promise I afterward learned began to
give them considerable uneasiness because as I grew
up I showed no disposition to ask. The schoolmaster,
Mr. Robert Martin, was applied to and induced to take
some notice of me. He took me upon an excursion one
day with some of my companions who attended school,
and great relief was experienced by my parents when
one day soon afterward I came and asked for permission to go to Mr. Martin's school.[1] I need not say the permission was duly granted. I had then entered upon my
eighth year, which subsequent experience leads me to

---

[1] It was known as Rolland School.

say is quite early enough for any child to begin attending school.

The school was a perfect delight to me, and if anything occurred which prevented my attendance I was unhappy. This happened every now and then because my morning duty was to bring water from the well at the head of Moodie Street. The supply was scanty and irregular. Sometimes it was not allowed to run until late in the morning and a score of old wives were sitting around, the turn of each having been previously secured through the night by placing a worthless can in the line. This, as might be expected, led to numerous contentions in which I would not be put down even by these venerable old dames. I earned the reputation of being "an awfu' laddie." In this way I probably developed the strain of argumentativeness, or perhaps combativeness, which has always remained with me.

In the performance of these duties I was often late for school, but the master, knowing the cause, forgave the lapses. In the same connection I may mention that I had often the shop errands to run after school, so that in looking back upon my life I have the satisfaction of feeling that I became useful to my parents even at the early age of ten. Soon after that the accounts of the various people who dealt with the shop were entrusted to my keeping so that I became acquainted, in a small way, with business affairs even in childhood.

One cause of misery there was, however, in my school experience. The boys nicknamed me "Martin's pet," and sometimes called out that dreadful epithet to me as I passed along the street. I did not know all that it meant, but it seemed to me a term of the utmost opprobrium, and I know that it kept me from responding as freely as I should otherwise have done to that excellent teacher, my only schoolmaster, to whom I owe a debt of gratitude which I regret I never had opportunity to do more than acknowledge before he died.

I may mention here a man whose influence over me cannot be overestimated, my Uncle Lauder, George Lauder's father.[1] My father was necessarily constantly at work in the loom shop and had little leisure to bestow upon me through the day. My uncle being a shopkeeper in the High Street was not thus tied down. Note the location for this was among the shopkeeping aristocracy, and high and varied degrees of aristocracy there were even among shopkeepers in Dunfermline. Deeply affected by my Aunt Seaton's death, which occurred about the beginning of my school life, he found his chief solace in the companionship of his only son, George, and myself. He possessed an extraordinary gift of dealing with children and taught us many things. Among others I remember how he taught us British history by imagining each of the monarchs in a certain place upon the walls of the room performing the act for which he was well known. Thus for me King John sits to this day above the mantelpiece signing the Magna Charta, and Queen Victoria is on the back of the door with her children on her knee.

It may be taken for granted that the omission which, years after, I found in the Chapter House at Westminster Abbey was fully supplied in our list of monarchs. A slab in a small chapel at Westminster says that the body of Oliver Cromwell was removed from there. In the list of the monarchs which I learned at my uncle's knee the grand republican monarch appeared writing his message to the Pope of Rome, informing His Holiness that "if

[1] The Lauder Technical College given by Mr. Carnegie to Dunfermline was named in honor of this uncle, George Lauder.

he did not cease persecuting the Protestants the thunder of Great Britain's cannon would be heard in the Vatican." It is needless to say that the estimate we formed of Cromwell was that he was worth them "a' thegither."

It was from my uncle I learned all that I know of the early history of Scotland — of Wallace and Bruce and Burns, of Blind Harry's history, of Scott, Ramsey, Tannahill, Hogg, and Fergusson. I can truly say in the words of Burns that there was then and there created in me a vein of Scottish prejudice (or patriotism) which will cease to exist only with life. Wallace, of course, was our hero. Everything heroic centered in him. Sad was the day when a wicked big boy at school told me that England was far larger than Scotland. I went to the uncle, who had the remedy.

"Not at all, Naig; if Scotland were rolled out flat as England, Scotland would be the larger, but would you have the Highlands rolled down?"

Oh, never! There was balm in Gilead for the wounded young patriot. Later the greater population of England was forced upon me, and again to the uncle I went.

"Yes, Naig, seven to one, but there were more than that odds against us at Bannockburn." And again there was joy in my heart — joy that there were more English men there since the glory was the greater.

This is something of a commentary upon the truth that war breeds war, that every battle sows the seeds of future battles, and that thus nations become traditional enemies. The experience of American boys is that of the Scotch. They grow up to read of Washington and Valley Forge, of Hessians hired to kill Americans, and they come to hate the very name of Englishman. Such was my experience with my American nephews. Scotland was all right, but England that had fought Scotland was the wicked partner. Not till they became men was the prejudice eradicated, and even yet some of it may linger.

Uncle Lauder has told me since that he often brought people into the room assuring them that he could make "Dod" (George Lauder) and me weep, laugh, or close our little fists ready to fight — in short, play upon all our moods through the influence of poetry and song. The betrayal of Wallace was his trump card which never failed to cause our little hearts to sob, a complete breakdown being the invariable result. Often as he told the story it never lost its hold. No doubt it received from time to time new embellishments. My uncle's stories never wanted "the hat and the stick" which Scott gave his. How wonderful is the influence of a hero upon children!

I spent many hours and evenings in the High Street with my uncle and "Dod," and thus began a lifelong brotherly alliance between the latter and myself. "Dod" and "Naig" we always were in the family. I could not say "George" in infancy and he could not get more than "Naig" out of Carnegie, and it has always been "Dod" and "Naig" with us. No other names would mean anything.

There were two roads by which to return from my uncle's house in the High Street to my home in Moodie Street at the foot of the town, one along the eerie churchyard of the Abbey among the dead, where there was no light; and the other along the lighted streets by way of the May Gate. When it became necessary for me to go home, my uncle, with a wicked pleasure, would ask which way I was going. Thinking what Wallace would do, I always replied I was going by the Abbey. I have the satisfaction of believing that never, not even upon one occasion, did I yield to the temptation to take the other turn and follow the lamps at the junction of the May Gate. I often passed along that churchyard and through the dark arch of the Abbey with my heart in my mouth. Trying to whistle and keep up my courage, I would plod through the darkness, falling back in all emergencies upon the thought of what Wallace would have done if he had met with any foe, natural or supernatural.

King Robert the Bruce never got justice from my cousin or myself in childhood. It was enough for us that he was a king while Wallace was the man of the people. Sir John Graham was our second. The intensity of a Scottish boy's patriotism, reared as I was, constitutes a real force in his life to the very end. If the source of my stock of that prime article — courage — were studied, I am sure the final analysis would find it founded upon Wallace, the hero of Scotland. It is a tower of strength for a boy to have a hero.

It gave me a pang to find when I reached America that there was any other country which pretended to have anything to be proud of. What was a country without Wallace, Bruce, and Burns? I find ill the untraveled Scotsman of to-day something still of this feeling. It remains for maturer years and wider knowledge to tell us that every nation has its heroes, its romance, its traditions, and its achievements; and while the true Scotsman will not find reason in after years to lower the estimate he has formed of his own country and of its position even among the larger nations of the earth, he will find ample reason to raise his opinion of other nations because they all have much to be proud of — quite enough to stimulate their sons so to act their parts as not to disgrace the land that gave them birth.

It was years before I could feel that the new land could be anything but a temporary abode. My heart was in Scotland. I resembled Principal Peterson's little boy who, when in Canada, in reply to a question, said he liked Canada "very well for a visit, but he could never live so far away from the remains of Bruce and Wallace."

CHAPTER II
Dunfermline and America

MY good Uncle Lauder justly set great value upon recitation in education, and many were the pennies which Dod and I received for this. In our little frocks or shirts, our sleeves rolled up, paper helmets and blackened faces, with laths for swords, my cousin and myself were kept constantly reciting Norval and Glenalvon, Roderick Dhu and James Fitz-James to our schoolmates and often to the older people.

I remember distinctly that in the celebrated dialogue between Norval and Glenalvon we had some qualms about repeating the phrase, — "and false as *hell.*" At first we made a slight cough over the objectionable word which always created amusement among the spectators. It was a great day for us when my uncle persuaded us that we could say "hell" without swearing. I am afraid we practiced it very often. I always played the part of Glenalvon and made a great mouthful of the word. It had for me the wonderful fascination attributed to forbidden fruit. I can well understand the story of Marjory Fleming, who being cross one morning when Walter Scott called and asked how she was, answered:

"I am very cross this morning, Mr. Scott. I just want to say 'damn' [with a swing], but I winna."

Thereafter the expression of the one fearful word was a great point. Ministers could say "damnation" in the pulpit without sin, and so we, too, had full range on "hell" in recitation. Another passage made a deep impression. In the fight between Norval and Glenalvon, Norval says, "When we contend again our strife is mortal." Using these words in an article written for the "North American Review" in 1897, my uncle came across them and immediately sat down and wrote me from Dunfermline that he knew where I had found the words. He was the only man living who did.

My power to memorize must have been greatly strengthened by the mode of teaching adopted by my uncle. I cannot name a more important means of benefiting young people than encouraging them to commit favorite pieces to memory and recite them often. Anything which pleased me I could learn with a rapidity which surprised partial friends. I could memorize anything whether it pleased me or not, but if it did not impress me strongly it passed away in a few hours.

One of the trials of my boy's life at school in Dunfermline was committing to memory two double verses of the Psalms which I had to recite daily. My plan was not to look at the psalm until I had started for school. It was not more than five or six minutes' slow walk, but I could readily master the task in that time, and, as the psalm was the first lesson, I was prepared and passed through the ordeal successfully. Had I been asked to repeat the psalm thirty minutes afterwards, the attempt would, I fear, have ended in disastrous failure.

The first penny I ever earned or ever received from any person beyond the family circle was one from my school-teacher, Mr. Martin, for repeating before the school Burns's poem, "Man was made to Mourn." In writing this I am reminded that in later years, dining with Mr. John Morley in London, the conversation turned upon the life of Wordsworth, and Mr. Morley said he had been searching his Burns for the poem to "Old Age," so much extolled by him, which he had not been able to find under that title. I had the pleasure of repeating part of it to him. He promptly handed me a second penny. Ah, great as Morley is, he wasn't my schoolteacher, Mr. Martin — the first "great" man I ever knew. Truly great was he to me. But a hero surely is "Honest John" Morley.

In religious matters we were not much hampered. While other boys and girls at school were compelled to learn the Shorter Catechism, Dod and I, by some arrangement the details of which I never clearly understood, were absolved. All of our family connections, Morrisons and Lauders, were advanced in their theological as in their political views, and had objections to the catechism, I have no doubt. We had not one orthodox Presbyterian in our family circle. My father, Uncle and Aunt Aitken, Uncle Lauder, and also my Uncle Carnegie, had fallen away from the tenets of Calvinism. At a later day most of them found refuge for a time in the doctrines of Swedenborg. My mother was always reticent upon religious subjects. She never mentioned these to me nor did she attend church, for she had no servant in those early days and did all the housework, including cooking our Sunday dinner. A great reader, always, Channing the Unitarian was in those days her special delight. She was a marvel!

During my childhood the atmosphere around me was in a state of violent disturbance in matters theological as well as political. Along with the most advanced ideas which were being agitated in the political world — the death of privilege, the equality of the citizen, Republicanism — I heard many disputations upon theological subjects which the impressionable child drank in to an extent quite unthought of by his elders. I well remember that the stern doctrines of Calvinism lay as a terrible nightmare upon me, but that state of mind was soon over, owing to the influences of which I have spoken. I grew up treasuring within me the fact that my father had risen and left the Presbyterian Church one day when the minister preached the doctrine of infant damnation. This was shortly after I had made my appearance.

Father could not stand it and said: "If that be your religion and that your God, I seek a better religion and a nobler God." He left the Presbyterian Church never to return, but he did not cease to attend various other churches. I saw him enter the closet every morning to pray and that impressed me. He was indeed a saint and always remained devout. All sects became to him as agencies for good. He had discovered that theologies were many, but religion was one. I was quite satisfied that my father knew better than the minister, who pictured not the Heavenly Father, but the cruel avenger of the Old Testament — an "Eternal Torturer" as Andrew D. White ventures to call him in his autobiography. Fortunately this conception of the Unknown is now largely of the past.

One of the chief enjoyments of my childhood was the keeping of pigeons and rabbits. I am grateful every time I think of the trouble my father took to build a suitable house for these pets. Our home became headquarters for my young companions. My mother was always looking to home influences as the best means of keeping her two boys in the right path. She used to say that the first step in this direction was to make home pleasant; and there was nothing she and my father would not do to please us and the neighbors' children who centered about us.

My first business venture was securing my companions' services for a season as an employer, the compensation being that the young rabbits, when such came, should be named after them. The Saturday holiday was generally spent by my flock in gathering food for the rabbits. My conscience reproves me to-day, looking back, when I think of the hard bargain I drove with my young playmates, many of whom were content to gather dandelions and clover for a whole season with me, conditioned upon this unique reward — the poorest return ever made to labor. Alas! what else had I to offer them! Not a penny.

I treasure the remembrance of this plan as the earliest evidence of organizing power upon the development of which my material success in life has hung — a success not to be attributed to what I have known or done myself, but to the faculty of knowing and choosing others who did know better than myself. Precious knowledge this for any man to possess. I did not understand steam machinery, but I tried to understand that much more complicated piece of mechanism — man. Stopping at a small Highland inn on our coaching trip in 1898, a gentleman came forward and introduced himself. He was Mr. MacIntosh, the great furniture manufacturer of Scotland — a fine character as I found out afterward. He said he had ventured to make himself known as he was one of the boys who had gathered, and sometimes he feared "conveyed," spoil for the rabbits, and had "one named after him." It may be imagined how glad I was to meet him — the only one of the rabbit boys I have met in after-life. I hope to keep his friendship to the last and see him often. [As I read this manuscript to-day, December 1, 1913, I have a very precious note from him, recalling old times when we were boys together. He has a reply by this time that will warm his heart as his note did mine.]

With the introduction and improvement of steam machinery, trade grew worse and worse in Dunfermline for the small manufacturers, and at last a letter was written to my mother's two sisters in Pittsburgh stating that the idea of our going to them was seriously entertained — not, as I remember hearing my parents say, to benefit their own condition, but for the sake of their two young sons. Satisfactory letters were received in reply. The decision was taken to sell the looms and furniture by auction. And my father's sweet voice sang often to mother, brother, and me:

> "To the West, to the West, to the land of the free,
> Where the mighty Missouri rolls down to the sea;
> Where a man is a man even though he must toil
> And the poorest may gather the fruits of the soil."

The proceeds of the sale were most disappointing. The looms brought hardly anything, and the result was that twenty pounds more were needed to enable the family to pay passage to America. Here let me record an act of friendship performed by a lifelong companion of my mother — who always attracted stanch friends because she was so stanch herself — Mrs. Henderson, by birth Ella Ferguson, the name by which she was known in our family. She boldly ventured to advance the needful twenty pounds, my Uncles Lauder and Morrison guaranteeing repayment. Uncle Lauder also lent his aid and advice, managing all the details for us, and on the 17th day of May, 1848, we left Dunfermline. My father's age was then forty-three, my mother's thirty-three. I was in my thirteenth year, my brother Tom in his fifth year — a beautiful white-haired child with lustrous black eyes, who everywhere attracted attention.

I had left school forever, with the exception of one winter's night-schooling in America, and later a French night-teacher for a time, and, strange to say, an elocutionist from whom I learned how to declaim. I could read, write, and cipher, and had begun the study of algebra and of Latin. A letter written to my Uncle Lauder during the voyage, and since returned, shows that I was then a better penman than now. I had wrestled with English grammar, and knew as little of what it was designed to teach as children usually do. I had read little except about Wallace, Bruce, and Burns; but knew many familiar pieces of poetry by heart. I should add to this the fairy tales of childhood, and especially the "Arabian Nights," by which I was carried into a new world. I was in dreamland as I devoured those stories.

On the morning of the day we started from beloved Dunfermline, in the omnibus that ran upon the coal railroad to Charleston, I remember that I stood with tearful eyes looking out of the window until Dunfermline vanished from view, the last structure to fade being the grand and sacred old Abbey. During my first fourteen years of absence my thought was almost daily, as it was that morning, "When shall I see you again?" Few days passed in which I did not see in my mind's eye the talismanic letters on the Abbey tower — "King Robert The Bruce." All my recollections of childhood, all I knew of fairyland, clustered around the old Abbey and its curfew bell, which tolled at eight o'clock every evening and was the signal for me to run to bed before it stopped. I have referred to that bell in my "American Four-in-Hand in Britain"[1] when passing the Abbey and I may as well quote from it now:

---

[1] *An American Four-in-Hand in Britain.* New York, 1886.

As we drove down the Pends I was standing on the front seat of the coach with Provost Walls, when I heard the first toll of the Abbey bell, tolled in honor of my mother and myself. My knees sank from under me, the tears came rushing before I knew it, and I turned round to tell the Provost that I must give in. For a moment I felt as if I were about to faint. Fortunately I saw that there was no crowd before us for a little distance. I had time to regain control, and biting my lips till they actually bled, I murmured to myself, "No matter, keep cool, you must go on"; but never can there come to my ears on earth, nor enter so deep into my soul, a sound that shall haunt and subdue me with its sweet, gracious, melting power as that did.

By that curfew bell I had been laid in my little couch to sleep the sleep of childish innocence. Father and mother, sometimes the one, sometimes the other, had told me as they bent lovingly over me night after night, what that bell said as it tolled. Many good words has that bell spoken to me through their translations. No wrong thing did I do through the day which that voice from all I knew of heaven and the great Father there did not tell me kindly about ere I sank to sleep, speaking the words so plainly that I knew that the power that moved it had seen all and was not angry, never angry, never, but so very, *very* sorry. Nor is that bell dumb to me to-day when I hear its voice. It still has its message, and now it sounded to welcome back the exiled mother and son under its precious care again.

The world has not within its power to devise, much less to bestow upon us, such reward as that which the Abbey bell gave when it tolled in our honor. But my brother Tom should have been there also; this was the thought that came. He, too, was beginning to know the wonders of that bell ere we were away to the newer land.

Rousseau wished to die to the strains of sweet music. Could I choose my accompaniment, I could wish to pass into the dim beyond with the tolling of the Abbey bell sounding in my ears, telling me of the race that had been run, and calling me, as it had called the little white-haired child, for the last time — *to sleep.*

I have had many letters from readers speaking of this passage in my book, some of the writers going so far as to say that tears fell as they read. It came from the heart and perhaps that is why it reached the hearts of others.

We were rowed over in a small boat to the Edinburgh steamer in the Firth of Forth. As I was about to be taken from the small boat to the steamer, I rushed to Uncle Lauder and clung round his neck, crying out: "I cannot leave you! I cannot leave you!" I was torn from him by a kind sailor who lifted me up on the deck of the steamer. Upon my return visit to Dunfermline this dear old fellow, when he came to see me, told me it was the saddest parting he had ever witnessed.

We sailed from the Broomielaw of Glasgow in the 800-ton sailing ship Wiscasset. During the seven weeks of the voyage, I came to know the sailors quite well, learned the names of the ropes, and was able to direct the passengers to answer the call of the boatswain, for the ship being undermanned, the aid of the passengers was urgently required. In consequence I was invited by the sailors to participate on Sundays, in the one delicacy of the sailors' mess, plum duff. I left the ship with sincere regret.

The arrival at New York was bewildering. I had been taken to see the Queen at Edinburgh, but that was the extent of my travels before emigrating. Glasgow we had not time to see before we sailed. New York was the first great hive of human industry among the inhabitants of which I had mingled, and the bustle and excitement of it overwhelmed me. The incident of our stay in New York which impressed me most occurred while I was walking through Bowling Green at Castle Garden. I was caught up in the arms of one of the Wiscasset sailors, Robert Barryman, who was decked out in regular Jack-ashore fashion, with blue jacket and white trousers. I thought him the most beautiful man I had ever seen.

He took me to a refreshment stand and ordered a glass of sarsaparilla for me, which I drank with as much relish as if it were the nectar of the gods. To this day nothing that I have ever seen of the kind rivals the image which remains in my mind of the gorgeousness of the highly ornamented brass vessel out of which that nectar came foaming. Often as I have passed the identical spot I see standing there the old woman's sarsaparilla stand, and I marvel what became of the dear old sailor. I have tried to trace him, but in vain, hoping that if found he might be enjoying a ripe old age, and that it might be in my power to add to the pleasure of his declining years. He was my ideal Tom Bowling, and when that fine old song is sung I always see as the "form of manly beauty" my dear old friend Barryman. Alas! ere this he's gone aloft. Well; by his kindness on the voyage he made one boy his devoted friend and admirer.

We knew only Mr. and Mrs. Sloane in New York — parents of the well-known John, Willie, and Henry Sloane. Mrs. Sloane (Euphemia Douglas) was my mother's companion in childhood in Dunfermline. Mr. Sloane and my father had been fellow weavers. We called upon them and were warmly welcomed. It was a genuine pleasure when Willie, his son, bought ground from me in 1900 opposite our New York residence for his two married daughters so that our children of the third generation became playmates as our mothers were of Scotland.

My father was induced by emigration agents in New York to take the Erie Canal by way of Buffalo and Lake Erie to Cleveland, and thence down the canal to Beaver — a journey which then lasted three weeks, and is made to-day by rail in ten hours. There was no railway communication then with Pittsburgh, nor indeed with any western town. The Erie Railway was under construction and we saw gangs of men at work upon it as we traveled. Nothing comes amiss to youth, and I look back upon my three weeks as a passenger upon the canal-boat with unalloyed pleasure. All that was disagreeable in my experience has long since faded from recollection, excepting the night we were compelled to remain upon the wharf-boat at Beaver waiting for the steamboat to take us up the Ohio to Pittsburgh. This was our first introduction to the mosquito in all its ferocity. My mother suffered so severely that in the morning she could hardly see. We were all frightful sights, but I do not remember that even the stinging misery of that night kept me from sleeping soundly. I could always sleep, never knowing "horrid night, the child of hell."

Our friends in Pittsburgh had been anxiously waiting to hear from us, and in their warm and affectionate greeting all our troubles were forgotten. We took up our residence with them in Allegheny City. A brother of my Uncle Hogan had built a small weaver's shop at the back end of a lot in Rebecca Street. This had a second story in which there were two rooms, and it was in these (free of rent, for my Aunt Aitken owned them) that my parents began housekeeping. My uncle soon gave up weaving and my father took his place and began making tablecloths, which he had not only to weave, but afterwards, acting as his own merchant, to travel and sell, as no dealers could be found to take them in quantity. He was compelled to market them himself, selling from door to door. The returns were meager in the extreme.

As usual, my mother came to the rescue. There was no keeping her down. In her youth she had learned to bind shoes in her father's business for pin-money, and the skill then acquired was now turned to account for the benefit of the family. Mr. Phipps, father of my friend and partner Mr. Henry Phipps, was, like my grandfather, a master shoemaker. He was our neighbor in Allegheny City. Work was obtained from him, and in addition to attending to her household duties — for, of course, we had no servant — this wonderful woman, my mother, earned four dollars a week by binding shoes. Midnight would often find her at work. In the intervals during the day and evening, when household cares would permit, and my young brother sat at her knee threading needles and waxing the thread for her, she recited to him, as she had to me, the gems of Scottish minstrelsy which she seemed to have by heart, or told him tales which failed not to contain a moral.

This is where the children of honest poverty have the most precious of all advantages over those of wealth. The mother, nurse, cook, governess, teacher, saint, all in one; the father, exemplar, guide, counselor, and friend! Thus were my brother and I brought up. What has the child of millionaire or nobleman that counts compared to such a heritage?

My mother was a busy woman, but all her work did not prevent her neighbors from soon recognizing her as a wise and kindly woman whom they could call upon for counselor help in times of trouble. Many have told me what my mother did for them. So it was in after years wherever we resided; rich and poor came to her with their trials and found good counsel. She towered among her neighbors wherever she went.

CHAPTER III
Pittsburgh and Work

THE great question now was, what could be found for me to do. I had just completed my thirteenth year, and I fairly panted to get to work that I might help the family to a start in the new land. The prospect of want had become to me a frightful nightmare. My thoughts at this period centered in the determination that we should make and save enough of money to produce three hundred dollars a year — twenty-five dollars monthly, which I figured was the sum required to keep us without being dependent upon others. Every necessary thing was very cheap in those days.

The brother of my Uncle Hogan would often ask what my parents meant to do with me, and one day there occurred the most tragic of all scenes I have ever witnessed. Never can I forget it. He said, with the kindest intentions in the world, to my mother, that I was a likely boy and apt to learn; and he believed that if a basket were fitted out for me with knickknacks to sell, I could peddle them around the wharves and make quite a considerable sum. I never knew what an enraged woman meant till then. My mother was sitting sewing at the moment, but she sprang to her feet with outstretched hands and shook them in his face.

"What! my son a peddler and go among rough men upon the wharves! I would rather throw him into the Allegheny River. Leave me!" she cried, pointing to the door, and Mr. Hogan went.

She stood a tragic queen. The next moment she had

broken down, but only for a few moments did tears fall and sobs come. Then she took her two boys in her arms and told us not to mind her foolishness. There were many things in the world for us to do and we could be useful men, honored and respected, if we always did what was right. It was a repetition of Helen Macgregor, in her reply to Osbaldistone in which she threatened to have her prisoners "chopped into as many pieces as there are checks in the tartan." But the reason for the outburst was different. It was not because the occupation suggested was peaceful labor, for we were taught that idleness was disgraceful; but because the suggested occupation was somewhat vagrant in character and not entirely respectable in her eyes. Better death. Yes, mother would have taken her two boys, one under each arm, and perished with them rather than they should mingle with low company in their extreme youth.

As I look back upon the early struggles this can be said: there was not a prouder family in the land. A keen sense of honor, independence, self-respect, pervaded the household. Walter Scott said of Burns that he had the most extraordinary eye he ever saw in a human being. I can say as much for my mother. As Burns has it:

> "Her eye even turned on empty space,
> Beamed keen with honor."

Anything low, mean, deceitful, shifty, coarse, underhand, or gossipy was foreign to that heroic soul. Tom and I could not help growing up respectable characters, having such a mother and such a father, for the father, too, was one of nature's noblemen, beloved by all, a saint.

Soon after this incident my father found it necessary

to give up hand-loom weaving and to enter the cotton factory of Mr. Blackstock, an old Scotsman in Allegheny City, where we lived. In this factory he also obtained for me a position as bobbin boy, and my first work was done there at one dollar and twenty cents per week. It was a hard life. In the winter father and I had to rise and break-fast in the darkness, reach the factory before it was day-light, and, with a short interval for lunch, work till after dark. The hours hung heavily upon me and in the work itself I took no pleasure; but the cloud had a silver lin-ing, as it gave me the feeling that I was doing something for my world — our family. I have made millions since, but none of those millions gave me such happiness as my first week's earnings. I was now a helper of the fam-ily, a breadwinner, and no longer a total charge upon my parents. Often had I heard my father's beautiful singing of "The Boatie Rows" and often I longed to fulfill the last lines of the verse:

> "When Aaleck, Jock, and Jeanettie,
> *Are up and got their lair,*[1]
> They'll serve to gar the boatie row,
> And lichten a' our care."

I was going to make our tiny craft skim. It should be noted here that Aaleck, Jock, and Jeanettie were first to get their education. Scotland was the first country that re-quired all parents, high or low, to educate their children, and established the parish public schools.

Soon after this Mr. John Hay, a fellow-Scotch manu-facturer of bobbins in Allegheny City, needed a boy, and asked whether I would not go into his service. I went, and received two dollars per week; but at first the work was even more irksome than the factory. I

[1] Education.

had to run a small steam-engine and to fire the boiler in the cellar of the bobbin factory. It was too much for me. I found myself night after night, sitting up in bed trying the steam gauges, fearing at one time that the steam was too low and that the workers above would complain that they had not power enough, and at another time that the steam was too high and that the boiler might burst.

But all this it was a matter of honor to conceal from my parents. They had their own troubles and bore them. I must play the man and bear mine. My hopes were high, and I looked every day for some change to take place. What it was to be I knew not, but that it would come I felt certain if I kept on. Besides, at this date I was not beyond asking myself what Wallace would have done and what a Scotsman ought to do. Of one thing I was sure, he ought never to give up.

One day the chance came. Mr. Hay had to make out some bills. He had no clerk, and was himself a poor penman. He asked me what kind of hand I could write, and gave me some writing to do. The result pleased him, and he found it convenient thereafter to let me make out his bills. I was also good at figures; and he soon found it to be to his interest — and besides, dear old man, I believe he was moved by good feeling toward the white-haired boy, for he had a kind heart and was Scotch and wished to relieve me from the engine — to put me at other things, less objectionable except in one feature.

It now became my duty to bathe the newly made spools in vats of oil. Fortunately there was a room reserved for this purpose and I was alone, but not all the resolution I could muster, nor all the indignation I felt at my own weakness, prevented my stomach from behaving in a most perverse way. I never succeeded in over-coming the nausea produced by the smell of the oil. Even Wallace and Bruce proved impotent here. But if I had to lose breakfast, or dinner, I had all the better appetite for supper, and the allotted work was done. A real disciple of Wallace or Bruce could not give up; he would die first.

My service with Mr. Hay was a distinct advance upon the cotton factory, and I also made the acquaintance of an employer who was very kind to me. Mr. Hay kept his books in single entry, and I was able to handle them for him; but hearing that all great firms kept their books in double entry, and after talking over the matter with my companions, John Phipps, Thomas N. Miller, and William Cowley, we all determined to attend night school during the winter and learn the larger system. So the four of us went to a Mr. Williams in Pittsburgh and learned double-entry bookkeeping.

One evening, early in 1850, when I returned home from work, I was told that Mr. David Brooks, manager of the telegraph office, had asked my Uncle Hogan if he knew where a good boy could be found to act as messenger. Mr. Brooks and my uncle were enthusiastic draught-players, and it was over a game of draughts that this important inquiry was made. Upon such trifles do the most momentous consequences hang. A word, a look, an accent, may affect the destiny not only of individuals, but of nations. He is a bold man who calls anything a trifle. Who was it who, being advised to disregard trifles, said he always would if anyone could tell him what a trifle was? The young should remember that upon trifles the best gifts of the gods often hang.

My uncle mentioned my name, and said he would see whether I would take the position. I remember so well the family council that was held. Of course I was wild with delight. No bird that ever was confined in a cage longed for freedom more than I. Mother favored, but father was disposed to deny my wish. It would prove too much for me, he said; I was too young and too small. For the two dollars and a half per week offered it was evident that a much larger boy was expected. Late at night I might be required to run out into the country with a telegram, and there would be dangers to encounter. Upon the whole my father said that it was best that I should remain where I was. He subsequently withdrew his objection, so far as to give me leave to try, and I believe he went to Mr. Hay and consulted with him. Mr. Hay thought it would be for my advantage, and although, as he said, it would be an inconvenience to him, still he advised that I should try, and if I failed he was kind enough to say that my old place would be open for me.

This being decided, I was asked to go over the river to Pittsburgh and call on Mr. Brooks. My father wished to go with me, and it was settled that he should accompany me as far as the telegraph office, on the corner of Fourth and Wood Streets. It was a bright, sunshiny morning and this augured well. Father and I walked over from Allegheny to Pittsburgh, a distance of nearly two miles from our house. Arrived at the door I asked father to wait outside. I insisted upon going alone upstairs to the second or operating floor to see the great man and learn my fate. I was led to this, perhaps, because I had by that time begun to consider myself something of an American. At first boys used to call me "Scotchie! Scotchie!" and I answered, "Yes, I'm Scotch and I am proud of the name." But in speech and in address the broad Scotch had been worn off to a slight extent, and I imagined that I could make a smarter show-ing if alone with Mr. Brooks than if my good old Scotch father were present, perhaps to smile at my airs.

I was dressed in my one white linen shirt, which was usually kept sacred for the Sabbath day, my blue round-about, and my whole Sunday suit. I had at that time, and for a few weeks after I entered the telegraph service, but one linen suit of summer clothing; and every Saturday night, no matter if that was my night on duty and I did not return till near midnight, my mother washed those clothes and ironed them, and I put them on fresh on Sab-bath morning. There was nothing that heroine did not do in the struggle we were making for elbow room in the western world. Father's long factory hours tried his strength, but he, too, fought the good fight like a hero and never failed to encourage me.

The interview was successful. I took care to explain that I did not know Pittsburgh, that perhaps I would not do, would not be strong enough; but all I wanted was a trial. He asked me how soon I could come, and I said that I could stay now if wanted. And, looking back over the circumstance, I think that answer might well be pon-dered by young men. It is a great mistake not to seize the opportunity. The position was offered to me; something might occur, some other boy might be sent for. Having got myself in I proposed to stay there if I could. Mr. Brooks very kindly called the other boy — for it was an additional messenger that was wanted — and asked him to show me about, and let me go with him and learn the business. I soon found opportunity to run down to the corner of the street and tell my father that it was all right, and to go home and tell mother that I had got the situation.

And that is how in 1850 I got my first real start in life.

From the dark cellar running a steam-engine at two dollars a week, begrimed with coal dirt, without a trace of the elevating influences of life, I was lifted into paradise, yes, heaven, as it seemed to me, with newspapers, pens, pencils, and sunshine about me. There was scarcely a minute in which I could not learn something or find out how much there was to learn and how little I knew. I felt that my foot was upon the ladder and that I was bound to climb.

I had only one fear, and that was that I could not learn quickly enough the addresses of the various business houses to which messages had to be delivered. I therefore began to note the signs of these houses up one side of the street and down the other. At nights I exercised my memory by naming in succession the various firms. Before long I could shut my eyes and, beginning at the foot of a business street, call off the names of the firms in proper order along one side to the top of the street, then crossing on the other side go down in regular order to the foot again.

The next step was to know the men themselves, for it gave a messenger a great advantage, and often saved a long journey, if he knew members or employees of firms. He might meet one of these going direct to his office. It was reckoned a great triumph among the boys to deliver a message upon the street. And there was the additional satisfaction to the boy himself, that a great man (and most men are great to messengers), stopped upon the street in this way, seldom failed to note the boy and compliment him.

The Pittsburgh of 1850 was very different from what it has since become. It had not yet recovered from the great fire which destroyed the entire business portion of the city on April 10, 1845. The houses were mainly of wood, a few only were of brick, and not one was fire-proof. The entire population in and around Pittsburgh was not over forty thousand. The business portion of the city did not extend as far as Fifth Avenue, which was then a very quiet street, remarkable only for having the theater upon it. Federal Street, Allegheny, consisted of straggling business houses with great open spaces between them, and I remember skating upon ponds in the very heart of the present Fifth Ward. The site of our Union Iron Mills was then, and many years later, a cabbage garden.

General Robinson, to whom I delivered many a telegraph message, was the first white child born west of the Ohio River. I saw the first telegraph line stretched from the east into the city; and, at a later date, I also saw the first locomotive, for the Ohio and Pennsylvania Railroad, brought by canal from Philadelphia and unloaded from a scow in Allegheny City. There was no direct railway communication to the East. Passengers took the canal to the foot of the Allegheny Mountains, over which they were transported to Hollidaysburg, a distance of thirty miles by rail; thence by canal again to Columbia, and then eighty-one miles by rail to Philadelphia — a journey which occupied three days.[1]

The great event of the day in Pittsburgh at that time was the arrival and departure of the steam packet to and from Cincinnati, for daily communication had been established. The business of the city was largely that of forwarding merchandise East and West, for it was the great transfer station from river to canal. A rolling mill

---

[1] "Beyond Philadelphia was the Camden and Amboy Railway; beyond Pittsburgh, the Fort Wayne and Chicago, separate organizations with which we had nothing to do." (*Problems of To-day*, by Andrew Carnegie, p. 187. New York, 1908.)

had begun to roll iron; but not a ton of pig metal was made, and not a ton of steel for many a year thereafter. The pig iron manufacture at first was a total failure because of the lack of proper fuel, although the most valuable deposit of coking coal in the world lay within a few miles, as much undreamt of for coke to smelt ironstone as the stores of natural gas which had for ages lain untouched under the city.

There were at that time not half a dozen "carriage" people in the town; and not for many years after was the attempt made to introduce livery, even for a coachman. As late as 1861, perhaps, the most notable financial event which had occurred in the annals of Pittsburgh was the retirement from business of Mr. Fahnestock with the enormous sum of $174,000, paid by his partners for his interest. How great a sum that seemed then and how trifling now!

My position as messenger boy soon made me acquainted with the few leading men of the city. The bar of Pittsburgh was distinguished. Judge Wilkins was at its head, and he and Judge MacCandless, Judge McClure, Charles Shaler and his partner, Edwin M. Stanton, afterwards the great War Secretary ("Lincoln's right-hand man") were all well known to me — the last-named especially, for he was good enough to take notice of me as a boy. In business circles among prominent men who still survive, Thomas M. Howe, James Park, C. G. Hussey, Benjamin F. Jones, William Thaw, John Chalfant, Colonel Herron were great men to whom the messenger boys looked as models, and not bad models either, as their lives proved. [Alas! all dead as I revise this paragraph in 1906, so steadily moves the solemn procession.]

My life as a telegraph messenger was in every respect

a happy one, and it was while in this position that I laid the foundation of my closest friendships. The senior messenger boy being promoted, a new boy was needed, and he came in the person of David McCargo, afterwards the well-known superintendent of the Allegheny Valley Railway. He was made my companion and we had to deliver all the messages from the Eastern line, while two other boys delivered the messages from the West. The Eastern and Western Telegraph Companies were then separate, although occupying the same building. "Davy" and I became firm friends at once, one great bond being that he was Scotch; for, although "Davy" was born in America, his father was quite as much a Scotsman, even in speech, as my own father.

A short time after "Davy's" appointment a third boy was required, and this time I was asked if I could find a suitable one. This I had no difficulty in doing in my chum, Robert Pitcairn, later on my successor as superintendent and general agent at Pittsburgh of the Pennsylvania Railroad. Robert, like myself, was not only Scotch, but Scotchborn, so that "Davy," "Bob," and "Andy" became the three Scotch boys who delivered all the messages of the Eastern Telegraph Line in Pittsburgh, for the then magnificent salary of two and a half dollars per week. It was the duty of the boys to sweep the office each morning, and this we did in turn, so it will be seen that we all began at the bottom. Hon. H. W. Oliver,[1] head of the great manufacturing firm of Oliver Brothers, and W. C. Morland,[2] City Solicitor, subsequently joined the corps and started in the same fashion. It is not the rich man's son that the young struggler for advancement has to fear in the race of life, nor his nephew, nor his cousin. Let him look out for the "dark

[1] Died 1904.
[2] Died 1889.

horse" in the boy who begins by sweeping out the office.

A messenger boy in those days had many pleasures. There were wholesale fruit stores, where a pocketful of apples was sometimes to be had for the prompt delivery of a message; bakers' and confectioners' shops, where sweet cakes were sometimes given to him. He met with very kind men, to whom he looked up with respect; they spoke a pleasant word and complimented him on his promptness, perhaps asked him to deliver a message on the way back to the office. I do not know a situation in which a boy is more apt to attract attention, which is all a really clever boy requires in order to rise. Wise men are always looking out for clever boys.

One great excitement of this life was the extra charge of ten cents which we were permitted to collect for messages delivered beyond a certain limit. These "dime messages," as might be expected, were anxiously watched, and quarrels arose among us as to the right of delivery. In some cases it was alleged boys had now and then taken a dime message out of turn. This was the only cause of serious trouble among us. By way of settlement I proposed that we should "pool" these messages and divide the cash equally at the end of each week. I was appointed treasurer. Peace and good-humor reigned ever afterwards. This pooling of extra earnings not being intended to create artificial prices was really cooperation. It was my first essay in financial organization.

The boys considered that they had a perfect right to spend these dividends, and the adjoining confectioner's shop had running accounts with most of them. The accounts were sometimes greatly overdrawn. The treasurer had accordingly to notify the confectioner, which he did in due form, that he would not be responsible for any debts contracted by the too hungry and greedy boys. Robert Pitcairn was the worst offender of all, apparently having not only one sweet tooth, but all his teeth of that character. He explained to me confidentially one day, when I scolded him, that he had live things in his stomach that gnawed his insides until fed upon sweets.

CHAPTER IV
Colonel Anderson and Books

WITH all their pleasures the messenger boys were hard worked. Every other evening they were required to be on duty until the office closed, and on these nights it was seldom that I reached home before eleven o'clock. On the alternating nights we were relieved at six. This did not leave much time for self-improvement, nor did the wants of the family leave any money to spend on books. There came, however, like a blessing from above, a means by which the treasures of literature were unfolded to me.

Colonel James Anderson — I bless his name as I write — announced that he would open his library of four hundred volumes to boys, so that any young man could take out, each Saturday afternoon, a book which could be exchanged for another on the succeeding Saturday. My friend, Mr. Thomas N. Miller, reminded me recently that Colonel Anderson's books were first opened to "working boys," and the question arose whether messenger boys, clerks, and others, who did not work with their hands, were entitled to books. My first communication to the press was a note, written to the "Pittsburgh Dispatch," urging that we should not be excluded; that although we did not now work with our hands, some of us had done so, and that we were really working boys.[1] Dear Colonel Anderson promptly en-

---

[1] The note was signed "Working Boy." The librarian responded in the columns of the *Dispatch* defending the rules, which he claimed meant that "a Working Boy should have a trade." Carnegie's rejoinder was signed "A Working Boy, though without a Trade," and a day or two thereafter the *Dispatch*

larged the classification. So my first appearance as a public writer was a success.

My dear friend, Tom Miller, one of the inner circle, lived near Colonel Anderson and introduced me to him, and in this way the windows were opened in the walls of my dungeon through which the light of knowledge streamed in. Every day's toil and even the long hours of night service were lightened by the book which I carried about with me and read in the intervals that could be snatched from duty. And the future was made bright by the thought that when Saturday came a new volume could be obtained. In this way I became familiar with Macaulay's essays and his history, and with Bancroft's "History of the United States," which I studied with more care than any other book I had then read. Lamb's essays were my special delight, but I had at this time no knowledge of the great master of all, Shakespeare, beyond the selected pieces in the school books. My taste for him I acquired a little later at the old Pittsburgh Theater.

John Phipps, James R. Wilson, Thomas N. Miller, William Cowley — members of our circle — shared with me the invaluable privilege of the use of Colonel Anderson's library. Books which it would have been impossible for me to obtain elsewhere were, by his wise generosity, placed within my reach; and to him I owe a taste for literature which I would not exchange for all the millions that were ever amassed by man. Life would be quite intolerable without it. Nothing contributed so much to keep my companions and myself clear of low fellowship and bad habits as the beneficence of the good

had an item on its editorial page which read: "Will 'a Working Boy without a Trade' please call at this office." (David Homer Bates in *Century Magazine*, July, 1908.)

Colonel. Later, when fortune smiled upon me, one of my first duties was the erection of a monument to my benefactor. It stands in front of the Hall and Library in Diamond Square, which I presented to Allegheny, and bears this inscription:

> To Colonel James Anderson, Founder of Free Libraries in Western Pennsylvania. He opened his Library to working boys and upon Saturday afternoons acted as librarian, thus dedicating not only his books but himself to the noble work. This monument is erected in grateful remembrance by Andrew Carnegie, one of the "working boys" to whom were thus opened the precious treasures of knowledge and imagination through which youth may ascend.

This is but a slight tribute and gives only a faint idea of the depth of gratitude which I feel for what he did for me and my companions. It was from my own early experience that I decided there was no use to which money could be applied so productive of good to boys and girls who have good within them and ability and ambition to develop it, as the founding of a public library in a community which is willing to support it as a municipal institution. I am sure that the future of those libraries I have been privileged to found will prove the correctness of this opinion. For if one boy in each library district, by having access to one of these libraries, is half as much benefited as I was by having access to Colonel Anderson's four hundred well-worn volumes, I shall consider they have not been established in vain.

"As the twig is bent the tree's inclined." The treasures of the world which books contain were opened to me at the right moment. The fundamental advantage of a library is that it gives nothing for nothing. Youths must acquire knowledge themselves. There is no escape from this. It gave me great satisfaction to discover, many years later, that my father was one of the five weavers in Dunfermline who gathered together the few books they had and formed the first circulating library in that town.

The history of that library is interesting. It grew, and was removed no less than seven times from place to place, the first move being made by the founders, who carried the books in their aprons and two coal scuttles from the hand-loom shop to the second resting-place. That my father was one of the founders of the first library in his native town, and that I have been fortunate enough to be the founder of the last one, is certainly to me one of the most interesting incidents of my life. I have said often, in public speeches, that I had never heard of a lineage for which I would exchange that of a library-founding weaver.[1] I followed my father in library founding unknowingly — I am tempted almost to say providentially — and it has been a source of intense satisfaction to me. Such a father as mine was a guide to be followed — one of the sweetest, purest, and kindest natures I have ever known.

I have stated that it was the theater which first stimulated my love for Shakespeare. In my messenger days the old Pittsburgh Theater was in its glory under the charge of Mr. Foster. His telegraphic business was done free, and the telegraph operators were given free admission to the theater in return. This privilege extended in some degree also to the messengers, who, I fear, sometimes withheld telegrams that arrived for him in the late afternoon until they could be presented at

[1] "It's a God's mercy we are all from honest weavers; let us pity those who haven't ancestors of whom they can be proud, dukes or duchesses though they be." (*Our Coaching Trip*, by Andrew Carnegie, New York, 1882.)

the door of the theater in the evening, with the timid request that the messenger might be allowed to slip up-stairs to the second tier — a request which was always granted. The boys exchanged duties to give each the coveted entrance in turn.

In this way I became acquainted with the world that lay behind the green curtain. The plays, generally, were of the spectacular order; without much literary merit, but well calculated to dazzle the eye of a youth of fifteen. Not only had I never seen anything so grand, but I had never seen anything of the kind. I had never been in a theater, or even a concert room, or seen any form of public amusement. It was much the same with "Davy" McCargo, "Harry" Oliver, and "Bob" Pitcairn. We all fell under the fascination of the footlights, and every opportunity to attend the theater was eagerly embraced.

A change in my tastes came when "Gust" Adams,[1] one of the most celebrated tragedians of the day, began to play in Pittsburgh a round of Shakespearean characters. Thenceforth there was nothing for me but Shakespeare. I seemed to be able to memorize him almost without effort. Never before had I realized what magic lay in words. The rhythm and the melody all seemed to find a resting-place in me, to melt into a solid mass which lay ready to come at call. It was a new language and its appreciation I certainly owe to dramatic representation, for, until I saw "Macbeth" played, my interest in Shakespeare was not aroused. I had not read the plays.

At a much later date, Wagner was revealed to me in "Lohengrin." I had heard at the Academy of Music in New York, little or nothing by him when the overture to "Lohengrin" thrilled me as a new revelation. Here

[1] Edwin Adams.

was a genius, indeed, differing from all before, a new ladder upon which to climb upward — like Shakespeare, a new friend.

I may speak here of another matter which belongs to this same period. A few persons in Allegheny — probably not above a hundred in all — had formed themselves into a Swedenborgian Society, in which our American relatives were prominent. My father attended that church after leaving the Presbyterian, and, of course, I was taken there. My mother, however, took no interest in Swedenborg. Although always inculcating respect for all forms of religion, and discouraging theological disputes, she maintained for herself a marked reserve. Her position might best be defined by the celebrated maxim of Confucius: "To perform the duties of this life well, troubling not about another, is the prime wisdom."

She encouraged her boys to attend church and Sunday School; but there was no difficulty in seeing that the writings of Swedenborg, and much of the Old and New Testaments had been discredited by her as unworthy of divine authorship or of acceptance as authoritative guides for the conduct of life. I became deeply interested in the mysterious doctrines of Swedenborg, and received the congratulations of my devout Aunt Aitken upon my ability to expound "spiritual sense." That dear old woman fondly looked forward to a time when I should become a shining light in the New Jerusalem, and I know it was sometimes not beyond the bounds of her imagination that I might blossom into what she called a "preacher of the Word."

As I more and more wandered from man-made theology these fond hopes weakened, but my aunt's interest in and affection for her first nephew, whom she had dandled on her knee in Scotland, never waned. My cousin, Leander Morris, whom she had some hopes of saving through the Swedenborgian revelation, grievously disappointed her by actually becoming a Baptist and being dipped. This was too much for the evangelist, although she should have remembered her father passed through that same experience and often preached for the Baptists in Edinburgh.

Leander's reception upon his first call after his fall was far from cordial. He was made aware that the family record had suffered by his backsliding when at the very portals of the New Jerusalem revealed by Swedenborg and presented to him by one of the foremost disciples — his aunt. He began deprecatingly:

"Why are you so hard on me, aunt? Look at Andy, he is not a member of any church and you don't scold him. Surely the Baptist Church is better than none."

The quick reply came:

"Andy! Oh! Andy, he's naked, but you are clothed in rags."

He never quite regained his standing with dear Aunt Aitken. I might yet be reformed, being unattached; but Leander had chosen a sect and that sect not of the New Jerusalem.

It was in connection with the Swedenborgian Society that a taste for music was first aroused in me. As an appendix to the hymn-book of the society there were short selections from the oratorios. I fastened instinctively upon these, and although denied much of a voice, yet credited with "expression," I was a constant attendant upon choir practice. The leader, Mr. Koethen, I have reason to believe, often pardoned the discords I produced in the choir because of my enthusiasm in the cause. When, at a later date, I became acquainted with the oratorios in full, it was a pleasure to find that several of those considered in musical circles as the gems of Handel's musical compositions were the ones that I as an ignorant boy had chosen as favorites. So the beginning of my musical education dates from the small choir of the Swedenborgian Society of Pittsburgh.

I must not, however, forget that a very good foundation was laid for my love of sweet sounds in the unsurpassed minstrelsy of my native land as sung by my father. There was scarcely an old Scottish song with which I was not made familiar, both words and tune. Folk-songs are the best possible foundation for sure progress to the heights of Beethoven and Wagner. My father being one of the sweetest and most pathetic singers I ever heard, I probably inherited his love of music and of song, though not given his voice. Confucius' exclamation often sounds in my ears: "Music, sacred tongue of God! I hear thee calling and I come."

An incident of this same period exhibits the liberality of my parents in another matter. As a messenger boy I had no holidays, with the exception of two weeks given me in the summer-time, which I spent boating on the river with cousins at my uncle's at East Liverpool, Ohio. I was very fond of skating, and in the winter about which I am speaking, the slack water of the river opposite our house was beautifully frozen over. The ice was in splendid condition, and reaching home late Saturday night the question arose whether I might be permitted to rise early in the morning and go skating before church hours. No question of a more serious character could have been submitted to ordinary Scottish parents. My mother was clear on the subject, that in the circumstances I should be allowed to skate as long as I liked. My father said he believed it was right I should go down and skate, but he hoped I would be back in time to go with him to church.

I suppose this decision would be arrived at to-day by nine hundred and ninety-nine out of every thousand homes in America, and probably also in the majority of homes in England, though not in Scotland. But those who hold to-day that the Sabbath in its fullest sense was made for man, and who would open picture galleries and museums to the public, and make the day somewhat of a day of enjoyment for the masses instead of pressing upon them the duty of mourning over sins largely imaginary, are not more advanced than were my parents forty years ago. They were beyond the orthodox of the period when it was scarcely permissible, at least among the Scotch, to take a walk for pleasure or read any but religious books on the Sabbath.

CHAPTER V
The Telegraph Office

I HAD served as messenger about a year, when Colonel John P. Glass, the manager of the downstairs office, who came in contact with the public, began selecting me occasionally to watch the office for a few minutes during his absence. As Mr. Glass was a highly popular man, and had political aspirations, these periods of absence became longer and more frequent, so that I soon became an adept in his branch of the work. I received messages from the public and saw that those that came from the operating-room were properly assigned to the boys for prompt delivery.

This was a trying position for a boy to fill, and at that time I was not popular with the other boys, who resented my exemption from part of my legitimate work. I was also taxed with being penurious in my habits — mean, as the boys had it. I did not spend my extra dimes, but they knew not the reason. Every penny that I could save I knew was needed at home. My parents were wise and nothing was withheld from me. I knew every week the receipts of each of the three who were working — my father, my mother, and myself. I also knew all the expenditures. We consulted upon the additions that could be made to our scanty stock of furniture and clothing and every new small article obtained was a source of joy. There never was a family more united.

Day by day, as mother could spare a silver half dollar, it was carefully placed in a stocking and hid until two hundred were gathered, when I obtained a draft to repay the twenty pounds so generously lent to us by her friend Mrs. Henderson. That was a day we celebrated. The Carnegie family was free from debt. Oh, the happiness of that day! The debt was, indeed, discharged, but the debt of gratitude remains that never can be paid. Old Mrs. Henderson lives to-day. I go to her house as to a shrine, to see her upon my visits to Dunfermline; and whatever happens she can never be forgotten. [As I read these lines, written some years ago, I moan, "Gone, gone with the others!" Peace to the ashes of a dear, good, noble friend of my mother's.]

The incident in my messenger life which at once lifted me to the seventh heaven, occurred one Saturday evening when Colonel Glass was paying the boys their month's wages. We stood in a row before the counter, and Mr. Glass paid each one in turn. I was at the head and reached out my hand for the first eleven and a quarter dollars as they were pushed out by Mr. Glass. To my surprise he pushed them past me and paid the next boy. I thought it was a mistake, for I had heretofore been paid first, but it followed in turn with each of the other boys. My heart began to sink within me. Disgrace seemed coming. What had I done or not done? I was about to be told that there was no more work for me. I was to disgrace the family. That was the keenest pang of all. When all had been paid and the boys were gone, Mr. Glass took me behind the counter and said that I was worth more than the other boys, and he had resolved to pay me thirteen and a half dollars a month.

My head swam; I doubted whether I had heard him correctly. He counted out the money. I don't know whether I thanked him; I don't believe I did. I took it and made one bound for the door and scarcely stopped until I got home. I remember distinctly running or rather bounding from end to end of the bridge across the Allegheny River — inside on the wagon track because the footwalk was too narrow. It was Saturday night. I handed over to mother, who was the treasurer of the family, the eleven dollars and a quarter and said nothing about the remaining two dollars and a quarter in my pocket — worth more to me then than all the millions I have made since.

Tom, a little boy of nine, and myself slept in the attic together, and after we were safely in bed I whispered the secret to my dear little brother. Even at his early age he knew what it meant, and we talked over the future. It was then, for the first time, I sketched to him how we would go into business together; that the firm of "Carnegie Brothers" would be a great one, and that father and mother should yet ride in their carriage. At the time that seemed to us to embrace everything known as wealth and most of what was worth striving for. The old Scotch woman, whose daughter married a merchant in London, being asked by her son-in-law to come to London and live near them, promising she should "ride in her carriage," replied:

"What good could it do me to ride in a carriage gin I could na be seen by the folk in Strathbogie?" Father and mother would not only be seen in Pittsburgh, but should visit Dunfermline, their old home, in style.

On Sunday morning with father, mother, and Tom at breakfast, I produced the extra two dollars and a quarter. The surprise was great and it took some moments for them to grasp the situation, but it soon dawned upon them. Then father's glance of loving pride and mother's blazing eye soon wet with tears, told their feeling. It was their boy's first triumph and proof positive that he was worthy of promotion. No subsequent success, or recognition of any kind, ever thrilled me as this did. I cannot even imagine one that could. Here was heaven upon earth. My whole world was moved to tears of joy.

Having to sweep out the operating-room in the mornings, the boys had an opportunity of practicing upon the telegraph instruments before the operators arrived. This was a new chance. I soon began to play with the key and to talk with the boys who were at the other stations who had like purposes to my own. Whenever one learns to do anything he has never to wait long for an opportunity of putting his knowledge to use.

One morning I heard the Pittsburgh call given with vigor. It seemed to me I could divine that some one wished greatly to communicate. I ventured to answer, and let the slip run. It was Philadelphia that wanted to send "a death message" to Pittsburgh immediately. Could I take it? I replied that I would try if they would send slowly. I succeeded in getting the message and ran out with it. I waited anxiously for Mr. Brooks to come in, and told him what I had dared to do. Fortunately, he appreciated it and complimented me, instead of scolding me for my temerity; yet dismissing me with the admonition to be very careful and not to make mistakes. It was not long before I was called sometimes to watch the instrument, while the operator wished to be absent, and in this way I learned the art of telegraphy.

We were blessed at this time with a rather indolent operator, who was only too glad to have me do his work. It was then the practice for us to receive the messages on a running slip of paper, from which the operator read to a copyist, but rumors had reached us that a man in the West had learned to read by sound and could really take a message by ear. This led me to practice the new method. One of the operators in the office, Mr. Maclean, became expert at it, and encouraged me by his success. I was surprised at the ease with which I learned the new language. One day, desiring to take a message in the absence of the operator, the old gentleman who acted as copyist resented my presumption and refused to "copy" for a messenger boy. I shut off the paper slip, took pencil and paper and began taking the message by ear. I shall never forget his surprise. He ordered me to give him back his pencil and pad, and after that there was never any difficulty between dear old Courtney Hughes and myself. He was my devoted friend and copyist.

Soon after this incident Joseph Taylor, the operator at Greensburg, thirty miles from Pittsburgh, wishing to be absent for two weeks, asked Mr. Brooks if he could not send some one to take his place. Mr. Brooks called me and asked whether I thought I could do the work. I replied at once in the affirmative.

"Well," he said, "we will send you out there for a trial."

I went out in the mail stage and had a most delightful trip. Mr. David Bruce, a well-known solicitor of Scottish ancestry, and his sister happened to be passengers. It was my first excursion, and my first glimpse of the country. The hotel at Greensburg was the first public house in which I had ever taken a meal. I thought the food wonderfully fine.

This was in 1852. Deep cuts and embankments near Greensburg were then being made for the Pennsylvania Railroad, and I often walked out in the early morning to see the work going forward, little dreaming that I was so soon to enter the service of that great corporation. This was the first responsible position I had occupied in the telegraph service, and I was so anxious to be at hand in case I should be needed, that one night very late I sat in the office during a storm, not wishing to cut off the connection. I ventured too near the key and for my boldness was knocked off my stool. A flash of lightning very nearly ended my career. After that I was noted in the office for caution during lightning storms. I succeeded in doing the small business at Greensburg to the satisfaction of my superiors, and returned to Pittsburgh surrounded with something like a halo, so far as the other boys were concerned. Promotion soon came. A new operator was wanted and Mr. Brooks telegraphed to my afterward dear friend James D. Reid, then general superintendent of the line, another fine specimen of the Scotsman, and took upon himself to recommend me as an assistant operator. The telegram from Louisville in reply stated that Mr. Reid highly approved of promoting "Andy," provided Mr. Brooks considered him competent. The result was that I began as a telegraph operator at the tremendous salary of twenty-five dollars per month, which I thought a fortune. To Mr. Brooks and Mr. Reid I owe my promotion from the messenger's station to the operating-room.[1] I was then in my seventeenth year and had served my apprenticeship. I was now performing a man's part, no longer a boy's — earning a dollar every working day.

[1] "I liked the boy's looks, and it was very easy to see that though he was little he was full of spirit. He had not been with me a month when he began to ask whether I would teach him to telegraph. I began to instruct him and found him an apt pupil." (James D. Reid, *The Telegraph in America*. New York, 1879.)

Reid was born near Dunfermline and forty years afterwards Mr. Carnegie was able to secure for him the appointment of United States Consul at Dunfermline.

The operating-room of a telegraph office is an excellent school for a young man. He there has to do with pencil and paper, with composition and invention. And there my slight knowledge of British and European affairs soon stood me in good stead. Knowledge is sure to prove useful in one way or another. It always tells. The foreign news was then received by wire from Cape Race, and the taking of successive "steamer news" was one of the most notable of our duties. I liked this better than any other branch of the work, and it was soon tacitly assigned to me.

The lines in those days worked poorly, and during a storm much had to be guessed at. My guessing powers were said to be phenomenal, and it was my favorite diversion to fill up gaps instead of interrupting the sender and spending minutes over a lost word or two. This was not a dangerous practice in regard to foreign news, for if any undue liberties were taken by the bold operator, they were not of a character likely to bring him into serious trouble. My knowledge of foreign affairs became somewhat extensive, especially regarding the affairs of Britain, and my guesses were quite safe, if I got the first letter or two right.

The Pittsburgh newspapers had each been in the habit of sending a reporter to the office to transcribe the press dispatches. Later on one man was appointed for all the papers and he suggested that multiple copies could readily be made of the news as received, and it was arranged that I should make five copies of all press dispatches for him as extra work for which he was to pay me a dollar per week. This, my first work for the press, yielded very modest remuneration, to be sure; but it made my salary thirty dollars per month, and every dollar counted in those days. The family was gradually gaining ground; already future millionairedom seemed dawning.

Another step which exercised a decided influence over me was joining the "Webster Literary Society" along with my companions, the trusty five already named. We formed a select circle and stuck closely together. This was quite an advantage for all of us. We had before this formed a small debating club which met in Mr. Phipps's father's room in which his few journeymen shoemakers worked during the day. Tom Miller recently alleged that I once spoke nearly an hour and a half upon the question, "Should the judiciary be elected by the people?" but we must mercifully assume his memory to be at fault. The "Webster" was then the foremost club in the city and proud were we to be thought fit for membership. We had merely been preparing ourselves in the cobbler's room.

I know of no better mode of benefiting a youth than joining such a club as this. Much of my reading became such as had a bearing on forthcoming debates and that gave clearness and fixity to my ideas. The self-possession I afterwards came to have before an audience may very safely be attributed to the experience of the "Webster Society." My two rules for speaking then (and now) were: Make yourself perfectly at home before your audience, and simply talk *to* them, not *at* them. Do not try to be somebody else; be your own self and *talk*, never "orate" until you can't help it.

I finally became an operator by sound, discarding printing entirely. The accomplishment was then so rare that people visited the office to be satisfied of the extraordinary feat. This brought me into such notice that when a great flood destroyed all telegraph communication between Steubenville and Wheeling, a distance of twenty-five miles, I was sent to the former town to receive the entire business then passing between the East and the West, and to send every hour or two the dispatches in small boats down the river to Wheeling. In exchange every returning boat brought rolls of dispatches which I wired East, and in this way for more than a week the entire telegraphic communication between the East and the West *via* Pittsburgh was maintained.

While at Steubenville I learned that my father was going to Wheeling and Cincinnati to sell the tablecloths he had woven. I waited for the boat, which did not arrive till late in the evening, and went down to meet him. I remember how deeply affected I was on finding that instead of taking a cabin passage, he had resolved not to pay the price, but to go down the river as a deck passenger. I was indignant that one of so fine a nature should be compelled to travel thus. But there was comfort in saying:

"Well, father, it will not be long before mother and you shall ride in your carriage."

My father was usually shy, reserved, and keenly sensitive, very saving of praise (a Scotch trait) lest his sons might be too greatly uplifted; but when touched he lost his self-control. He was so upon this occasion, and grasped my hand with a look which I often see and can never forget. He murmured slowly:

"Andra, I am proud of you."

The voice trembled and he seemed ashamed of himself for saying so much. The tear had to be wiped from his eye, I fondly noticed, as he bade me good-night and told me to run back to my office. Those words rang in my ear and warmed my heart for years and years. We understood each other. How reserved the Scot is! Where he feels most he expresses least. Quite right. There are holy depths which it is sacrilege to disturb. Silence is more eloquent than words. My father was one of the most lovable of men, beloved of his companions, deeply religious, although non-sectarian and non-theological, not much of a man of the world, but a man all over for heaven. He was kindness itself, although reserved. Alas! he passed away soon after returning from this Western tour just as we were becoming able to give him a life of leisure and comfort.

After my return to Pittsburgh it was not long before I made the acquaintance of an extraordinary man, Thomas A. Scott, one to whom the term "genius" in his department may safely be applied. He had come to Pittsburgh as superintendent of that division of the Pennsylvania Railroad. Frequent telegraphic communication was necessary between him and his superior, Mr. Lombaert, general superintendent at Altoona. This brought him to the telegraph office at nights, and upon several occasions I happened to be the operator. One day I was surprised by one of his assistants, with whom I was acquainted, telling me that Mr. Scott had asked him whether he thought that I could be obtained as his clerk and telegraph operator, to which this young man told me he had replied:

"That is impossible. He is now an operator."

But when I heard this I said at once:

"Not so fast. He can have me. I want to get out of a mere office life. Please go and tell him so."

The result was I was engaged February 1, 1853, at a salary of thirty-five dollars a month as Mr. Scott's clerk and operator. A raise in wages from twenty-five to thirty-five dollars per month was the greatest I had ever known. The public telegraph line was temporarily put into Mr. Scott's office at the outer depot and the Pennsylvania Railroad Company was given permission to use the wire at seasons when such use would not interfere with the general public business, until their own line, then being built, was completed.

CHAPTER VI
Railroad Service

FROM the operating-room of the telegraph office I had now stepped into the open world, and the change at first was far from agreeable. I had just reached my eighteenth birthday, and I do not see how it could be possible for any boy to arrive at that age much freer from a knowledge of anything but what was pure and good. I do not believe, up to that time, I had ever spoken a bad word in my life and seldom heard one. I knew nothing of the base and the vile. Fortunately I had always been brought in contact with good people.

I was now plunged at once into the company of coarse men, for the office was temporarily only a portion of the shops and the headquarters for the freight conductors, brakemen, and firemen. All of them had access to the same room with Superintendent Scott and myself, and they availed themselves of it. This was a different world, indeed, from that to which I had been accustomed. I was not happy about it. I ate, necessarily, of the fruit of the tree of knowledge of good and evil for the first time. But there were still the sweet and pure surroundings of home, where nothing coarse or wicked ever entered, and besides, there was the world in which I dwelt with my companions, all of them refined young men, striving to improve themselves and become respected citizens. I passed through this phase of my life detesting what was foreign to my nature and my early education. The experience with coarse men was probably beneficial because it gave me a "scunner" (disgust), to use a

Scotism, at chewing or smoking tobacco, also at swearing or the use of improper language, which fortunately remained with me through life.

I do not wish to suggest that the men of whom I have spoken were really degraded or bad characters. The habit of swearing, with coarse talk, chewing and smoking tobacco, and snuffing were more prevalent then than to-day and meant less than in this age. Railroading was new, and many rough characters were attracted to it from the river service. But many of the men were fine young fellows who have lived to be highly respectable citizens and to occupy responsible positions. And I must say that one and all of them were most kind to me. Many are yet living from whom I hear occasionally and regard with affection. A change came at last when Mr. Scott had his own office which he and I occupied.

I was soon sent by Mr. Scott to Altoona to get the monthly pay-rolls and checks. The railroad line was not completed over the Allegheny Mountains at that time, and I had to pass over the inclined planes which made the journey a remarkable one to me. Altoona was then composed of a few houses built by the company. The shops were under construction and there was nothing of the large city which now occupies the site. It was there that I saw for the first time the great man in our railroad field — Mr. Lombaert, general superintendent. His secretary at that time was my friend, Robert Pitcairn, for whom I had obtained a situation on the railroad, so that "Davy," "Bob," and "Andy" were still together in the same service. We had all left the telegraph company for the Pennsylvania Railroad Company.

Mr. Lombaert was very different from Mr. Scott;

he was not sociable, but rather stern and unbending. Judge then of Robert's surprise, and my own, when, after saying a few words to me, Mr. Lombaert added: "You must come down and take tea with us to-night." I stammered out something of acceptance and awaited the appointed hour with great trepidation. Up to this time I considered that invitation the greatest honor I had received. Mrs. Lombaert was exceedingly kind, and Mr. Lombaert's introduction of me to her was: "This is Mr. Scott's 'Andy.'" I was very proud indeed of being recognized as belonging to Mr. Scott.

An incident happened on this trip which might have blasted my career for a time. I started next morning for Pittsburgh with the pay-rolls and checks, as I thought, securely placed under my waistcoat, as it was too large a package for my pockets. I was a very enthusiastic railroader at that time and preferred riding upon the engine. I got upon the engine that took me to Hollidaysburg where the State railroad over the mountain was joined up. It was a very rough ride, indeed, and at one place, uneasily feeling for the pay-roll package, I was horrified to find that the jolting of the train had shaken it out. I had lost it!

There was no use in disguising the fact that such a failure would ruin me. To have been sent for the pay-rolls and checks and to lose the package, which I should have "grasped as my honor," was a dreadful showing. I called the engineer and told him it must have been shaken out within the last few miles. Would he reverse his engine and run back for it? Kind soul, he did so. I watched the line, and on the very banks of a large stream, within a few feet of the water, I saw that package lying. I could scarcely believe my eyes. I ran down and grasped it. It was all right. Need I add that it never passed out of my firm grasp again until it was safe in Pittsburgh? The engineer and fireman were the only persons who knew of my carelessness, and I had their assurance that it would not be told.

It was long after the event that I ventured to tell the story. Suppose that package had fallen just a few feet farther away and been swept down by the stream, how many years of faithful service would it have required upon my part to wipe out the effect of that one piece of carelessness! I could no longer have enjoyed the confidence of those whose confidence was essential to success had fortune not favored me. I have never since believed in being too hard on a young man, even if he does commit a dreadful mistake or two; and I have always tried in judging such to remember the difference it would have made in my own career but for an accident which restored to me that lost package at the edge of the stream a few miles from Hollidaysburg. I could go straight to the very spot to-day, and often as I passed over that line afterwards I never failed to see that light-brown package lying upon the bank. It seemed to be calling:

"All right, my boy! The good gods were with you, but don't do it again!"

At an early age I became a strong anti-slavery partisan and hailed with enthusiasm the first national meeting of the Republican Party in Pittsburgh, February 22, 1856, although too young to vote. I watched the prominent men as they walked the streets, lost in admiration for Senators Wilson, Hale, and others. Some time before I had organized among the railroad men a club of a hundred for the "New York Weekly Tribune," and ventured occasionally upon short notes to the great editor, Horace Greeley, who did so much to arouse the people to action upon this vital question.

The first time I saw my work in type in the then flaming organ of freedom certainly marked a stage in my career. I kept that "Tribune" for years. Looking back to-day one cannot help regretting so high a price as the Civil War had to be paid to free our land from the curse, but it was not slavery alone that needed abolition. The loose Federal system with State rights so prominent would inevitably have prevented, or at least long delayed, the formation of one solid, all-powerful, central government. The tendency under the Southern idea was centrifugal. To-day it is centripetal, all drawn toward the center under the sway of the Supreme Court, the decisions of which are, very properly, half the dicta of lawyers and half the work of statesmen. Uniformity in many fields must be secured. Marriage, divorce, bankruptcy, railroad supervision, control of corporations, and some other departments should in some measure be brought under one head. [Re-reading this paragraph to-day, July, 1907, written many years ago, it seems prophetic. These are now burning questions.]

It was not long after this that the railroad company constructed its own telegraph line. We had to supply it with operators. Most of these were taught in our offices at Pittsburgh. The telegraph business continued to increase with startling rapidity. We could scarcely provide facilities fast enough. New telegraph offices were required. My fellow messenger-boy, "Davy" McCargo, I appointed superintendent of the telegraph department March 11, 1859. I have been told that "Davy" and myself are entitled to the credit of being the first to employ young women as telegraph operators in the United States upon railroads, or perhaps in any branch. At all events, we placed girls in various offices as pupils, taught and then put them in charge of offices as occasion required. Among the first of these was my cousin, Miss Maria Hogan. She was the operator at the freight station in Pittsburgh, and with her were placed successive pupils, her office becoming a school. Our experience was that young women operators were more to be relied upon than young men. Among all the new occupations invaded by women I do not know of any better suited for them than that of telegraph operator.

Mr. Scott was one of the most delightful superiors that anybody could have and I soon became warmly attached to him. He was my great man and all the hero worship that is inherent in youth I showered upon him. I soon began placing him in imagination in the presidency of the great Pennsylvania Railroad — a position which he afterwards attained. Under him I gradually performed duties not strictly belonging to my department and I can attribute my decided advancement in the service to one well-remembered incident.

The railway was a single line. Telegraph orders to trains often became necessary, although it was not then a regular practice to run trains by telegraph. No one but the superintendent himself was permitted to give a train order on any part of the Pennsylvania system, or indeed of any other system, I believe, at that time. It was then a dangerous expedient to give telegraphic orders, for the whole system of railway management was still in its infancy, and men had not yet been trained for it. It was necessary for Mr. Scott to go out night after night to break-downs or wrecks to superintend the clearing of the line. He was necessarily absent from the office on many mornings.

One morning I reached the office and found that a serious accident on the Eastern Division had delayed the express passenger train westward, and that the passenger train eastward was proceeding with a flagman in advance at every curve. The freight trains in both directions were all standing still upon the sidings. Mr. Scott was not to be found. Finally I could not resist the temptation to plunge in, take the responsibility, give "train orders," and set matters going. "Death or Westminster Abbey," flashed across my mind. I knew it was dismissal, disgrace, perhaps criminal punishment for me if I erred. On the other hand, I could bring in the wearied freight-train men who had lain out all night. I could set everything in motion. I knew I could. I had often done it in wiring Mr. Scott's orders. I knew just what to do, and so I began. I gave the orders in his name, started every train, sat at the instrument watching every tick, carried the trains along from station to station, took extra precautions, and had everything running smoothly when Mr. Scott at last reached the office. He had heard of the delays. His first words were:

"Well! How are matters?"

He came to my side quickly, grasped his pencil and began to write his orders. I had then to speak, and timidly said:

"Mr. Scott, I could not find you anywhere and I gave these orders in your name early this morning."

"Are they going all right? Where is the Eastern Express?"

I showed him the messages and gave him the position of every train on the line—freights, ballast trains, everything—showed him the answers of the various conductors, the latest reports at the stations where the various trains had passed. All was right. He looked in my face for a second. I scarcely dared look in his. I did not know what was going to happen. He did not say one word, but again looked carefully over all that had taken place. Still he said nothing. After a little he moved away from my desk to his own, and that was the end of it. He was afraid to approve what I had done, yet he had not censured me. If it came out all right, it was all right; if it came out all wrong, the responsibility was mine. So it stood, but I noticed that he came in very regularly and in good time for some mornings after that.

Of course I never spoke to anyone about it. None of the trainmen knew that Mr. Scott had not personally given the orders. I had almost made up my mind that if the like occurred again, I would not repeat my proceeding of that morning unless I was authorized to do so. I was feeling rather distressed about what I had done until I heard from Mr. Franciscus, who was then in charge of the freighting department at Pittsburgh, that Mr. Scott, the evening after the memorable morning, had said to him:

"Do you know what that little white-haired Scotch devil of mine did?"

"No."

"I'm blamed if he didn't run every train on the division in my name without the slightest authority."

"And did he do it all right?" asked Franciscus.

"Oh, yes, all right."

This satisfied me. Of course I had my cue for the next occasion, and went boldly in. From that date it was very seldom that Mr. Scott gave a train order.

The greatest man of all on my horizon at this time was John Edgar Thomson, president of the Pennsylvania, and for whom our steel-rail mills were afterward named. He was the most reserved and silent of men, next to General Grant, that I ever knew, although General

Grant was more voluble when at home with friends. He walked about as if he saw nobody when he made his periodical visits to Pittsburgh. This reserve I learned afterwards was purely the result of shyness. I was surprised when in Mr. Scott's office he came to the telegraph instrument and greeted me as "Scott's Andy." But I learned afterwards that he had heard of my train-running exploit. The battle of life is already half won by the young man who is brought personally in contact with high officials; and the great aim of every boy should be to do something beyond the sphere of his duties — something which attracts the attention of those over him.

Some time after this Mr. Scott wished to travel for a week or two and asked authority from Mr. Lombaert to leave me in charge of the division. Pretty bold man he was, for I was then not very far out of my teens. It was granted. Here was the coveted opportunity of my life. With the exception of one accident caused by the inexcusable negligence of a ballast-train crew, everything went well in his absence. But that this accident should occur was gall and wormwood to me. Determined to fulfill all the duties of the station I held a court-martial, examined those concerned, dismissed peremptorily the chief offender, and suspended two others for their share in the catastrophe. Mr. Scott after his return of course was advised of the accident, and proposed to investigate and deal with the matter. I felt I had gone too far, but having taken the step, I informed him that all that had been settled. I had investigated the matter and punished the guilty. Some of these appealed to Mr. Scott for a reopening of the case, but this I never could have agreed to, had it been pressed. More by look I think than by word Mr. Scott understood my feelings upon this delicate point, and acquiesced.

It is probable he was afraid I had been too severe and very likely he was correct. Some years after this, when I, myself, was superintendent of the division I always had a soft spot in my heart for the men then suspended for a time. I had felt qualms of conscience about my action in this, my first court. A new judge is very apt to stand so straight as really to lean a little backward. Only experience teaches the supreme force of gentleness. Light but certain punishment, when necessary, is most effective. Severe punishments are not needed and a judicious pardon, for the first offense at least, is often best of all.

As the half-dozen young men who constituted our inner circle grew in knowledge, it was inevitable that the mysteries of life and death, the here and the hereafter, should cross our path and have to be grappled with. We had all been reared by good, honest, self-respecting parents, members of one or another of the religious sects. Through the influence of Mrs. McMillan, wife of one of the leading Presbyterian ministers of Pittsburgh, we were drawn into the social circle of her husband's church. [As I read this on the moors, July 16, 1912, I have before me a note from Mrs. McMillan from London in her eightieth year. Two of her daughters were married in London last week to university professors, one remains in Britain, the other has accepted an appointment in Boston. Eminent men both. So draws our English-speaking race together.] Mr. McMillan was a good strict Calvinist of the old school, his charming wife a born leader of the young. We were all more at home with her and enjoyed ourselves more at her home gatherings than elsewhere. This led to some of us occasionally attending her church.

A sermon of the strongest kind upon predestination which Miller heard there brought the subject of theology upon us and it would not down. Mr. Miller's people were strong Methodists, and Tom had known little of dogmas. This doctrine of predestination, including infant damnation — some born to glory and others to the opposite — appalled him. To my astonishment I learnt that, going to Mr. McMillan after the sermon to talk over the matter, Tom had blurted out at the finish,

"Mr. McMillan, if your idea were correct, your God would be a perfect devil," and left the astonished minister to himself.

This formed the subject of our Sunday afternoon conferences for many a week. Was that true or not, and what was to be the consequence of Tom's declaration? Should we no longer be welcome guests of Mrs. McMillan? We could have spared the minister, perhaps, but none of us relish the idea of banishment from his wife's delightful reunions. There was one point clear. Carlyle's struggles over these matters had impressed us and we could follow him in his resolve: "If it be incredible, in God's name let it be discredited." It was only the truth that could make us free, and the truth, the whole truth, we should pursue.

Once introduced, of course, the subject remained with us, and one after the other the dogmas were voted down as the mistaken ideas of men of a less enlightened age. I forget who first started us with a second axiom. It was one we often dwelt upon: "A forgiving God would be the noblest work of man." We accepted as proven that each stage of civilization creates its own God, and that as man ascends and becomes better his conception of the Unknown likewise improves. Thereafter we all became less theological, but I am sure more truly religious. The crisis passed. Happily we were not excluded from Mrs. McMillan's society. It was a notable day, however, when we resolved to stand by Miller's statement, even if it involved banishment and worse. We young men were getting to be pretty wild boys about theology, although more truly reverent about religion.

The first great loss to our circle came when John Phipps was killed by a fall from a horse. This struck home to all of us, yet I remember I could then say to myself: "John has, as it were, just gone home to England where he was born. We are all to follow him soon and live forever together." I had then no doubts. It was not a hope I was pressing to my heart, but a certainty. Happy those who in their agony have such a refuge. We should all take Plato's advice and never give up everlasting hope, "alluring ourselves as with enchantments, for the hope is noble and the reward is great." Quite right. It would be no greater miracle that brought us into another world to live forever with our dearest than that which has brought us into this one to live a lifetime with them. Both are equally incomprehensible to finite beings. Let us therefore comfort ourselves with everlasting hope, "as with enchantments," as Plato recommends, never forgetting, however, that we all have our duties here and that the kingdom of heaven is within us. It also passed into an axiom with us that he who proclaims there is no hereafter is as foolish as he who proclaims there is, since neither can know, though all may and should hope. Meanwhile "Home our heaven" instead of "Heaven our home" was our motto.

During these years of which I have been writing, the

family fortunes had been steadily improving. My thirty-five dollars a month had grown to forty, an unsolicited advance having been made by Mr. Scott. It was part of my duty to pay the men every month.[1] We used checks upon the bank and I drew my salary invariably in two twenty-dollar gold pieces. They seemed to me the prettiest works of art in the world. It was decided in family council that we could venture to buy the lot and the two small frame houses upon it, in one of which we had lived, and the other, a four-roomed house, which till then had been occupied by my Uncle and Aunt Hogan, who had removed elsewhere. It was through the aid of my dear Aunt Aitken that we had been placed in the small house above the weaver's shop, and it was now our turn to be able to ask her to return to the house that formerly had been her own. In the same way after we had occupied the four-roomed house, Uncle Hogan having passed away, we were able to restore Aunt Hogan to her old home when we removed to Altoona. One hundred dollars cash was paid upon purchase, and the total price, as I remember, was seven hundred dollars. The struggle then was to make up the semi-annual payments of interest and as great an amount of the principal as we could save. It was not long before the debt was cleared off and we were property-holders, but before that was accomplished, the first sad break occurred in our family, in my father's death, October 2, 1855. Fortunately for the three remaining members life's duties were pressing. Sorrow and duty contended and we had to work. The expenses

[1] "I remember well when I used to write out the monthly pay-roll and came to Mr. Scott's name for $125. I wondered what he did with it all. I was then getting thirty-five." (Andrew Carnegie in speech at Reunion of U.S. Military Telegraph Corps, March 28, 1907.)

connected with his illness had to be saved and paid and we had not up to this time much store in reserve.

And here comes in one of the sweet incidents of our early life in America. The principal member of our small Swedenborgian Society was Mr. David McCandless. He had taken some notice of my father and mother, but beyond a few passing words at church on Sundays, I do not remember that they had ever been brought in close contact. He knew Aunt Aitken well, however, and now sent for her to say that if my mother required any money assistance at this sad period he would be very pleased to advance whatever was necessary. He had heard much of my heroic mother and that was sufficient.

One gets so many kind offers of assistance when assistance is no longer necessary, or when one is in a position which would probably enable him to repay a favor, that it is delightful to record an act of pure and disinterested benevolence. Here was a poor Scottish woman bereft of her husband, with her eldest son just getting a start and a second in his early teens, whose misfortunes appealed to this man, and who in the most delicate manner sought to mitigate them. Although my mother was able to decline the proffered aid, it is needless to say that Mr. McCandless obtained a place in our hearts sacred to himself. I am a firm believer in the doctrine that people deserving necessary assistance at critical periods in their career usually receive it. There are many splendid natures in the world — men and women who are not only willing, but anxious to stretch forth a helping hand to those they know to be worthy. As a rule, those who show willingness to help themselves need not fear about obtaining the help of others.

Father's death threw upon me the management of affairs to a greater extent than ever. Mother kept on the binding of shoes; Tom went steadily to the public school; and I continued with Mr. Scott in the service of the railroad company. Just at this time Fortunatus knocked at our door. Mr. Scott asked me if I had five hundred dollars. If so, he said he wished to make an investment for me. Five hundred cents was much nearer my capital. I certainly had not fifty dollars saved for investment, but I was not going to miss the chance of becoming financially connected with my leader and great man. So I said boldly I thought I could manage that sum. He then told me that there were ten shares of Adams Express stock that he could buy, which had belonged to a station agent, Mr. Reynolds, of Wilkinsburg. Of course this was reported to the head of the family that evening, and she was not long in suggesting what might be done. When did she ever fail? We had then paid five hundred dollars upon the house, and in some way she thought this might be pledged as security for a loan.

My mother took the steamer the next morning for East Liverpool, arriving at night, and through her brother there the money was secured. He was a justice of the peace, a well-known resident of that then small town, and had numerous sums in hand from farmers for investment. Our house was mortgaged and mother brought back the five hundred dollars which I handed over to Mr. Scott, who soon obtained for me the coveted ten shares in return. There was, unexpectedly, an additional hundred dollars to pay as a premium, but Mr. Scott kindly said I could pay that when convenient, and this of course was an easy matter to do.

This was my first investment. In those good old days

monthly dividends were more plentiful than now and Adams Express paid a monthly dividend. One morning a white envelope was lying upon my desk, addressed in a big John Hancock hand, to "Andrew Carnegie, Esquire." "Esquire" tickled the boys and me inordinately. At one corner was seen the round stamp of Adams Express Company. I opened the envelope. All it contained was a check for ten dollars upon the Gold Exchange Bank of New York. I shall remember that check as long as I live, and that John Hancock signature of "J. C. Babcock, Cashier." It gave me the first penny of revenue from capital — something that I had not worked for with the sweat of my brow. "Eureka!" I cried. "Here's the goose that lays the golden eggs."

It was the custom of our party to spend Sunday afternoons in the woods. I kept the first check and showed it as we sat under the trees in a favorite grove we had found near Wood's Run. The effect produced upon my companions was overwhelming. None of them had imagined such an investment possible. We resolved to save and to watch for the next opportunity for investment in which all of us should share, and for years afterward we divided our trifling investments and worked together almost as partners.

Up to this time my circle of acquaintances had not enlarged much. Mrs. Franciscus, wife of our freight agent, was very kind and on several occasions asked me to her house in Pittsburgh. She often spoke of the first time I rang the bell of the house in Third Street to deliver a message from Mr. Scott. She asked me to come in; I bashfully declined and it required coaxing upon her part to overcome my shyness. She was never able for years to induce me to partake of a meal in her house. I had great timidity about going into other people's houses, until late in life; but Mr. Scott would occasionally insist upon my going to his hotel and taking a meal with him, and these were great occasions for me. Mr. Franciscus's was the first considerable house, with the exception of Mr. Lombaert's at Altoona, I had ever entered, as far as I recollect. Every house was fashionable in my eyes that was upon any one of the principal streets, provided it had a hall entrance.

I had never spent a night in a strange house in my life until Mr. Stokes of Greensburg, chief counsel of the Pennsylvania Railroad, invited me to his beautiful home in the country to pass a Sunday. It was an odd thing for Mr. Stokes to do, for I could little interest a brilliant and educated man like him. The reason for my receiving such an honor was a communication I had written for the "Pittsburgh Journal." Even in my teens I was a scribbler for the press. To be an editor was one of my ambitions. Horace Greeley and the "Tribune" was my ideal of human triumph. Strange that there should have come a day when I could have bought the "Tribune"; but by that time the pearl had lost its luster. Our air castles are often within our grasp late in life, but then they charm not.

The subject of my article was upon the attitude of the city toward the Pennsylvania Railroad Company. It was signed anonymously and I was surprised to find it got a prominent place in the columns of the "Journal," then owned and edited by Robert M. Riddle. I, as operator, received a telegram addressed to Mr. Scott and signed by Mr. Stokes, asking him to ascertain from Mr. Riddle who the author of that communication was. I knew that Mr. Riddle could not tell the author, because he did not know him; but at the same time I was afraid that if Mr. Scott called upon him he would hand him the manuscript, which Mr. Scott would certainly recognize at a glance. I therefore made a clean breast of it to Mr. Scott and told him I was the author. He seemed incredulous. He said he had read it that morning and wondered who had written it. His incredulous look did not pass me unnoticed. The pen was getting to be a weapon with me. Mr. Stokes's invitation to spend Sunday with him followed soon after, and the visit is one of the bright spots in my life. Henceforth we were great friends.

The grandeur of Mr. Stokes's home impressed me, but the one feature of it that eclipsed all else was a marble mantel in his library. In the center of the arch, carved in the marble, was an open book with this inscription:

> "He that cannot reason is a fool,
> He that will not a bigot,
> He that dare not a slave."

These noble words thrilled me. I said to myself, "Some day, some day, I'll have a library" (that was a look ahead) "and these words shall grace the mantel as here." And so they do in New York and Skibo to-day.

Another Sunday which I spent at his home after an interval of several years was also noteworthy. I had then become the superintendent of the Pittsburgh Division of the Pennsylvania Railroad. The South had seceded. I was all aflame for the flag. Mr. Stokes, being a leading Democrat, argued against the right of the North to use force for the preservation of the Union. He gave vent to sentiments which caused me to lose my self-control, and I exclaimed:

"Mr. Stokes, we shall be hanging men like you in less than six weeks."

I hear his laugh as I write, and his voice calling to his wife in the adjoining room:

"Nancy, Nancy, listen to this young Scotch devil. He says they will be hanging men like me in less than six weeks."

Strange things happened in those days. A short time after, that same Mr. Stokes was applying to me in Washington to help him to a major's commission in the volunteer forces. I was then in the Secretary of War's office, helping to manage the military railroads and telegraphs for the Government. This appointment he secured and ever after was Major Stokes, so that the man who doubted the right of the North to fight for the Union had himself drawn sword in the good cause. Men at first argued and theorized about Constitutional rights. It made all the difference in the world when the flag was fired upon. In a moment everything was ablaze — paper constitutions included. The Union and Old Glory! That was all the people cared for, but that was enough. The Constitution was intended to insure one flag, and as Colonel Ingersoll proclaimed: "There was not air enough on the American continent to float two."

CHAPTER VII
Superintendent of the Pennsylvania

MR. SCOTT was promoted to be the general superintendent of the Pennsylvania Railroad in 1856, taking Mr. Lombaert's place; and he took me, then in my twenty-third year, with him to Altoona. This breaking-up of associations in Pittsburgh was a sore trial, but nothing could be allowed to interfere for a moment with my business career. My mother was satisfied upon this point, great as the strain was upon her. Besides, "follow my leader" was due to so true a friend as Mr. Scott had been.

His promotion to the superintendency gave rise to some jealousy; and besides that, he was confronted with a strike at the very beginning of his appointment. He had lost his wife in Pittsburgh a short time before and had his lonely hours. He was a stranger in Altoona, his new headquarters, and there was none but myself seemingly of whom he could make a companion. We lived for many weeks at the railway hotel together before he took up housekeeping and brought his children from Pittsburgh, and at his desire I occupied the same large bedroom with him. He seemed anxious always to have me near him.

The strike became more and more threatening. I remember being wakened one night and told that the freight-train men had left their trains at Mifflin; that the line was blocked on this account and all traffic stopped. Mr. Scott was then sleeping soundly. It seemed to me a pity to disturb him, knowing how overworked and overanxious he was; but he awoke and I suggested that I should go up and attend to the matter. He seemed to murmur assent, not being more than half awake. So I went to the office and in his name argued the question with the men and promised them a hearing next day at Altoona. I succeeded in getting them to resume their duties and to start the traffic.

Not only were the trainmen in a rebellious mood, but the men in the shops were rapidly organizing to join with the disaffected. This I learned in a curious manner. One night, as I was walking home in the dark, I became aware that a man was following me. By and by he came up to me and said:

"I must not be seen with you, but you did me a favor once and I then resolved if ever I could serve you I would do it. I called at the office in Pittsburgh and asked for work as a blacksmith. You said there was no work then at Pittsburgh, but perhaps employment could be had at Altoona, and if I would wait a few minutes you would ask by telegraph. You took the trouble to do so, examined my recommendations, and gave me a pass and sent me here. I have a splendid job. My wife and family are here and I was never so well situated in my life. And now I want to tell you something for your good."

I listened and he went on to say that a paper was being rapidly signed by the shopmen, pledging themselves to strike on Monday next. There was no time to be lost. I told Mr. Scott in the morning and he at once had printed notices posted in the shops that all men who had signed the paper, pledging themselves to strike, were dismissed and they should call at the office to be paid. A list of the names of the signers had come into our possession in the meantime, and this fact was announced. Consternation followed and the threatened strike was broken.

I have had many incidents, such as that of the blacksmith, in my life. Slight attentions or a kind word to the humble often bring back reward as great as it is unlooked for. No kind action is ever lost. Even to this day I occasionally meet men whom I had forgotten, who recall some trifling attention I have been able to pay them, especially when in charge at Washington of government railways and telegraphs during the Civil War, when I could pass people within the lines — a father helped to reach a wounded or sick son at the front, or enabled to bring home his remains, or some similar service. I am indebted to these trifles for some of the happiest attentions and the most pleasing incidents of my life. And there is this about such actions: they are disinterested, and the reward is sweet in proportion to the humbleness of the individual whom you have obliged. It counts many times more to do a kindness to a poor working-man than to a millionaire, who may be able some day to repay the favor. How true Wordsworth's lines:

> "That best portion of a good man's life —
> His little, nameless, unremembered acts
> Of kindness and of love."

The chief happening, judged by its consequences, of the two years I spent with Mr. Scott at Altoona, arose from my being the principal witness in a suit against the company, which was being tried at Greensburg by the brilliant Major Stokes, my first host. It was feared that I was about to be subpoenaed by the plaintiff, and the Major, wishing a postponement of the case, asked Mr. Scott to send me out of the State as rapidly as possible. This was a happy change for me, as I was enabled to visit my two bosom companions, Miller and Wilson, then in the railway service at Crestline, Ohio.

On my way thither, while sitting on the end seat of the rear car watching the line, a farmer-looking man approached me. He carried a small green bag in his hand. He said the brakeman had informed him I was connected with the Pennsylvania Railroad. He wished to show me the model of a car which he had invented for night traveling. He took a small model out of the bag, which showed a section of a sleeping-car.

This was the celebrated T. T. Woodruff, the inventor of that now indispensable adjunct of civilization — the sleeping-car. Its importance flashed upon me. I asked him if he would come to Altoona if I sent for him, and I promised to lay the matter before Mr. Scott at once upon my return. I could not get that sleeping-car idea out of my mind, and was most anxious to return to Altoona that I might press my views upon Mr. Scott. When I did so, he thought I was taking time by the forelock, but was quite receptive and said I might telegraph for the patentee. He came and contracted to place two of his cars upon the line as soon as they could be built. After this Mr. Woodruff, greatly to my surprise, asked me if I would not join him in the new enterprise and offered me an eighth interest in the venture.

I promptly accepted his offer, trusting to be able to make payments somehow or other. The two cars were to be paid for by monthly installments after delivery. When the time came for making the first payment, my portion was two hundred and seventeen and a half dollars. I boldly decided to apply to the local banker, Mr. Lloyd, for a loan of that sum. I explained the matter to him, and I remember that he put his great arm (he was six feet three or four) around me, saying:

"Why, of course I will lend it. You are all right, Andy."

And here I made my first note, and actually got a banker to take it. A proud moment that in a young man's career! The sleeping-cars were a great success and their monthly receipts paid the monthly installments. The first considerable sum I made was from this source. [To-day, July 19, 1909, as I re-read this, how glad I am that I have recently heard from Mr. Lloyd's married daughter telling me of her father's deep affection for me, thus making me very happy, indeed.]

One important change in our life at Altoona, after my mother and brother arrived, was that, instead of continuing to live exclusively by ourselves, it was considered necessary that we should have a servant. It was with the greatest reluctance my mother could be brought to admit a stranger into the family circle. She had been everything and had done everything for her two boys. This was her life, and she resented with all a strong woman's jealousy the introduction of a stranger who was to be permitted to do anything whatever in the home. She had cooked and served her boys, washed their clothes and mended them, made their beds, cleaned their home. Who dare rob her of those motherly privileges! But nevertheless we could not escape the inevitable servant girl. One came, and others followed, and with these came also the destruction of much of that genuine family happiness which flows from exclusiveness. Being served by others is a poor substitute for a mother's labor of love. The ostentatious meal prepared by a strange cook whom one seldom sees, and served by hands paid for the task, lacks the sweetness of that which a mother's hands lay before you as the expression and proof of her devotion.

Among the manifold blessings I have to be thankful for is that neither nurse nor governess was my companion in infancy. No wonder the children of the poor are distinguished for the warmest affection and the closest adherence to family ties and are characterized by a filial regard far stronger than that of those who are mistakenly called more fortunate in life. They have passed the impressionable years of childhood and youth in constant loving contact with father and mother, to each they are all in all, no third person coming between. The child that has in his father a teacher, companion, and counselor, and whose mother is to him a nurse, seamstress, governess, teacher, companion, heroine, and saint all in one, has a heritage to which the child of wealth remains a stranger.

There comes a time, although the fond mother cannot see it, when a grown son has to put his arms around his saint and kissing her tenderly try to explain to her that it would be much better were she to let him help her in some ways; that, being out in the world among men and dealing with affairs, he sometimes sees changes which it would be desirable to make; that the mode of life delightful for young boys should be changed in some respects and the house made suitable for their friends to enter. Especially should the slaving mother live the life of ease hereafter, reading and visiting more and entertaining dear friends — in short, rising to her proper and deserved position as Her Ladyship.

Of course the change was very hard upon my mother, but she finally recognized the necessity for it, probably realized for the first time that her eldest son was getting on. "Dear Mother," I pleaded, my arms still around her, "you have done everything for and have been everything to Tom and me, and now do let me do something for you; let us be partners and let us always think what is best for each other. The time has come for you to play the lady and some of these days you are to ride in your carriage; meanwhile do get that girl in to help you. Tom and I would like this."

The victory was won, and my mother began to go out with us and visit her neighbors. She had not to learn self-possession nor good manners, these were innate; and as for education, knowledge, rare good sense, and kindliness, seldom was she to meet her equal. I wrote "never" instead of "seldom" and then struck it out. Nevertheless my private opinion is reserved.

Life at Altoona was made more agreeable for me through Mr. Scott's niece, Miss Rebecca Stewart, who kept house for him. She played the part of elder sister to me to perfection, especially when Mr. Scott was called to Philadelphia or elsewhere. We were much together, often driving in the afternoons through the woods. The intimacy did not cease for many years, and re-reading some of her letters in 1906 I realized more than ever my indebtedness to her. She was not much beyond my own age, but always seemed a great deal older. Certainly she was more mature and quite capable of playing the elder sister's part. It was to her I looked up in those days as the perfect lady. Sorry am I our paths parted so widely in later years. Her daughter married the Earl of Sussex and her home in late years has been abroad. [July 19, 1909, Mrs. Carnegie and I found my elder-sister friend April last, now in widowhood, in Paris, her sister and also her daughter all well and happy. A great pleasure, indeed. There are no substitutes for the true friends of youth.]

Mr. Scott remained at Altoona for about three years when deserved promotion came to him. In 1859 he was made vice-president of the company, with his office in Philadelphia. What was to become of me was a serious question. Would he take me with him or must I remain at Altoona with the new official? The thought was to me unbearable. To part with Mr. Scott was hard enough; to serve a new official in his place I did not believe possible. The sun rose and set upon his head so far as I was concerned. The thought of my promotion, except through him, never entered my mind.

He returned from his interview with the president at Philadelphia and asked me to come into the private room in his house which communicated with the office. He told me it had been settled that he should remove to Philadelphia. Mr. Enoch Lewis, the division superintendent, was to be his successor. I listened with great interest as he approached the inevitable disclosure as to what he was going to do with me. He said finally:

"Now about yourself. Do you think you could manage the Pittsburgh Division?"

I was at an age when I thought I could manage anything. I knew nothing that I would not attempt, but it had never occurred to me that anybody else, much less Mr. Scott, would entertain the idea that I was as yet fit to do anything of the kind proposed. I was only twenty-four years old, but my model then was Lord John Russell, of whom it was said he would take the command of the Channel Fleet to-morrow. So would Wallace or Bruce. I told Mr. Scott I thought I could.

"Well," he said, "Mr. Potts" (who was then superintendent of the Pittsburgh Division) "is to be promoted to the transportation department in Philadelphia and I recommended you to the president as his successor. He agreed to give you a trial. What salary do you think you should have?"

"Salary," I said, quite offended; "what do I care for salary? I do not want the salary; I want the position.

It is glory enough to go back to the Pittsburgh Division in your former place. You can make my salary just what you please and you need not give me any more than what I am getting now."

That was sixty-five dollars a month.

"You know," he said, "I received fifteen hundred dollars a year when I was there; and Mr. Potts is receiving eighteen hundred. I think it would be right to start you at fifteen hundred dollars, and after a while if you succeed you will get the eighteen hundred. Would that be satisfactory?"

"Oh, please," I said, "don't speak to me of money!"

It was not a case of mere hire and salary, and then and there my promotion was sealed. I was to have a department to myself, and instead of signing "T. A. S." orders between Pittsburgh and Altoona would now be signed "A. C." That was glory enough for me.

The order appointing me superintendent of the Pittsburgh Division was issued December 1, 1859. Preparations for removing the family were made at once. The change was hailed with joy, for although our residence in Altoona had many advantages, especially as we had a large house with some ground about it in a pleasant part of the suburbs and therefore many of the pleasures of country life, all these did not weigh as a feather in the scale as against the return to old friends and associations in dirty, smoky Pittsburgh. My brother Tom had learned telegraphy during his residence in Altoona and he returned with me and became my secretary.

The winter following my appointment was one of the most severe ever known. The line was poorly constructed, the equipment inefficient and totally inadequate for the business that was crowding upon it. The rails were laid upon huge blocks of stone, cast-iron chairs for holding the rails were used, and I have known as many as forty-seven of these to break in one night. No wonder the wrecks were frequent. The superintendent of a division in those days was expected to run trains by telegraph at night, to go out and remove all wrecks, and indeed to do anything. At one time for eight days I was constantly upon the line, day and night, at one wreck or obstruction after another. I was probably the most inconsiderate superintendent that ever was entrusted with the management of a great property, for, never knowing fatigue myself, being kept up by a sense of responsibility probably, I overworked the men and was not careful enough in considering the limits of human endurance. I have always been able to sleep at any time. Snatches of half an hour at intervals during the night in a dirty freight car were sufficient.

The Civil War brought such extraordinary demands on the Pennsylvania line that I was at last compelled to organize a night force; but it was with difficulty I obtained the consent of my superiors to entrust the charge of the line at night to a train dispatcher. Indeed, I never did get their unequivocal authority to do so, but upon my own responsibility I appointed perhaps the first night train dispatcher that ever acted in America — at least he was the first upon the Pennsylvania system.

Upon our return to Pittsburgh in 1860 we rented a house in Hancock Street, now Eighth Street, and resided there for a year or more. Any accurate description of Pittsburgh at that time would be set down as a piece of the grossest exaggeration. The smoke permeated and penetrated everything. If you placed your hand on the balustrade of the stair it came away black; if you washed face and hands they were as dirty as ever in an hour. The soot gathered in the hair and irritated the skin, and

for a time after our return from the mountain atmosphere of Altoona, life was more or less miserable. We
soon began to consider how we could get to the country, and fortunately at that time Mr. D. A. Stewart, then
freight agent for the company, directed our attention
to a house adjoining his residence at Homewood. We
moved there at once and the telegraph was brought
in, which enabled me to operate the division from the
house when necessary.

Here a new life was opened to us. There were country
lanes and gardens in abundance. Residences had from
five to twenty acres of land about them. The Homewood
Estate was made up of many hundreds of acres, with
beautiful woods and glens and a running brook. We, too,
had a garden and a considerable extent of ground around
our house. The happiest years of my mother's life were
spent here among her flowers and chickens and the surroundings of country life. Her love of flowers was a passion. She was scarcely ever able to gather a flower. Indeed I remember she once reproached me for pulling up
a weed, saying "it was something green." I have inherited
this peculiarity and have often walked from the house
to the gate intending to pull a flower for my button-hole
and then left for town unable to find one I could destroy.

With this change to the country came a whole host
of new acquaintances. Many of the wealthy families of
the district had their residences in this delightful sub-
urb. It was, so to speak, the aristocratic quarter. To the
entertainments at these great houses the young superintendent was invited. The young people were musical and we had musical evenings a plenty. I heard subjects discussed which I had never known before, and
I made it a rule when I heard these to learn something

about them at once. I was pleased every day to feel that I
was learning something new.

It was here that I first met the Vandevort brothers, Benjamin and John. The latter was my traveling-companion
on various trips which I took later in life. "Dear Vandy" appears as my chum in "Round the World." Our neighbors,
Mr. and Mrs. Stewart, became more and more dear to us,
and the acquaintance we had before ripened into lasting
friendship. One of my pleasures is that Mr. Stewart subsequently embarked in business with us and became a partner, as "Vandy" did also. Greatest of all the benefits of our
new home, however, was making the acquaintance of the
leading family of Western Pennsylvania, that of the Honorable Judge Wilkins. The Judge was then approaching
his eightieth year, tall, slender, and handsome, in full possession of all his faculties, with a courtly grace of manner,
and the most wonderful store of knowledge and reminis-
cence of any man I had yet been privileged to meet. His
wife, the daughter of George W. Dallas, Vice-President
of the United States, has ever been my type of gracious
womanhood in age — the most beautiful, most charming
venerable old lady I ever knew or saw. Her daughter, Miss
Wilkins, with her sister, Mrs. Saunders, and her children
resided in the stately mansion at Homewood, which was
to the surrounding district what the baronial hall in Britain is or should be to its district — the center of all that
was cultured, refined, and elevating.

To me it was especially pleasing that I seemed to be
a welcome guest there. Musical parties, charades, and
theatricals in which Miss Wilkins took the leading parts
furnished me with another means of self-improvement.
The Judge himself was the first man of historical note
whom I had ever known. I shall never forget the im-

pression it made upon me when in the course of conversation, wishing to illustrate a remark, he said: "President Jackson once said to me," or, "I told the Duke of Wellington so and so." The Judge in his earlier life (1834) had been Minister to Russia under Jackson, and in the same easy way spoke of his interview with the Czar. It seemed to me that I was touching history itself. The house was a new atmosphere, and my intercourse with the family was a powerful stimulant to the desire for improvement of my mind and manners.

The only subject upon which there was always a decided, though silent, antagonism between the Wilkins family and myself was politics. I was an ardent Free-Soiler in days when to be an abolitionist was somewhat akin to being a republican in Britain. The Wilkinses were strong Democrats with leanings toward the South, being closely connected with leading Southern families. On one occasion at Homewood, on entering the drawing-room, I found the family excitedly conversing about a terrible incident that had recently occurred.

"What do you think!" said Mrs. Wilkins to me; "Dallas" (her grandson) "writes me that he has been compelled by the commandant of West Point to sit next a negro! Did you ever hear the like of that? Is it not disgraceful? Negroes admitted to West Point!"

"Oh!" I said, "Mrs. Wilkins, there is something even worse than that. I understand that some of them have been admitted to heaven!"

There was a silence that could be felt. Then dear Mrs. Wilkins said gravely:

"That is a different matter, Mr. Carnegie."

By far the most precious gift ever received by me up to that time came about in this manner. Dear Mrs. Wilkins began knitting an afghan, and during the work many were the inquiries as to whom it was for. No, the dear queenly old lady would not tell; she kept her secret all the long months until, Christmas drawing near, the gift finished and carefully wrapped up, and her card with a few loving words enclosed, she instructed her daughter to address it to me. It was duly received in New York. Such a tribute from such a lady! Well, that afghan, though often shown to dear friends, has not been much used. It is sacred to me and remains among my precious possessions.

I had been so fortunate as to meet Leila Addison while living in Pittsburgh, the talented daughter of Dr. Addison, who had died a short time before. I soon became acquainted with the family and record with grateful feelings the immense advantage which that acquaintance also brought to me. Here was another friendship formed with people who had all the advantages of the higher education. Carlyle had been Mrs. Addison's tutor for a time, for she was an Edinburgh lady. Her daughters had been educated abroad and spoke French, Spanish, and Italian as fluently as English. It was through intercourse with this family that I first realized the indescribable yet immeasurable gulf that separates the highly educated from people like myself. But "the wee drap o' Scotch bluid atween us" proved its potency as usual.

Miss Addison became an ideal friend because she undertook to improve the rough diamond, if it were indeed a diamond at all. She was my best friend, because my severest critic. I began to pay strict attention to my language, and to the English classics, which I now read with great avidity. I began also to notice how much better it was to be gentle in tone and manner, polite and courteous to all — in short, better behaved. Up to this time I had been, perhaps, careless in dress and rather affected it. Great heavy boots, loose collar, and general roughness of attire were then peculiar to the West and in our circle considered manly. Anything that could be labeled foppish was looked upon with contempt. I remember the first gentleman I ever saw in the service of the railway company who wore kid gloves. He was the object of derision among us who aspired to be manly men. I was a great deal the better in all these respects after we moved to Homewood, owing to the Addisons.

CHAPTER VIII
Civil War Period

IN 1861 the Civil War broke out and I was at once summoned to Washington by Mr. Scott, who had been appointed Assistant Secretary of War in charge of the Transportation Department. I was to act as his assistant in charge of the military railroads and telegraphs of the Government and to organize a force of railway men. It was one of the most important departments of all at the beginning of the war.

The first regiments of Union troops passing through Baltimore had been attacked, and the railway line cut between Baltimore and Annapolis Junction, destroying communication with Washington. It was therefore necessary for me, with my corps of assistants, to take train at Philadelphia for Annapolis, a point from which a branch line extended to the Junction, joining the main line to Washington. Our first duty was to repair this branch and make it passable for heavy trains, a work of some days. General Butler and several regiments of troops arrived a few days after us, and we were able to transport his whole brigade to Washington.

I took my place upon the first engine which started for the Capital, and proceeded very cautiously. Some distance from Washington I noticed that the telegraph wires had been pinned to the ground by wooden stakes. I stopped the engine and ran forward to release them, but I did not notice that the wires had been pulled to one side before staking. When released, in their spring upwards, they struck me in the face, knocked me over, and cut a gash in my cheek which bled profusely. In this condition I entered the city of Washington with the first troops, so that with the exception of one or two soldiers, wounded a few days previously in passing through the streets of Baltimore, I can justly claim that I "shed my blood for my country" among the first of its defenders. I gloried in being useful to the land that had done so much for me, and worked, I can truly say, night and day, to open communication to the South.

I soon removed my headquarters to Alexandria,[1] Virginia, and was stationed there when the unfortunate battle of Bull Run was fought. We could not believe the reports that came to us, but it soon became evident that we must rush every engine and car to the front to bring back our defeated forces. The closest point then was Burke Station. I went out there and loaded up train after train of the poor wounded volunteers. The rebels were reported to be close upon us and we were finally compelled to close Burke Station, the operator and myself leaving on the last train for Alexandria where the effect of panic was evident upon every side. Some of our railway men were missing, but the number at the mess on the following morning showed that, compared with other branches of the service, we had cause for congratulation. A few conductors and engineers had obtained boats and crossed the Potomac, but the great body of

[1] "When Carnegie reached Washington his first task was to establish a ferry to Alexandria and to extend the Baltimore and Ohio Railroad track from the old depot in Washington, along Maryland Avenue to and across the Potomac, so that locomotives and cars might be crossed for use in Virginia. Long Bridge, over the Potomac, had to be rebuilt, and I recall the fact that under the direction of Carnegie and R. F. Morley the railroad between Washington and Alexandria was completed in the remarkably short period of seven days. All hands, from Carnegie down, worked day and night to accomplish the task." (Bates, *Lincoln in the Telegraph Office*, p. 22. New York, 1907.)

the men remained, although the roar of the guns of the pursuing enemy was supposed to be heard in every sound during the night. Of our telegraphers not one was missing the next morning.

Soon after this I returned to Washington and made my headquarters in the War Building with Colonel Scott. As I had charge of the telegraph department, as well as the railways, this gave me an opportunity of seeing President Lincoln, Mr. Seward, Secretary Cameron, and others; and I was occasionally brought in personal contact with these men, which was to me a source of great interest. Mr. Lincoln would occasionally come to the office and sit at the desk awaiting replies to telegrams, or perhaps merely anxious for information.

All the pictures of this extraordinary man are like him. He was so marked of feature that it was impossible for anyone to paint him and not produce a likeness. He was certainly one of the most homely men I ever saw when his features were in repose; but when excited or telling a story, intellect shone through his eyes and illuminated his face to a degree which I have seldom or never seen in any other. His manners were perfect because natural; and he had a kind word for everybody, even the youngest boy in the office. His attentions were not graduated. They were the same to all, as deferential in talking to the messenger boy as to Secretary Seward. His charm lay in the total absence of manner. It was not so much, perhaps, what he said as the way in which he said it that never failed to win one. I have often regretted that I did not note down carefully at the time some of his curious sayings, for he said even common things in an original way. I never met a great man who so thoroughly made himself one with all men as Mr. Lincoln. As Secretary Hay so well says, "It is impossible to imagine anyone a valet to Mr. Lincoln; he would have been his companion." He was the most perfect democrat, revealing in every word and act the equality of men.

When Mason and Slidell in 1861 were taken from the British ship Trent there was intense anxiety upon the part of those who, like myself, knew what the right of asylum on her ships meant to Britain. It was certain war or else a prompt return of the prisoners. Secretary Cameron being absent when the Cabinet was summoned to consider the question, Mr. Scott was invited to attend as Assistant Secretary of War. I did my best to let him understand that upon this issue Britain would fight beyond question, and urged that he stand firm for surrender, especially since it had been the American doctrine that ships should be immune from search. Mr. Scott, knowing nothing of foreign affairs, was disposed to hold the captives, but upon his return from the meeting he told me that Seward had warned the Cabinet it meant war, just as I had said. Lincoln, too, was at first inclined to hold the prisoners, but was at last converted to Seward's policy. The Cabinet, however, had decided to postpone action until the morrow, when Cameron and other absentees would be present. Mr. Scott was requested by Seward to meet Cameron on arrival and get him right on the subject before going to the meeting, for he was expected to be in no surrendering mood. This was done and all went well next day.

The general confusion which reigned at Washington at this time had to be seen to be understood. No description can convey my initial impression of it. The first time I saw General Scott, then Commander-in-Chief, he was being helped by two men across the pavement from his office into his carriage. He was an old, decrepit man, paralyzed not only in body, but in mind; and it was upon this noble relic of the past that the organization of the forces of the Republic depended. His chief commissary, General Taylor, was in some degree a counterpart of Scott. It was our business to arrange with these, and others scarcely less fit, for the opening of communications and for the transportation of men and supplies. They were seemingly one and all martinets who had passed the age of usefulness. Days would elapse before a decision could be obtained upon matters which required prompt action. There was scarcely a young active officer at the head of any important department — at least I cannot recall one. Long years of peace had fossilized the service.

The same cause had produced like results, I understood, in the Navy Department, but I was not brought in personal contact with it. The navy was not important at the beginning, it was the army that counted. Nothing but defeat was to be looked for until the heads of the various departments were changed, and this could not be done in a day. The impatience of the country at the apparent delay in producing an effective weapon for the great task thrown upon the Government was no doubt natural, but the wonder to me is that order was so soon evolved from the chaos which prevailed in every branch of the service.

As far as our operations were concerned we had one great advantage. Secretary Cameron authorized Mr. Scott (he had been made a Colonel) to do what he thought necessary without waiting for the slow movements of the officials under the Secretary of War. Of this authority unsparing use was made, and the important part played by the railway and telegraph department of the Government from the very beginning of the war is to be attributed to the fact that we had the cordial support of Secretary Cameron. He was then in the possession of all his faculties and grasped the elements of the problem far better than his generals and heads of departments. Popular clamor compelled Lincoln to change him at last, but those who were behind the scenes well knew that if other departments had been as well managed as was the War Department under Cameron, all things considered, much of disaster would have been avoided.

Lochiel, as Cameron liked to be called, was a man of sentiment. In his ninetieth year he visited us in Scotland and, passing through one of our glens, sitting on the front seat of our four-in-hand coach, he reverently took off his hat and bareheaded rode through the glen, overcome by its grandeur. The conversation turned once upon the efforts which candidates for office must themselves put forth and the fallacy that office seeks the man, except in very rare emergencies. Apropos of this Lochiel told this story about Lincoln's second term:

One day at Cameron's country home near Harrisburg, Pennsylvania, he received a telegram saying that President Lincoln would like to see him. Accordingly he went to Washington. Lincoln began:

"Cameron, the people about me are telling me that it is my patriotic duty to become a candidate for a second term, that I am the only man who can save my country, and so on; and do you know I'm just beginning to be fool enough to believe them a little. What do you say, and how could it be managed?"

"Well, Mr. President, twenty-eight years ago President Jackson sent for me as you have now done and told me just the same story. His letter reached me in New Orleans and I traveled ten days to reach Washington.

I told President Jackson I thought the best plan would be to have the Legislature of one of the States pass resolutions insisting that the pilot should not desert the ship during these stormy times, and so forth. If one State did this I thought others would follow. Mr. Jackson concurred and I went to Harrisburg, and had such a resolution prepared and passed. Other States followed as I expected and, as you know, he won a second term."

"Well," said Lincoln, "could you do that now?"

"No," said I, "I am too near to you, Mr. President; but if you desire I might get a friend to attend to it, I think."

"Well," said President Lincoln, "I leave the matter with you."

"I sent for Foster here" (who was his companion on the coach and our guest) "and asked him to look up the Jackson resolutions. We changed them a little to meet new conditions and passed them. The like result followed as in the case of President Jackson. Upon my next visit to Washington I went in the evening to the President's public reception. When I entered the crowded and spacious East Room, being like Lincoln very tall, the President recognized me over the mass of people and holding up both white-gloved hands which looked like two legs of mutton, called out: 'Two more in to-day, Cameron, two more.' That is, two additional States had passed the Jackson-Lincoln resolutions."

Apart from the light this incident throws upon political life, it is rather remarkable that the same man should have been called upon by two presidents of the United States, twenty-eight years apart, under exactly similar circumstances and asked for advice, and that, the same expedient being employed, both men became candidates and both secured second terms. As was once explained upon a memorable occasion: "There's figuring in all them things."

When in Washington I had not met General Grant, because he was in the West up to the time of my leaving, but on a journey to and from Washington he stopped at Pittsburgh to make the necessary arrangements for his removal to the East. I met him on the line upon both occasions and took him to dine with me in Pittsburgh. There were no dining-cars then. He was the most ordinary-looking man of high position I had ever met, and the last that one would select at first glance as a remarkable man. I remember that Secretary of War Stanton said that when he visited the armies in the West, General Grant and his staff entered his car; he looked at them, one after the other, as they entered and seeing General Grant, said to himself, "Well, I do not know which is General Grant, but there is one that cannot be." Yet this was he. [Reading this years after it was written, I laugh. It is pretty hard on the General, for I have been taken for him more than once.]

In those days of the war much was talked about "strategy" and the plans of the various generals. I was amazed at General Grant's freedom in talking to me about such things. Of course he knew that I had been in the War Office, and was well known to Secretary Stanton,[1] and had some knowledge of what was going on; but my surprise can be imagined when he said to me:

"Well, the President and Stanton want me to go East and take command there, and I have agreed to

[1] Mr. Carnegie gave to Stanton's college, Kenyon, $80,000, and on April 26, 1906, delivered at the college an address on the great War Secretary. It has been published under the title *Edwin M. Stanton, an Address by Andrew Carnegie on Stanton Memorial Day at Kenyon College.* (New York, 1906.)

do it. I am just going West to make the necessary arrangements."

I said, "I suspected as much."

"I am going to put Sherman in charge," he said.

"That will surprise the country," I said, "for I think the impression is that General Thomas should succeed."

"Yes, I know that," he said, "but I know the men and Thomas will be the first to say that Sherman is the man for the work. There will be no trouble about that. The fact is the western end is pretty far down, and the next thing we must do is to push the eastern end down a little."

That was exactly what he did. And that was Grant's way of putting strategy into words. It was my privilege to become well acquainted with him in after years. If ever a man was without the slightest trace of affectation, Grant was that man. Even Lincoln did not surpass him in that: but Grant was a quiet, slow man while Lincoln was always alive and in motion. I never heard Grant use a long or grand word, or make any attempt at "manner," but the general impression that he was always reticent is a mistake. He was a surprisingly good talker sometimes and upon occasion liked to talk. His sentences were always short and to the point, and his observations upon things remarkably shrewd. When he had nothing to say he said nothing. I noticed that he was never tired of praising his subordinates in the war. He spoke of them as a fond father speaks of his children.

The story is told that during the trials of war in the West, General Grant began to indulge too freely in liquor. His chief of staff, Rawlins, boldly ventured to tell him so. That this was the act of a true friend Grant fully recognized.

"You do not mean that? I was wholly unconscious of it. I am surprised!" said the General.

"Yes, I do mean it. It is even beginning to be a subject of comment among your officers."

"Why did you not tell me before? I'll never drink a drop of liquor again."

He never did. Time after time in later years, dining with the Grants in New York, I have seen the General turn down the wine-glasses at his side. That indomitable will of his enabled him to remain steadfast to his resolve, a rare case as far as my experience goes. Some have refrained for a time. In one noted case one of our partners refrained for three years, but alas, the old enemy at last recaptured its victim.

Grant, when President, was accused of being pecuniarily benefited by certain appointments, or acts, of his administration, while his friends knew that he was so poor that he had been compelled to announce his intention of abandoning the customary state dinners, each one of which, he found, cost eight hundred dollars — a sum which he could not afford to pay out of his salary. The increase of the presidential salary from $25,000 to $50,000 a year enabled him, during his second term, to save a little, although he cared no more about money than about uniforms. At the end of his first term I know he had nothing. Yet I found, when in Europe, that the impression was widespread among the highest officials there that there was something in the charge that General Grant had benefited pecuniarily by appointments. We know in America how little weight to attach to these charges, but it would have been well for those who made them so recklessly to have considered what effect they would produce upon public opinion in other lands.

The cause of democracy suffers more in Britain to-day from the generally received opinion that American politics are corrupt, and therefore that republicanism necessarily produces corruption, than from any other one cause. Yet, speaking with some knowledge of politics in both lands, I have not the slightest hesitation in saying that for every ounce of corruption of public men in the new land of republicanism there is one in the old land of monarchy, only the forms of corruption differ. Titles are the bribes in the monarchy, not dollars. Office is a common and proper reward in both. There is, however, this difference in favor of the monarchy; titles are given openly and are not considered by the recipients or the mass of the people as bribes.

When I was called to Washington in 1861, it was supposed that the war would soon be over; but it was seen shortly afterwards that it was to be a question of years. Permanent officials in charge would be required. The Pennsylvania Railroad Company was unable to spare Mr. Scott, and Mr. Scott, in turn, decided that I must return to Pittsburgh, where my services were urgently needed, owing to the demands made upon the Pennsylvania by the Government. We therefore placed the department at Washington in the hands of others and returned to our respective positions.

After my return from Washington reaction followed and I was taken with my first serious illness. I was completely broken down, and after a struggle to perform my duties was compelled to seek rest. One afternoon, when on the railway line in Virginia, I had experienced something like a sunstroke, which gave me considerable trouble. It passed off, however, but after that I found I could not stand heat and had to be careful to keep out of the sun — a hot day wilting me completely. [That is the reason why the cool Highland air in summer has been to me a panacea for many years. My physician has insisted that I must avoid our hot American summers.]

Leave of absence was granted me by the Pennsylvania Railroad Company, and the long-sought opportunity to visit Scotland came. My mother, my bosom friend Tom Miller, and myself, sailed in the steamship Etna, June 28, 1862, I in my twenty-seventh year; and on landing in Liverpool we proceeded at once to Dunfermline. No change ever affected me so much as this return to my native land. I seemed to be in a dream. Every mile that brought us nearer to Scotland increased the intensity of my feelings. My mother was equally moved, and I remember, when her eyes first caught sight of the familiar yellow bush, she exclaimed:

"Oh! there's the broom, the broom!"

Her heart was so full she could not restrain her tears, and the more I tried to make light of it or to soothe her, the more she was overcome. For myself, I felt as if I could throw myself upon the sacred soil and kiss it.[1]

In this mood we reached Dunfermline. Every object we passed was recognized at once, but everything seemed so small, compared with what I had imagined it, that I was completely puzzled. Finally, reaching Uncle Lauder's and getting into the old room where he had taught Dod and myself so many things, I exclaimed:

"You are all here; everything is just as I left it, but you are now all playing with toys."

---

[1] "It's a God's mercy I was born a Scotchman, for I do not see how I could ever have been contented to be anything else. The little dour deevil, set in her own ways, and getting them, too, level-headed and shrewd, with an eye to the main chance always and yet so lovingly weak, so fond, so led away by song or story, so easily touched to fine issues, so leal, so true. Ah! you suit me, Scotia, and proud am I that I am your son." (Andrew Carnegie, *Our Coaching Trip*, p. 152. New York, 1882.)

The High Street, which I had considered not a bad Broadway, uncle's shop, which I had compared with some New York establishments, the little mounds about the town, to which we had run on Sundays to play, the distances, the height of the houses, all had shrunk. Here was a city of the Lilliputians. I could almost touch the eaves of the house in which I was born, and the sea — to walk to which on a Saturday had been considered quite a feat — was only three miles distant. The rocks at the seashore, among which I had gathered wilks (whelks) seemed to have vanished, and a tame flat shoal remained. The schoolhouse, around which had centered many of my schoolboy recollections — my only Alma Mater — and the playground, upon which mimic battles had been fought and races run, had shrunk into ridiculously small dimensions. The fine residences, Broomhall, Fordell, and especially the conservatories at Donibristle, fell one after the other into the petty and insignificant. What I felt on a later occasion on a visit to Japan, with its small toy houses, was something like a repetition of the impression my old home made upon me.

Everything was there in miniature. Even the old well at the head of Moodie Street, where I began my early struggles, was changed from what I had pictured it. But one object remained all that I had dreamed of it. There was no disappointment in the glorious old Abbey and its Glen. It was big enough and grand enough, and the memorable carved letters on the top of the tower — "King Robert The Bruce" — filled my eye and my heart as fully as of old. Nor was the Abbey bell disappointing, when I heard it for the first time after my return. For this I was grateful. It gave me a rallying point, and around the old Abbey, with its Palace ruins and the

Glen, other objects adjusted themselves in their true proportions after a time.

My relatives were exceedingly kind, and the oldest of all, my dear old Auntie Charlotte, in a moment of exultation exclaimed:

"Oh, you will just be coming back here some day and *keep a shop in the High Street.*"

To keep a shop in the High Street was her idea of triumph. Her son-in-law and daughter, both my full cousins, though unrelated to each other, had risen to this sublime height, and nothing was too great to predict for her promising nephew. There is an aristocracy even in shopkeeping, and the family of the greengrocer of the High Street mingles not upon equal terms with him of Moodie Street.

Auntie, who had often played my nurse, liked to dwell upon the fact that I was a screaming infant that had to be fed with two spoons, as I yelled whenever one left my mouth. Captain Jones, our superintendent of the steel works at a later day, described me as having been born "with two rows of teeth and holes punched for more," so insatiable was my appetite for new works and increased production. As I was the first child in our immediate family circle, there were plenty of now venerable relatives begging to be allowed to play nurse, my aunties among them. Many of my childhood pranks and words they told me in their old age. One of them that the aunties remembered struck me as rather precocious.

I had been brought up upon wise saws and one that my father had taught me was soon given direct application. As a boy, returning from the seashore three miles distant, he had to carry me part of the way upon his back. Going up a steep hill in the gloaming he remarked upon the heavy load, hoping probably I would propose to walk a bit. The response, however, which he received was:

"Ah, faither, never mind, patience and perseverance make the man, ye ken."

He toiled on with his burden, but shaking with laughter. He was hoist with his own petard, but his burden grew lighter all the same. I am sure of this.

My home, of course, was with my instructor, guide, and inspirer, Uncle Lauder — he who had done so much to make me romantic, patriotic, and poetical at eight. Now I was twenty-seven, but Uncle Lauder still remained Uncle Lauder. He had not shrunk, no one could fill his place. We had our walks and talks constantly and I was "Naig" again to him. He had never had any name for me but that and never did have. My dear, dear uncle, and more, much more than uncle to me.[1]

I was still dreaming and so excited that I could not sleep and had caught cold in the bargain. The natural result of this was a fever. I lay in uncle's house for six weeks, a part of that time in a critical condition. Scottish medicine was then as stern as Scottish theology (both are now much softened), and I was bled. My thin American blood was so depleted that when I was pronounced convalescent it was long before I could stand upon my feet. This illness put an end to my visit, but by the time I had reached America again, the ocean voyage had done me so much good I was able to resume work.

I remember being deeply affected by the reception I met with when I returned to my division. The men of the eastern end had gathered together with a cannon and while the train passed I was greeted with a salvo.

[1] "This uncle, who loved liberty because it is the heritage of brave souls, in the dark days of the American Civil War stood almost alone in his community for the cause which Lincoln represented." (Hamilton Wright Mabie in *Century Magazine*, vol. 64, p. 958.)

This was perhaps the first occasion upon which my subordinates had an opportunity of making me the subject of any demonstration, and their reception made a lasting impression. I knew how much I cared for them and it was pleasing to know that they reciprocated my feelings. Working-men always do reciprocate kindly feeling. If we truly care for others we need not be anxious about their feelings for us. Like draws to like.

CHAPTER IX
Bridge-Building

DURING the Civil War the price of iron went up to something like $130 per ton. Even at that figure it was not so much a question of money as of delivery. The railway lines of America were fast becoming dangerous for want of new rails, and this state of affairs led me to organize in 1864 a rail-making concern at Pittsburgh. There was no difficulty in obtaining partners and capital, and the Superior Rail Mill and Blast Furnaces were built.

In like manner the demand for locomotives was very great, and with Mr. Thomas N. Miller[1] I organized in 1866 the Pittsburgh Locomotive Works, which has been a prosperous and creditable concern — locomotives made there having obtained an enviable reputation throughout the United States. It sounds like a fairy tale to-day to record that in 1906 the one-hundred-dollar shares of this company sold for three thousand dollars — that is, thirty dollars for one. Large annual dividends had been paid regularly and the company had been very successful — sufficient proof of the policy: "Make nothing but the very best." We never did.

When at Altoona I had seen in the Pennsylvania Railroad Company's works the first small bridge built of iron. It proved a success. I saw that it would never do to depend further upon wooden bridges for permanent

---

[1] Mr. Carnegie had previous to this — as early as 1861 — been associated with Mr. Miller in the Sun City Forge Company, doing a small iron business.

railway structures. An important bridge on the Pennsylvania Railroad had recently burned and the traffic had been obstructed for eight days. Iron was the thing. I proposed to H. J. Linville, who had designed the iron bridge, and to John L. Piper and his partner, Mr. Schiffler, who had charge of bridges on the Pennsylvania line, that they should come to Pittsburgh and I would organize a company to build iron bridges. It was the first company of its kind. I asked my friend, Mr. Scott, of the Pennsylvania Railroad, to go with us in the venture, which he did. Each of us paid for a one fifth interest, or $1250. My share I borrowed from the bank. Looking back at it now the sum seemed very small, but "tall oaks from little acorns grow."

In this way was organized in 1862 the firm of Piper and Schiffler which was merged into the Keystone Bridge Company in 1863 — a name which I remember I was proud of having thought of as being most appropriate for a bridge-building concern in the State of Pennsylvania, the Keystone State. From this beginning iron bridges came generally into use in America, indeed, in the world at large so far as I know. My letters to iron manufacturers in Pittsburgh were sufficient to insure the new company credit. Small wooden shops were erected and several bridge structures were undertaken. Cast-iron was the principal material used, but so well were the bridges built that some made at that day and since strengthened for heavier traffic, still remain in use upon various lines.

The question of bridging the Ohio River at Steubenville came up, and we were asked whether we would undertake to build a railway bridge with a span of three hundred feet over the channel. It seems ridiculous at the present day to think of the serious doubts entertained about our ability to do this; but it must be remembered this was before the days of steel and almost before the use of wrought-iron in America. The top cords and supports were all of cast-iron. I urged my partners to try it anyhow, and we finally closed a contract, but I remember well when President Jewett[1] of the railway company visited the works and cast his eyes upon the piles of heavy cast-iron lying about, which were parts of the forthcoming bridge, that he turned to me and said:

"I don't believe these heavy castings can be made to stand up and carry themselves, much less carry a train across the Ohio River."

The Judge, however, lived to believe differently. The bridge remained until recently, though strengthened to carry heavier traffic. We expected to make quite a sum by this first important undertaking, but owing to the inflation of the currency, which occurred before the work was finished, our margin of profit was almost swallowed up. It is an evidence of the fairness of President Edgar Thomson, of the Pennsylvania that, upon learning the facts of the case, he allowed an extra sum to secure us from loss. The subsequent position of affairs, he said, was not contemplated by either party when the contract was made. A great and a good man was Edgar Thomson, a close bargainer for the Pennsylvania Railroad, but ever mindful of the fact that the spirit of the law was above the letter.

In Linville, Piper, and Schiffler, we had the best talent of that day—Linville an engineer, Piper a hustling, active mechanic, and Schiffler sure and steady. Colonel Piper was an exceptional man. I heard President Thomson of the Pennsylvania once say he would rather have him at a burnt bridge than all the

[1] Thomas L. Jewett, President of the Panhandle.

engineering corps. There was one subject upon which the Colonel displayed great weakness (fortunately for us) and that was the horse. Whenever a business discussion became too warm, and the Colonel showed signs of temper, which was not seldom, it was a sure cure to introduce that subject. Everything else would pass from his mind; he became absorbed in the fascinating topic of horseflesh. If he had overworked himself, and we wished to get him to take a holiday, we sent him to Kentucky to look after a horse or two that one or the other of us was desirous of obtaining, and for the selection of which we would trust no one but himself. But his craze for horses sometimes brought him into serious difficulties. He made his appearance at the office one day with one half of his face as black as mud could make it, his clothes torn, and his hat missing, but still holding the whip in one hand. He explained that he had attempted to drive a fast Kentucky colt; one of the reins had broken and he had lost his "steerage-way," as he expressed it.

He was a grand fellow, "Pipe" as we called him, and when he took a fancy to a person, as he did to me, he was for and with him always. In later days when I removed to New York he transferred his affections to my brother, whom he invariably called Thomas, instead of Tom. High as I stood in his favor, my brother afterwards stood higher. He fairly worshiped him, and anything that Tom said was law and gospel. He was exceedingly jealous of our other establishments, in which he was not directly interested, such as our mills which supplied the Keystone Works with iron. Many a dispute arose between the mill managers and the Colonel as to quality, price, and so forth. On one occasion he came to my brother to complain that a bargain which he had made for the supply of iron for a year had not been copied correctly. The prices were "net," and nothing had been said about "net" when the bargain was made. He wanted to know just what that word "net" meant.

"Well, Colonel," said my brother, "it means that nothing more is to be added."

"All right, Thomas," said the Colonel, entirely satisfied.

There is much in the way one puts things. "Nothing to be deducted" might have caused a dispute.

He was made furious one day by Bradstreet's volume which gives the standing of business concerns. Never having seen such a book before, he was naturally anxious to see what rating his concern had. When he read that the Keystone Bridge Works were "BC," which meant "Bad Credit," it was with difficulty he was restrained from going to see our lawyers to have a suit brought against the publishers. Tom, however, explained to him that the Keystone Bridge Works were in bad credit because they never borrowed anything, and he was pacified. No debt was one of the Colonel's hobbies. Once, when I was leaving for Europe, when many firms were hard up and some failing around us, he said to me:

"The sheriff can't get us when you are gone if I don't sign any notes, can he?"

"No," I said, "he can't."

"All right, we'll be here when you come back."

Talking of the Colonel reminds me of another unusual character with whom we were brought in contact in these bridge-building days. This was Captain Eads, of St. Louis,[1] an original genius *minus* scientific knowledge to guide his erratic ideas of things mechanical.

---

[1] Captain James B. Eads, afterward famous for his jetty system in the Mississippi River.

He was seemingly one of those who wished to have everything done upon his own original plans. That a thing had been done in one way before was sufficient to cause its rejection. When his plans for the St. Louis Bridge were presented to us, I handed them to the one man in the United States who knew the subject best — our Mr. Linville. He came to me in great concern, saying:

"The bridge if built upon these plans will not stand up; it will not carry its own weight."

"Well," I said, "Captain Eads will come to see you and in talking over matters explain this to him gently, get it into proper shape, lead him into the straight path and say nothing about it to others."

This was successfully accomplished; but in the construction of the bridge poor Piper was totally unable to comply with the extraordinary requirements of the Captain. At first he was so delighted with having received the largest contract that had yet been let that he was all graciousness to Captain Eads. It was not even "Captain" at first, but "'Colonel' Eads, how do you do? Delighted to see you." By and by matters became a little complicated. We noticed that the greeting became less cordial, but still it was "Good-morning, Captain Eads." This fell till we were surprised to hear "Pipe" talking of "Mr. Eads." Before the troubles were over, the "Colonel" had fallen to "Jim Eads," and to tell the truth, long before the work was out of the shops, "Jim" was now and then preceded by a big "D." A man may be possessed of great ability, and be a charming, interesting character, as Captain Eads undoubtedly was, and yet not be able to construct the first bridge of five hundred feet span over the Mississippi River,[1] without

[1] The span was 515 feet, and at that time considered the finest metal arch in the world.

availing himself of the scientific knowledge and practical experience of others.

When the work was finished, I had the Colonel with me in St. Louis for some days protecting the bridge against a threatened attempt on the part of others to take possession of it before we obtained full payment. When the Colonel had taken up the planks at both ends, and organized a plan of relieving the men who stood guard, he became homesick and exceedingly anxious to return to Pittsburgh. He had determined to take the night train and I was at a loss to know how to keep him with me until I thought of his one vulnerable point. I told him, during the day, how anxious I was to obtain a pair of horses for my sister. I wished to make her a present of a span, and I had heard that St. Louis was a noted place for them. Had he seen anything superb?

The bait took. He launched forth into a description of several spans of horses he had seen and stables he had visited. I asked him if he could possibly stay over and select the horses. I knew very well that he would wish to see them and drive them many times which would keep him busy. It happened just as I expected. He purchased a splendid pair, but then another difficulty occurred about transporting them to Pittsburgh. He would not trust them by rail and no suitable boat was to leave for several days. Providence was on my side evidently. Nothing on earth would induce that man to leave the city until he saw those horses fairly started and it was an even wager whether he would not insist upon going up on the steamer with them himself. We held the bridge. "Pipe" made a splendid Horatius. He was one of the best men and one of the most valuable partners I ever was favored with, and richly deserved the rewards which he did so much to secure.

The Keystone Bridge Works have always been a source of satisfaction to me. Almost every concern that had undertaken to erect iron bridges in America had failed. Many of the structures themselves had fallen and some of the worst railway disasters in America had been caused in that way. Some of the bridges had given way under wind pressure but nothing has ever happened to a Keystone bridge, and some of them have stood where the wind was not tempered. There has been no luck about it. We used only the best material and enough of it, making our own iron and later our own steel. We were our own severest inspectors, and would build a safe structure or none at all. When asked to build a bridge which we knew to be of insufficient strength or of unscientific design, we resolutely declined. Any piece of work bearing the stamp of the Keystone Bridge Works (and there are few States in the Union where such are not to be found) we were prepared to underwrite. We were as proud of our bridges as Carlyle was of the bridge his father built across the Annan. "An honest brig," as the great son rightly said.

This policy is the true secret of success. Uphill work it will be for a few years until your work is proven, but after that it is smooth sailing. Instead of objecting to inspectors they should be welcomed by all manufacturing establishments. A high standard of excellence is easily maintained, and men are educated in the effort to reach excellence. I have never known a concern to make a decided success that did not do good, honest work, and even in these days of the fiercest competition, when everything would seem to be a matter of price, there lies still at the root of great business success the very much more important factor of quality. The effect of attention to quality, upon every man in the service, from the president of the concern down to the humblest laborer, cannot be overestimated. And bearing on the same question, clean, fine workshops and tools, well-kept yards and surroundings are of much greater importance than is usually supposed.

I was very much pleased to hear a remark, made by one of the prominent bankers who visited the Edgar Thomson Works during a Bankers' Convention held at Pittsburgh. He was one of a party of some hundreds of delegates, and after they had passed through the works he said to our manager:

"Somebody appears to belong to these works."

He put his finger there upon one of the secrets of success. They did belong to somebody. The president of an important manufacturing work once boasted to me that their men had chased away the first inspector who had ventured to appear among them, and that they had never been troubled with another since. This was said as a matter of sincere congratulations, but I thought to myself: "This concern will never stand the strain of competition; it is bound to fail when hard times come." The result proved the correctness of my belief. The surest foundation of a manufacturing concern is quality. After that, and a long way after, comes cost.

I gave a great deal of personal attention for some years to the affairs of the Keystone Bridge Works, and when important contracts were involved often went myself to meet the parties. On one such occasion in 1868, I visited Dubuque, Iowa, with our engineer, Walter Katte. We were competing for the building of the most important railway bridge that had been built up to that time, a bridge across the wide Mississippi at Dubuque, to span which was considered a great undertaking. We found the river frozen and crossed it upon a sleigh drawn by four horses.

That visit proved how much success turns upon trifles. We found we were not the lowest bidder. Our chief rival was a bridge-building concern in Chicago to which the board had decided to award the contract. I lingered and talked with some of the directors. They were delightfully ignorant of the merits of cast- and wrought-iron. We had always made the upper cord of the bridge of the latter, while our rivals' was made of cast-iron. This furnished my text. I pictured the result of a steamer striking against the one and against the other. In the case of the wrought-iron cord it would probably only bend; in the case of the cast-iron it would certainly break and down would come the bridge. One of the directors, the well-known Perry Smith, was fortunately able to enforce my argument, by stating to the board that what I said was undoubtedly the case about cast-iron. The other night he had run his buggy in the dark against a lamp-post which was of cast-iron and the lamp-post had broken to pieces. Am I to be censured if I had little difficulty here in recognizing something akin to the hand of Providence, with Perry Smith the manifest agent?

"Ah, gentlemen," I said, "there is the point. A little more money and you could have had the indestructible wrought-iron and your bridge would stand against any steamboat. We never have built and we never will build a cheap bridge. Ours don't fall."

There was a pause; then the president of the bridge company, Mr. Allison, the great Senator, asked if I would excuse them for a few moments. I retired. Soon they recalled me and offered the contract, provided we took the lower price, which was only a few thousand dollars less. I agreed to the concession. That cast-iron lamp-post so opportunely smashed gave us one of our most profitable contracts and, what is more, obtained for us the reputation of having taken the Dubuque bridge against all competitors. It also laid the foundation for me of a lifelong, unbroken friendship with one of America's best and most valuable public men, Senator Allison.

The moral of that story lies on the surface. If you want a contract, be on the spot when it is let. A smashed lamp-post or something equally unthought of may secure the prize if the bidder be on hand. And if possible stay on hand until you can take the written contract home in your pocket. This we did at Dubuque, although it was suggested we could leave and it would be sent after us to execute. We preferred to remain, being anxious to see more of the charms of Dubuque.

After building the Steubenville Bridge, it became a necessity for the Baltimore and Ohio Railroad Company to build bridges across the Ohio River at Parkersburg and Wheeling, to prevent their great rival, the Pennsylvania Railroad Company, from possessing a decided advantage. The days of ferryboats were then fast passing away. It was in connection with the contracts for these bridges that I had the pleasure of making the acquaintance of a man, then of great position, Mr. Garrett, president of the Baltimore and Ohio.

We were most anxious to secure both bridges and all the approaches to them, but I found Mr. Garrett decidedly of the opinion that we were quite unable to do so much work in the time specified. He wished to build the approaches and the short spans in his own shops, and asked me if we would permit him to use our patents. I replied that we would feel highly honored by the Baltimore and Ohio doing so. The stamp of approval of the Baltimore and Ohio Railroad would be worth ten times the patent fees. He could use all, and everything, we had.

There was no doubt as to the favorable impression that made upon the great railway magnate. He was much pleased and, to my utter surprise, took me into his private room and opened up a frank conversation upon matters in general. He touched especially upon his quarrels with the Pennsylvania Railroad people, with Mr. Thomson and Mr. Scott, the president and vice president, whom he knew to be my special friends. This led me to say that I had passed through Philadelphia on my way to see him and had been asked by Mr. Scott where I was going.

"I told him that I was going to visit you to obtain the contracts for your great bridges over the Ohio River. Mr. Scott said it was not often that I went on a fool's errand, but that I was certainly on one now; that Mr. Garrett would never think for a moment of giving me his contracts, for everyone knew that I was, as a former employee, always friendly to the Pennsylvania Railroad. Well, I said, we shall build Mr. Garrett's bridges."

Mr. Garrett promptly replied that when the interests of his company were at stake it was the best always that won. His engineers had reported that our plans were the best and that Scott and Thomson would see that he had only one rule — the interests of his company. Although he very well knew that I was a Pennsylvania Railroad man, yet he felt it his duty to award us the work.

The negotiation was still unsatisfactory to me, because we were to get all the difficult part of the work —

the great spans of which the risk was then considerable — while Mr. Garrett was to build all the small and
profitable spans at his own shops upon our plans and
patents. I ventured to ask whether he was dividing the
work because he honestly believed we could not open his
bridges for traffic as soon as his masonry would permit.
He admitted he was. I told him that he need not have any
fear upon that point.

"Mr. Garrett," I said, "would you consider my personal
bond a good security?"

"Certainly," he said.

"Well, now," I replied, "bind me! I know what I am doing. I will take the risk. How much of a bond do you want
me to give you that your bridges will be opened for traffic at the specified time if you give us the entire contract,
provided you get your masonry ready?"

"Well, I would want a hundred thousand dollars from
you, young man."

"All right," I said, "prepare your bond. Give us the work.
Our firm is not going to let me lose a hundred thousand
dollars. You know that."

"Yes," he said, "I believe if you are bound for a hundred
thousand dollars your company will work day and night
and I will get my bridges."

This was the arrangement which gave us what were then
the gigantic contracts of the Baltimore and Ohio Railroad.
It is needless to say that I never had to pay that bond. My
partners knew much better than Mr. Garrett the conditions of his work. The Ohio River was not to be trifled with,
and long before his masonry was ready we had relieved
ourselves from all responsibility upon the bond by placing
the superstructure on the banks awaiting the completion
of the substructure which he was still building.

Mr. Garrett was very proud of his Scottish blood, and Burns having been once touched upon between us we became firm friends. He afterwards took me to his fine mansion in the country. He was one of the few Americans who then lived in the grand style of a country gentleman, with many hundreds of acres of beautiful land, park-like drives, a stud of thoroughbred horses, with cattle, sheep, and dogs, and a home that realized what one had read of the country life of a nobleman in England.

At a later date he had fully determined that his railroad company should engage in the manufacture of steel rails and had applied for the right to use the Bessemer patents. This was a matter of great moment to us. The Baltimore and Ohio Railroad Company was one of our best customers, and we were naturally anxious to prevent the building of steel-rail rolling mills at Cumberland. It would have been a losing enterprise for the Baltimore and Ohio, for I was sure it could buy its steel rails at a much cheaper rate than it could possibly make the small quantity needed for itself. I visited Mr. Garrett to talk the matter over with him. He was then much pleased with the foreign commerce and the lines of steamships which made Baltimore their port. He drove me, accompanied by several of his staff, to the wharves where he was to decide about their extension, and as the foreign goods were being discharged from the steamship side and placed in the railway cars, he turned to me and said:

"Mr. Carnegie, you can now begin to appreciate the magnitude of our vast system and understand why it is necessary that we should make everything for ourselves, even our steel rails. We cannot depend upon private concerns to supply us with any of the principal articles we consume. We shall be a world to ourselves."

"Well," I said, "Mr. Garrett, it is all very grand, but really your 'vast system' does not overwhelm me. I read your last annual report and saw that you collected last year for transporting the goods of others the sum of fourteen millions of dollars. The firms I control dug the material from the hills, made their own goods, and sold them to a much greater value than that. You are really a very small concern compared with Carnegie Brothers and Company."

My railroad apprenticeship came in there to advantage. We heard no more of the Baltimore and Ohio Railroad Company entering into competition with us. Mr. Garrett and I remained good friends to the end. He even presented me with a Scotch collie dog of his own rearing. That I had been a Pennsylvania Railroad man was drowned in the "wee drap o' Scotch bluid atween us."

CHAPTER X
The Iron Works

THE Keystone Works have always been my pet as being the parent of all the other works. But they had not been long in existence before the advantage of wrought-over cast-iron became manifest. Accordingly, to insure uniform quality, and also to make certain shapes which were not then to be obtained, we determined to embark in the manufacture of iron. My brother and I became interested with Thomas N. Miller, Henry Phipps, and Andrew Kloman in a small iron mill. Miller was the first to embark with Kloman and he brought Phipps in, lending him eight hundred dollars to buy a one-sixth interest, in November, 1861.

I must not fail to record that Mr. Miller was the pioneer of our iron manufacturing projects. We were all indebted to Tom, who still lives (July 20, 1911) and sheds upon us the sweetness and light of a most lovable nature, a friend who grows more precious as the years roll by. He has softened by age, and even his outbursts against theology as antagonistic to true religion are in his fine old age much less alarming. We are all prone to grow philosophic in age, and perhaps this is well. [In re-reading this — July 19, 1912 — in our retreat upon the high moors at Aultnagar, I drop a tear for my bosom friend, dear Tom Miller, who died in Pittsburgh last winter. Mrs. Carnegie and I attended his funeral. Henceforth life lacks something, lacks much — my first partner in early years, my dearest friend in old age. May I go where he is, wherever that may be.]

Andrew Kloman had a small steel-hammer in Allegheny City. As a superintendent of the Pennsylvania Railroad I had found that he made the best axles. He was a great mechanic — one who had discovered, what was then unknown in Pittsburgh, that whatever was worth doing with machinery was worth doing well. His German mind made him thorough. What he constructed cost enormously, but when once started it did the work it was intended to do from year's end to year's end. In those early days it was a question with axles generally whether they would run any specified time or break. There was no analysis of material, no scientific treatment of it.

How much this German created! He was the first man to introduce the cold saw that cut cold iron the exact lengths. He invented upsetting machines to make bridge links, and also built the first "universal" mill in America. All these were erected at our works. When Captain Eads could not obtain the couplings for the St. Louis Bridge arches (the contractors failing to make them) and matters were at a standstill, Kloman told us that he could make them and why the others had failed. He succeeded in making them. Up to that date they were the largest semicircles that had ever been rolled. Our confidence in Mr. Kloman may be judged from the fact that when he said he could make them we unhesitatingly contracted to furnish them.

I have already spoken of the intimacy between our family and that of the Phippses. In the early days my chief companion was the elder brother, John. Henry was several years my junior, but had not failed to attract my attention as a bright, clever lad. One day he asked his brother John to lend him a quarter of a dollar. John saw that he had important use for it and handed him the shining quarter without inquiry. Next morning an advertisement appeared in the "Pittsburgh Dispatch":

"A willing boy wishes work."

This was the use the energetic and willing Harry had made of his quarter, probably the first quarter he had ever spent at one time in his life. A response came from the well-known firm of Dilworth and Bidwell. They asked the "willing boy" to call. Harry went and obtained a position as errand boy, and as was then the custom, his first duty every morning was to sweep the office. He went to his parents and obtained their consent, and in this way the young lad launched himself upon the sea of business. There was no holding back a boy like that. It was the old story. He soon became indispensable to his employers, obtained a small interest in a collateral branch of their business; and then, ever on the alert, it was not many years before he attracted the attention of Mr. Miller, who made a small investment for him with Andrew Kloman. That finally resulted in the building of the iron mill in Twenty-Ninth Street. He had been a schoolmate and great crony of my brother Tom. As children they had played together, and throughout life, until my brother's death in 1886, these two formed, as it were, a partnership within a partnership. They invariably held equal interests in the various firms with which they were connected. What one did the other did.

The errand boy is now one of the richest men in the United States and has begun to prove that he knows how to expend his surplus. Years ago he gave beautiful conservatories to the public parks of Allegheny and Pittsburgh. That he specified "that these should be open upon Sunday" shows that he is a man of his time. This clause in the gift created much excitement. Ministers denounced him from the pulpit and assemblies of the church passed resolutions declaring against the desecration of the Lord's Day. But the people rose, *en masse*, against this narrow-minded contention and the Council of the city accepted the gift with acclamation. The sound common sense of my partner was well expressed when he said in reply to a remonstrance by ministers:

"It is all very well for you, gentlemen, who work one day in the week and are masters of your time the other six during which you can view the beauties of Nature — all very well for you — but I think it shameful that you should endeavor to shut out from the toiling masses all that is calculated to entertain and instruct them during the only day which you well know they have at their disposal."

These same ministers have recently been quarreling in their convention at Pittsburgh upon the subject of instrumental music in churches. But while they are debating whether it is right to have organs in churches, intelligent people are opening museums, conservatories, and libraries upon the Sabbath; and unless the pulpit soon learns how to meet the real wants of the people in this life (where alone men's duties lie) much better than it is doing at present, these rival claimants for popular favor may soon empty their churches.

Unfortunately Kloman and Phipps soon differed with Miller about the business and forced him out. Being convinced that Miller was unfairly treated, I united with him in building new works. These were the Cyclops Mills of 1864. After they were set running it became possible, and therefore advisable, to unite the old and the new works, and the Union Iron Mills were formed by their consolidation in 1867. I did not believe that Mr. Miller's reluctance to associate again with his former partners, Phipps and Kloman, could not be overcome, because they would not control the Union Works. Mr. Miller, my brother, and I would hold the controlling interest. But Mr. Miller proved obdurate and begged me to buy his interest, which I reluctantly did after all efforts had failed to induce him to let bygones be bygones. He was Irish, and the Irish blood when aroused is uncontrollable. Mr. Miller has since regretted (to me) his refusal of my earnest request, which would have enabled the pioneer of all of us to reap what was only his rightful reward — millionairedom for himself and his followers.

We were young in manufacturing then and obtained for the Cyclops Mills what was considered at the time an enormous extent of land — seven acres. For some years we offered to lease a portion of the ground to others. It soon became a question whether we could continue the manufacture of iron within so small an area. Mr. Kloman succeeded in making iron beams and for many years our mill was far in advance of any other in that respect. We began at the new mill by making all shapes which were required, and especially such as no other concern would undertake, depending upon an increasing demand in our growing country for things that were only rarely needed at first. What others could not or would not do we would attempt, and this was a rule of our business which was strictly adhered to. Also we would make nothing except of excellent quality. We always accommodated our customers, even although at some expense to ourselves, and in cases of dispute we gave the other party the benefit of the doubt and settled. These were our rules. We had no lawsuits.

As I became acquainted with the manufacture of iron I was greatly surprised to find that the cost of each of the various processes was unknown. Inquiries made of the leading manufacturers of Pittsburgh proved this. It was a lump business, and until stock was taken and the books balanced at the end of the year, the manufacturers were in total ignorance of results. I heard of men who thought their business at the end of the year would show a loss and had found a profit, and *vice-versa*. I felt as if we were moles burrowing in the dark, and this to me was intolerable. I insisted upon such a system of weighing and accounting being introduced throughout our works as would enable us to know what our cost was for each process and especially what each man was doing, who saved material, who wasted it, and who produced the best results.

To arrive at this was a much more difficult task than one would imagine. Every manager in the mills was naturally against the new system. Years were required before an accurate system was obtained, but eventually, by the aid of many clerks and the introduction of weighing scales at various points in the mill, we began to know not only what every department was doing, but what each one of the many men working at the furnaces was doing, and thus to compare one with another. One of the chief sources of success in manufacturing is the introduction and strict maintenance of a perfect system of accounting so that responsibility for money or materials can be brought home to every man. Owners who, in the office, would not trust a clerk with five dollars without having a check upon him, were supplying tons of material daily to men in the mills without exacting an account of their stewardship by weighing what each returned in the finished form.

The Siemens Gas Furnace had been used to some extent in Great Britain for heating steel and iron, but it was supposed to be too expensive. I well remember the criticisms made by older heads among the Pittsburgh manufacturers about the extravagant expenditure we were making upon these new-fangled furnaces. But in the heating of great masses of material, almost half the waste could sometimes be saved by using the new furnaces. The expenditure would have been justified, even if it had been doubled. Yet it was many years before we were followed in this new departure; and in some of those years the margin of profit was so small that the most of it was made up from the savings derived from the adoption of the improved furnaces.

Our strict system of accounting enabled us to detect the great waste possible in heating large masses of iron. This improvement revealed to us a valuable man in a clerk, William Borntraeger, a distant relative of Mr. Kloman, who came from Germany. He surprised us one day by presenting a detailed statement showing results for a period, which seemed incredible. All the needed labor in preparing this statement he had performed at night unasked and unknown to us. The form adapted was uniquely original. Needless to say, William soon became superintendent of the works and later a partner, and the poor German lad died a millionaire. He well deserved his fortune.

It was in 1862 that the great oil wells of Pennsylvania attracted attention. My friend Mr. William Coleman, whose daughter became, at a later date, my sister-in-law, was deeply interested in the discovery, and nothing would do but that I should take a trip with him to the oil regions. It was a most interesting excursion. There had been a rush to the oil fields and the influx was so great that it was impossible for all to obtain shelter. This, however, to the class of men who flocked thither, was but a slight drawback. A few hours sufficed to knock up a shanty, and it was surprising in how short a time they were able to surround themselves with many of the comforts of life. They were men above the average, men who had saved considerable sums and were able to venture something in the search for fortune.

What surprised me was the good humor which prevailed everywhere. It was a vast picnic, full of amusing incidents. Everybody was in high glee; fortunes were supposedly within reach; everything was booming. On the tops of the derricks floated flags on which strange mottoes were displayed. I remember looking down toward the river and seeing two men working their treadles boring for oil upon the banks of the stream, and inscribed upon their flag was "Hell or China." They were going down, no matter how far.

The adaptability of the American was never better displayed than in this region. Order was soon evolved out of chaos. When we visited the place not long after we were serenaded by a brass band the players of which were made up of the new inhabitants along the creek. It would be safe to wager that a thousand Americans in a new land would organize themselves, establish schools, churches, newspapers, and brass bands — in short, provide themselves with all the appliances of civilization — and go ahead developing their country before an equal number of British would have discovered who among them was the highest in hereditary rank and had the best claims to leadership owing to his grandfather. There is but one rule among Americans — the tools of those who can use them.

To-day Oil Creek is a town of many thousand inhabitants, as is also Titusville at the other end of the creek. The district which began by furnishing a few barrels of oil every season, gathered with blankets from the surface of the creek by the Seneca Indians, has now several towns and refineries, with millions of dollars of capital. In those early days all the arrangements were of the crudest character. When the oil was obtained it was run into flat-bottomed boats which leaked badly. Water ran into the boats and the oil overflowed into the river. The creek was dammed at various places, and upon a stipulated day and hour the dams were opened and upon the flood the oil boats floated to the Allegheny River, and thence to Pittsburgh.

In this way not only the creek, but the Allegheny River, became literally covered with oil. The loss involved in transportation to Pittsburgh was estimated at fully a third of the total quantity, and before the oil boats started it is safe to say that another third was lost by leakage. The oil gathered by the Indians in the early days was bottled in Pittsburgh and sold at high prices as medicine — a dollar for a small vial. It had general reputation as a sure cure for rheumatic tendencies. As it became plentiful and cheap its virtues vanished. What fools we mortals be!

The most celebrated wells were upon the Storey farm. Upon these we obtained an option of purchase for forty thousand dollars. We bought them. Mr. Coleman, ever ready at suggestion, proposed to make a lake of oil by excavating a pool sufficient to hold a hundred thousand barrels (the waste to be made good every day by running streams of oil into it), and to hold it for the not far distant day when, as we then expected, the oil supply would cease. This was promptly acted upon, but after losing many thousands of barrels waiting for the expected day (which has not yet arrived) we abandoned the reserve. Coleman predicted that when the supply stopped, oil would bring ten dollars a barrel and there-fore we would have a million dollars worth in the lake. We did not think then of Nature's storehouse below which still keeps on yielding many thousands of barrels per day without apparent exhaustion.

This forty-thousand-dollar investment proved for us the best of all so far. The revenues from it came at the most opportune time.[1] The building of the new mill in Pittsburgh required not only all the capital we could gather, but the use of our credit, which I consider, look-ing backward, was remarkably good for young men.

Having become interested in this oil venture, I made several excursions to the district and also, in 1864, to an oil field in Ohio where a great well had been struck which yielded a peculiar quality of oil well fitted for lubricating purposes. My journey thither with Mr. Coleman and Mr. David Ritchie was one of the strangest experiences I ever had. We left the railway line some hundreds of miles from Pittsburgh and plunged through a sparsely inhabited district to the waters of Duck Creek to see the monster well. We bought it before leaving.

It was upon our return that adventures began. The weather had been fine and the roads quite passable dur-ing our journey thither, but rain had set in during our stay. We started back in our wagon, but before going far fell into difficulties. The road had become a mass of soft, tenacious mud and our wagon labored fearfully. The rain fell in torrents, and it soon became evident that

[1] The wells on the Storey farm paid in one year a million dollars in cash and dividends, and the farm itself eventually became worth, on a stock basis, five million dollars.

we were in for a night of it. Mr. Coleman lay at full length on one side of the wagon, and Mr. Ritchie on the other, and I, being then very thin, weighing not much more than a hundred pounds, was nicely sandwiched between the two portly gentlemen. Every now and then the wagon proceeded a few feet heaving up and down in the most outrageous manner, and finally sticking fast. In this fashion we passed the night. There was in front a seat across the wagon, under which we got our heads, and in spite of our condition the night was spent in uproarious merriment.

By the next night we succeeded in reaching a country town in the worst possible plight. We saw the little frame church of the town lighted and heard the bell ringing. We had just reached our tavern when a committee appeared stating that they had been waiting for us and that the congregation was assembled. It appears that a noted exhorter had been expected who had no doubt been delayed as we had been. I was taken for the absentee minister and asked how soon I would be ready to accompany them to the meeting-house. I was almost prepared with my companions to carry out the joke (we were in for fun), but I found I was too exhausted with fatigue to attempt it. I had never before come so near occupying a pulpit.

My investments now began to require so much of my personal attention that I resolved to leave the service of the railway company and devote myself exclusively to my own affairs. I had been honored a short time before this decision by being called by President Thomson to Philadelphia. He desired to promote me to the office of assistant general superintendent with headquarters at Altoona under Mr. Lewis. I declined, telling him that I had decided to give up the railroad service altogether, that I was determined to make a fortune and I saw no means of doing this honestly at any salary the railroad company could afford to give, and I would not do it by indirection. When I lay down at night I was going to get a verdict of approval from the highest of all tribunals, the judge within.

I repeated this in my parting letter to President Thomson, who warmly congratulated me upon it in his letter of reply. I resigned my position March 28, 1865, and received from the men on the railway a gold watch. This and Mr. Thomson's letter I treasure among my most precious mementos.

The following letter was written to the men on the Division:

PENNSYLVANIA RAILROAD COMPANY
SUPERINTENDENT'S OFFICE, PITTSBURGH DIVISION
PITTSBURGH, *March 28, 1865*

To the Officers and Employees of the Pittsburgh Division
GENTLEMEN:

I cannot allow my connection with you to cease without some expression of the deep regret felt at parting.

Twelve years of pleasant intercourse have served to inspire feelings of personal regard for those who have so faithfully labored with me in the service of the Company. The coming change is painful only as I reflect that in consequence thereof I am not to be in the future, as in the past, intimately associated with you and with many others in the various departments, who have through business intercourse, become my personal friends. I assure you although the official relations hitherto existing between us must soon close, I can never fail to feel and evince the liveliest interest in the welfare of such as have been identified with the Pittsburgh Division in times past, and who are, I trust, for many years to come to contribute to the success of the Pennsylvania Railroad Company, and share in its justly deserved prosperity.

Thanking you most sincerely for the uniform kindness

shown toward me, for your zealous efforts made at all times to meet my wishes, and asking for my successor similar support at your hands, I bid you all farewell.

Very respectfully
(Signed)   ANDREW CARNEGIE

Thenceforth I never worked for a salary. A man must necessarily occupy a narrow field who is at the beck and call of others. Even if he becomes president of a great corporation he is hardly his own master, unless he hold control of the stock. The ablest presidents are hampered by boards of directors and shareholders, who can know but little of the business. But I am glad to say that among my best friends to-day are those with whom I labored in the service of the Pennsylvania Railroad Company.

In the year 1867, Mr. Phipps, Mr. J. W. Vandevort, and myself revisited Europe, traveling extensively through England and Scotland, and made the tour of the Continent. "Vandy" had become my closest companion. We had both been fired by reading Bayard Taylor's "Views Afoot." It was in the days of the oil excitement and shares were going up like rockets. On Sunday, lying in the grass, I said to "Vandy":

"If you could make three thousand dollars would you spend it in a tour through Europe with me?"

"Would a duck swim or an Irishman eat potatoes?" was his reply.

The sum was soon made in oil stock by the investment of a few hundred dollars which "Vandy" had saved. This was the beginning of our excursion. We asked my partner, Harry Phipps, who was by this time quite a capitalist, to join the party. We visited most of the capitals of Europe, and in all the enthusiasm of youth climbed every spire, slept on mountain-tops, and carried our luggage in knapsacks upon our backs. We ended our journey upon Vesuvius, where we resolved some day to go around the world.

This visit to Europe proved most instructive. Up to this time I had known nothing of painting or sculpture, but it was not long before I could classify the works of the great painters. One may not at the time justly appreciate the advantage he is receiving from examining the great masterpieces, but upon his return to America he will find himself unconsciously rejecting what before seemed truly beautiful, and judging productions which come before him by a new standard. That which is truly great has so impressed itself upon him that what is false or pretentious proves no longer attractive.

My visit to Europe also gave me my first great treat in music. The Handel Anniversary was then being celebrated at the Crystal Palace in London, and I had never up to that time, nor have I often since, felt the power and majesty of music in such high degree. What I heard at the Crystal Palace and what I subsequently heard on the Continent in the cathedrals, and at the opera, certainly enlarged my appreciation of music. At Rome the Pope's choir and the celebrations in the churches at Christmas and Easter furnished, as it were, a grand climax to the whole.

These visits to Europe were also of great service in a commercial sense. One has to get out of the swirl of the great Republic to form a just estimate of the velocity with which it spins. I felt that a manufacturing concern like ours could scarcely develop fast enough for the wants of the American people, but abroad nothing seemed to be going forward. If we excepted a few of the capitals of Europe, everything on the Continent seemed to be almost at a standstill, while the Republic represented throughout its entire extent such a scene as there must have been at the Tower of Babel, as pictured in the story-books — hundreds rushing to and fro, each more active than his neighbor, and all engaged in constructing the mighty edifice.

It was Cousin "Dod" (Mr. George Lauder) to whom we were indebted for a new development in our mill operations — the first of its kind in America. He it was who took our Mr. Coleman to Wigan in England and explained the process of washing and coking the dross from coal mines. Mr. Coleman had constantly been telling us how grand it would be to utilize what was then being thrown away at our mines, and was indeed an expense to dispose of. Our Cousin "Dod" was a mechanical engineer, educated under Lord Kelvin at Glasgow University, and as he corroborated all that Mr. Coleman stated, in December, 1871, I undertook to advance the capital to build works along the line of the Pennsylvania Railroad. Contracts for ten years were made with the leading coal companies for their dross and with the railway companies for transportation, and Mr. Lauder, who came to Pittsburgh and superintended the whole operation for years, began the construction of the first coal-washing machinery in America. He made a success of it — he never failed to do that in any mining or mechanical operation he undertook — and he soon cleared the cost of the works. No wonder that at a later date my partners desired to embrace the coke works in our general firm and thus capture not only these, but Lauder also. "Dod" had won his spurs.

The ovens were extended from time to time until we had five hundred of them, washing nearly fifteen hundred tons of coal daily. I confess I never pass these coal ovens at Larimer's Station without feeling that if he who makes two blades of grass grow where one grew before is a public benefactor and lays the race under obligation, those who produce superior coke from material that has been for all previous years thrown over the bank as worthless, have great cause for self-congratulation. It is fine to make something out of nothing; it is also something to be the first firm to do this upon our continent.

We had another valuable partner in a second cousin of mine, a son of Cousin Morrison of Dunfermline. Walking through the shops one day, the superintendent asked me if I knew I had a relative there who was proving an exceptional mechanic. I replied in the negative and asked that I might speak with him on our way around. We met. I asked his name.

"Morrison," was the reply, "son of Robert" — my cousin Bob.

"Well, how did you come here?"

"I thought we could better ourselves," he said.

"Who have you with you?"

"My wife," was the reply.

"Why didn't you come first to see your relative who might have been able to introduce you here?"

"Well, I didn't feel I needed help if I only got a chance."

There spoke the true Morrison, taught to depend on himself, and independent as Lucifer. Not long afterwards I heard of his promotion to the superintendency of our newly acquired works at Duquesne, and from that position he steadily marched upward. He is to-day a blooming, but still sensible, millionaire. We are all proud of Tom Morrison. [A note received from him yesterday invites Mrs. Carnegie and myself to be his guests during our coming visit of a few days at the annual celebration of the Carnegie Institute.]

I was always advising that our iron works should be extended and new developments made in connection with the manufacture of iron and steel, which I saw was only in its infancy. All apprehension of its future development was dispelled by the action of America with regard to the tariff upon foreign imports. It was clear to my mind that the Civil War had resulted in a fixed determination upon the part of the American people to build a nation within itself, independent of Europe in all things essential to its safety. America had been obliged to import all her steel of every form and most of the iron needed, Britain being the chief seller. The people demanded a home supply and Congress granted the manufacturers a tariff of twenty-eight per cent *ad valorem* on steel rails — the tariff then being equal to about twenty-eight dollars per ton. Rails were selling at about a hundred dollars per ton, and other rates in proportion.

Protection has played a great part in the development of manufacturing in the United States. Previous to the Civil War it was a party question, the South standing for free trade and regarding a tariff as favorable only to the North. The sympathy shown by the British Government for the Confederacy, culminating in the escape of the Alabama and other privateers to prey upon American commerce, aroused hostility against that Government, notwithstanding the majority of her common people favored the United States. The tariff became no longer a party question, but a national policy, approved by both parties. It had become a patriotic duty to develop vital resources. No less than ninety Northern Democrats in Congress, including the Speaker of the House, agreed upon that point.

Capital no longer hesitated to embark in manufacturing, confident as it was that the nation would protect it as long as necessary. Years after the war, demands for a reduction of the tariff arose and it was my lot to be drawn into the controversy. It was often charged that bribery of Congressmen by manufacturers was common. So far as I know there was no foundation for this. Certainly the manufacturers never raised any sums beyond those needed to maintain the Iron and Steel Association, a matter of a few thousand dollars per year. They did, however, subscribe freely to a campaign when the issue was Protection *versus* Free Trade.

The duties upon steel were successively reduced, with my cordial support, until the twenty-eight dollars duty on rails became only one fourth or seven dollars per ton. [To-day (1911) the duty is only about one half of that, and even that should go in the next revision.] The effort of President Cleveland to pass a more drastic new tariff was interesting. It cut too deep in many places and its passage would have injured more than one manufacturer. I was called to Washington, and tried to modify and, as I believe, improve, the Wilson Bill. Senator Gorman, Democratic leader of the Senate, Governor Flower of New York, and a number of the ablest Democrats were as sound protectionists in moderation as I was. Several of these were disposed to oppose the Wilson Bill as being unnecessarily severe and certain to cripple some of our domestic industries. Senator Gorman said to me he wished as little as I did to injure any home producer, and he thought his colleagues had confidence in and would be guided by me as to iron and steel rates, provided that large reductions were made and that the Republican Senators would stand unitedly for a bill of that character. I remember his words, "I can afford to fight the President and beat him, but I can't afford to fight him and be beaten."

Governor Flower shared these views. There was little trouble in getting our party to agree to the large reductions I proposed. The Wilson-Gorman Tariff Bill was adopted. Meeting Senator Gorman later, he explained that he had to give way on cotton ties to secure several Southern Senators. Cotton ties had to be free. So tariff legislation goes.

I was not sufficiently prominent in manufacturing to take part in getting the tariff established immediately after the war, so it happened that my part has always been to favor reduction of duties, opposing extremes — the unreasonable protectionists who consider the higher the duties the better and declaim against any reduction, and the other extremists who denounce all duties and would adopt unrestrained free trade.

We could now (1907) abolish all duties upon steel and iron without injury, essential as these duties were at the beginning. Europe has not much surplus production, so that should prices rise exorbitantly here only a small amount could be drawn from there and this would instantly raise prices in Europe, so that our home manufacturers could not be seriously affected. Free trade would only tend to prevent exorbitant prices here for a time when the demand was excessive. Home iron and steel manufacturers have nothing to fear from free trade. [I recently (1910) stated this in evidence before the Tariff Commission at Washington.]

CHAPTER XI

New York as Headquarters

O UR business continued to expand and required frequent visits on my part to the East, especially to New York, which is as London to Britain — the headquarters of all really important enterprises in America. No large concern could very well get on without being represented there. My brother and Mr. Phipps had full grasp of the business at Pittsburgh. My field appeared to be to direct the general policy of the companies and negotiate the important contracts.

My brother had been so fortunate as to marry Miss Lucy Coleman, daughter of one of our most valued partners and friends. Our family residence at Homewood was given over to him, and I was once more compelled to break old associations and leave Pittsburgh in 1867 to take up my residence in New York. The change was hard enough for me, but much harder for my mother; but she was still in the prime of life and we could be happy anywhere so long as we were together. Still she did feel the leaving of our home very much. We were perfect strangers in New York, and at first took up our quarters in the St. Nicholas Hotel, then in its glory. I opened an office in Broad Street.

For some time the Pittsburgh friends who came to New York were our chief source of happiness, and the Pittsburgh papers seemed necessary to our existence. I made frequent visits there and my mother often accompanied me, so that our connection with the old home was still maintained. But after a time new friendships were formed and new interests awakened and New York began to be called home. When the proprietors of the St. Nicholas opened the Windsor Hotel uptown, we took up our residence there and up to the year 1887 that was our New York home. Mr. Hawk, the proprietor, became one of our valued friends and his nephew and namesake still remains so.

Among the educative influences from which I derived great advantage in New York, none ranks higher than the Nineteenth Century Club organized by Mr. and Mrs. Courtlandt Palmer. The club met at their house once a month for the discussion of various topics and soon attracted many able men and women. It was to Madame Botta I owed my election to membership — a remarkable woman, wife of Professor Botta, whose drawing room became more of a salon than any in the city, if indeed it were not the only one resembling a salon at that time. I was honored by an invitation one day to dine at the Bottas' and there met for the first time several distinguished people, among them one who became my lifelong friend and wise counselor, Andrew D. White, then president of Cornell University, afterwards Ambassador to Russia and Germany, and our chief delegate to the Hague Conference.

Here in the Nineteenth Century Club was an arena, indeed. Able men and women discussed the leading topics of the day in due form, addressing the audience one after another. The gatherings soon became too large for a private room. The monthly meetings were then held in the American Art Galleries. I remember the first evening I took part as one of the speakers the subject was "The Aristocracy of the Dollar." Colonel Thomas Wentworth Higginson was the first speaker. This was my introduction to a New York audience.

Thereafter I spoke now and then. It was excellent training, for one had to read and study for each appearance.

I had lived long enough in Pittsburgh to acquire the manufacturing, as distinguished from the speculative, spirit. My knowledge of affairs, derived from my position as telegraph operator, had enabled me to know the few Pittsburgh men or firms which then had dealings upon the New York Stock Exchange, and I watched their careers with deep interest. To me their operations seemed simply a species of gambling. I did not then know that the credit of all these men or firms was seriously impaired by the knowledge (which it is almost impossible to conceal) that they were given to speculation. But the firms were then so few that I could have counted them on the fingers of one hand. The Oil and Stock Exchanges in Pittsburgh had not as yet been founded and brokers' offices with wires in connection with the stock exchanges of the East were unnecessary. Pittsburgh was emphatically a manufacturing town.

I was surprised to find how very different was the state of affairs in New York. There were few even of the business men who had not their ventures in Wall Street to a greater or less extent. I was besieged with inquiries from all quarters in regard to the various railway enterprises with which I was connected. Offers were made to me by persons who were willing to furnish capital for investment and allow me to manage it — the supposition being that from the inside view which I was enabled to obtain I could invest for them successfully. Invitations were extended to me to join parties who intended quietly to buy up the control of certain properties. In fact the whole speculative field was laid out before me in its most seductive guise.

All these allurements I declined. The most notable

offer of this kind I ever received was one morning in the Windsor Hotel soon after my removal to New York. Jay Gould, then in the height of his career, approached me and said he had heard of me and he would purchase control of the Pennsylvania Railroad Company and give me one half of all profits if I would agree to devote myself to its management. I thanked him and said that, although Mr. Scott and I had parted company in business matters, I would never raise my hand against him. Subsequently Mr. Scott told me he had heard I had been selected by New York interests to succeed him. I do not know how he had learned this, as I had never mentioned it. I was able to reassure him by saying that the only railroad company I would be president of would be one I owned.

Strange what changes the whirligig of time brings in. It was my part one morning in 1900, some thirty years afterwards, to tell the son of Mr. Gould of his father's offer and to say to him:

"Your father offered me control of the great Pennsylvania system. Now I offer his son in return the control of an international line from ocean to ocean."

The son and I agreed upon the first step — that was the bringing of his Wabash line to Pittsburgh. This was successfully done under a contract given the Wabash of one third of the traffic of our steel company. We were about to take up the eastern extension from Pittsburgh to the Atlantic when Mr. Morgan approached me in March, 1901, through Mr. Schwab, and asked if I really wished to retire from business. I answered in the affirmative and that put an end to our railway operations.

I have never bought or sold a share of stock speculatively in my life, except one small lot of Pennsylvania

Railroad shares that I bought early in life for investment and for which I did not pay at the time because bankers offered to carry it for me at a low rate. I have adhered to the rule never to purchase what I did not pay for, and never to sell what I did not own. In those early days, however, I had several interests that were taken over in the course of business. They included some stocks and securities that were quoted on the New York Stock Exchange, and I found that when I opened my paper in the morning I was tempted to look first at the quotations of the stock market. As I had determined to sell all my interests in every outside concern and concentrate my attention upon our manufacturing concerns in Pittsburgh, I further resolved not even to own any stock that was bought and sold upon any stock exchange. With the exception of trifling amounts which came to me in various ways I have adhered strictly to this rule.

Such a course should commend itself to every man in the manufacturing business and to all professional men. For the manufacturing man especially the rule would seem all-important. His mind must be kept calm and free if he is to decide wisely the problems which are continually coming before him. Nothing tells in the long run like good judgment, and no sound judgment can remain with the man whose mind is disturbed by the mercurial changes of the Stock Exchange. It places him under an influence akin to intoxication. What is not, he sees, and what he sees, is not. He cannot judge of relative values or get the true perspective of things. The molehill seems to him a mountain and the mountain a molehill, and he jumps at conclusions which he should arrive at by reason. His mind is upon the stock quotations and not upon the points that require calm thought.

Speculation is a parasite feeding upon values, creating none.

My first important enterprise after settling in New York was undertaking to build a bridge across the Mississippi at Keokuk.[1] Mr. Thomson, president, of the Pennsylvania Railroad, and I contracted for the whole structure, foundation, masonry, and superstructure, taking bonds and stocks in payment. The undertaking was a splendid success in every respect, except financially. A panic threw the connecting railways into bankruptcy. They were unable to pay the stipulated sums. Rival systems built a bridge across the Mississippi at Burlington and a railway down the west side of the Mississippi to Keokuk. The handsome profits which we saw in prospect were never realized. Mr. Thomson and myself, however, escaped loss, although there was little margin left.

The superstructure for this bridge was built at our Keystone Works in Pittsburgh. The undertaking required me to visit Keokuk occasionally, and there I made the acquaintance of clever and delightful people, among them General and Mrs. Reid, and Mr. and Mrs. Leighton. Visiting Keokuk with some English friends at a later date, the impression they received of society in the Far West, on what to them seemed the very outskirts of civilization, was surprising. A reception given to us one evening by General Reid brought together an assembly creditable to any town in Britain. More than one of the guests had distinguished himself during the war and had risen to prominence in the national councils.

The reputation obtained in the building of the Keokuk bridge led to my being applied to by those who were in charge of the scheme for bridging the Mississippi at

---

[1] It was an iron bridge 2300 feet in length with a 380-foot span.

St. Louis, to which I have already referred. This was connected with my first large financial transaction. One day in 1869 the gentleman in charge of the enterprise, Mr. Macpherson (he was very Scotch), called at my New York office and said they were trying to raise capital to build the bridge. He wished to know if I could not enlist some of the Eastern railroad companies in the scheme. After careful examination of the project I made the contract for the construction of the bridge on behalf of the Keystone Bridge Works. I also obtained an option upon four million dollars of first mortgage bonds of the bridge company and set out for London in March, 1869, to negotiate their sale.

During the voyage I prepared a prospectus which I had printed upon my arrival in London, and, having upon my previous visit made the acquaintance of Junius S. Morgan, the great banker, I called upon him one morning and opened negotiations. I left with him a copy of the prospectus, and upon calling next day was delighted to find that Mr. Morgan viewed the matter favorably. I sold him part of the bonds with the option to take the remainder; but when his lawyers were called in for advice a score of changes were required in the wording of the bonds. Mr. Morgan said to me that as I was going to Scotland I had better go now; I could write the parties in St. Louis and ascertain whether they would agree to the changes proposed. It would be time enough, he said, to close the matter upon my return three weeks hence.

But I had no idea of allowing the fish to play so long, and informed him that I would have a telegram in the morning agreeing to all the changes. The Atlantic cable had been open for some time, but it is doubtful if it had yet carried so long a private cable as I sent that day.

It was an easy matter to number the lines of the bond and then going carefully over them to state what changes, omissions, or additions were required in each line. I showed Mr. Morgan the message before sending it and he said:

"Well, young man, if you succeed in that you deserve a red mark."

When I entered the office next morning, I found on the desk that had been appropriated to my use in Mr. Morgan's private office the colored envelope which contained the answer. There it was: "Board meeting last night; changes all approved." "Now, Mr. Morgan," I said, "we can proceed, assuming that the bond is as your lawyers desire." The papers were soon closed.

While I was in the office Mr. Sampson, the financial editor of "The Times," came in. I had an interview with him, well knowing that a few words from him would go far in lifting the price of the bonds on the Exchange. American securities had recently been fiercely attacked, owing to the proceedings of Fisk and Gould in connection with the Erie Railway Company, and their control of the judges in New York, who seemed to do their bidding. I knew this would be handed out as an objection, and therefore I met it at once. I called Mr. Sampson's attention to the fact that the charter of the St. Louis Bridge Company was from the National Government. In case of necessity appeal lay directly to the Supreme Court of the United States, a body vying with their own high tribunals. He said he would be delighted to give prominence to this commendable feature. I described the bridge as a toll-gate on the continental highway and this appeared to please him. It was all plain and easy sailing, and when he left the office, Mr. Morgan clapped me on the shoulder and said:

"Thank you, young man; you have raised the price of those bonds five per cent this morning."

"All right, Mr. Morgan," I replied; "now show me how I can raise them five per cent more for you."

The issue was a great success, and the money for the St. Louis Bridge was obtained. I had a considerable margin of profit upon the negotiation. This was my first financial negotiation with the bankers of Europe. Mr. Pullman told me a few days later that Mr. Morgan at a dinner party had told the telegraphic incident and predicted, "That young man will be heard from."

After closing with Mr. Morgan, I visited my native town, Dunfermline, and at that time made the town a gift of public baths. It is notable largely because it was the first considerable gift I had ever made. Long before that I had, at my Uncle Lauder's suggestion, sent a subscription to the fund for the Wallace Monument on Stirling Heights overlooking Bannockburn. It was not much, but I was then in the telegraph office and it was considerable out of a revenue of thirty dollars per month with family expenses staring us in the face. Mother did not grudge it; on the contrary, she was a very proud woman that her son's name was seen on the list of contributors, and her son felt he was really beginning to be something of a man. Years afterward my mother and I visited Stirling, and there unveiled, in the Wallace Tower, a bust of Sir Walter Scott, which she had presented to the monument committee. We had then made great progress, at least financially, since the early subscription. But distribution had not yet begun.[1]

[1] The ambitions of Mr. Carnegie at this time (1868) are set forth in the following memorandum made by him. It has only recently come to light:

St. Nicholas Hotel, New York, December, 1868.

Thirty-three and an income of $50,000 per annum! By this time two years I can so arrange all my business as to secure at least $50,000 per annum.

So far with me it had been the age of accumulation.

While visiting the Continent of Europe in 1867 and deeply interested in what I saw, it must not be thought that my mind was not upon affairs at home. Frequent letters kept me advised of business matters. The question of railway communication with the Pacific had been brought to the front by the Civil War, and Congress had passed an act to encourage the construction of a line. The first sod had just been cut at Omaha and it was intended that the line should ultimately be pushed through to San Francisco. One day while in Rome it struck me that this might be done much sooner than was then anticipated. The nation, having made up its mind that its territory must be bound together, might be trusted to see that no time was lost in accomplishing it. I wrote my friend Mr. Scott, suggesting that we should obtain the contract to place sleeping-cars upon the great California line. His reply contained these words:

"Well, young man, you do take time by the forelock."

Beyond this never earn — make no effort to increase fortune, but spend the surplus each year for benevolent purposes. Cast aside business forever, except for others.

Settle in Oxford and get a thorough education, making the acquaintance of literary men — this will take three years' active work — pay especial attention to speaking in public. Settle then in London and purchase a controlling interest in some newspaper or live review and give the general management of it attention, taking a part in public matters, especially those connected with education and improvement of the poorer classes.

Man must have an idol — the amassing of wealth is one of the worst species of idolatry — no idol more debasing than the worship of money. Whatever I engage in I must push inordinately; therefore should I be careful to choose that life which will be the most elevating in its character. To continue much longer overwhelmed by business cares and with most of my thoughts wholly upon the way to make more money in the shortest time, must degrade me beyond hope of permanent recovery. I will resign business at thirty-five, but during the ensuing two years I wish to spend the afternoons in receiving instruction and in reading systematically.

Nevertheless, upon my return to America, I pursued the idea. The sleeping-car business, in which I was interested, had gone on increasing so rapidly that it was impossible to obtain cars enough to supply the demand. This very fact led to the forming of the present Pullman Company. The Central Transportation Company was simply unable to cover the territory with sufficient rapidity, and Mr. Pullman beginning at the greatest of all railway centers in the world — Chicago — soon rivaled the parent concern. He had also seen that the Pacific Railroad would be the great sleeping-car line of the world, and I found him working for what I had started after. He was, indeed, a lion in the path. Again, one may learn, from an incident which I had from Mr. Pullman himself, by what trifles important matters are sometimes determined.

The president of the Union Pacific Railway was passing through Chicago. Mr. Pullman called upon him and was shown into his room. Lying upon the table was a telegram addressed to Mr. Scott, saying, "Your proposition for sleeping-cars is accepted." Mr. Pullman read this involuntarily and before he had time to refrain. He could not help seeing it where it lay. When President Durrant entered the room he explained this to him and said:

"I trust you will not decide this matter until I have made a proposition to you."

Mr. Durrant promised to wait. A meeting of the board of directors of the Union Pacific Company was held soon after this in New York. Mr. Pullman and myself were in attendance, both striving to obtain the prize which neither he nor I undervalued. One evening we began to mount the broad staircase in the St. Nicholas Hotel at the same time. We had met before, but were not well acquainted. I said, however, as we walked up the stairs:

"Good-evening, Mr. Pullman! Here we are together, and are we not making a nice couple of fools of ourselves?" He was not disposed to admit anything and said:

"What do you mean?"

I explained the situation to him. We were destroying by our rival propositions the very advantages we desired to obtain.

"Well," he said, "what do you propose to do about it?"

"Unite," I said. "Make a joint proposition to the Union Pacific, your party and mine, and organize a company."

"What would you call it?" he asked.

"The Pullman Palace Car Company," I replied.

This suited him exactly; and it suited me equally well.

"Come into my room and talk it over," said the great sleeping-car man.

I did so, and the result was that we obtained the contract jointly. Our company was subsequently merged in the general Pullman Company and we took stock in that company for our Pacific interests. Until compelled to sell my shares during the subsequent financial panic of 1873 to protect our iron and steel interests, I was, I believe, the largest shareholder in the Pullman Company.

This man Pullman and his career are so thoroughly American that a few words about him will not be out of place. Mr. Pullman was at first a working carpenter, but when Chicago had to be elevated he took a contract on his own account to move or elevate houses for a stipulated sum. Of course he was successful, and from this small beginning he became one of the principal and best-known contractors in that line. If a great hotel was to be raised ten feet without disturbing its hundreds of guests or interfering in any way with its business, Mr. Pullman was the man. He was one of those rare characters who can see the drift of things, and was always to be found, so to speak, swimming in the main current where movement was the fastest. He soon saw, as I did, that the sleeping-car was a positive necessity upon the American continent. He began to construct a few cars at Chicago and to obtain contracts upon the lines centering there.

The Eastern concern was in no condition to cope with that of an extraordinary man like Mr. Pullman. I soon recognized this, and although the original patents were with the Eastern company and Mr. Woodruff himself, the original patentee, was a large shareholder, and although we might have obtained damages for infringement of patent after some years of litigation, yet the time lost before this could be done would have been sufficient to make Pullman's the great company of the country. I therefore earnestly advocated that we should unite with Mr. Pullman, as I had united with him before in the Union Pacific contract. As the personal relations between Mr. Pullman and some members of the Eastern company were unsatisfactory, it was deemed best that I should undertake the negotiations, being upon friendly footing with both parties. We soon agreed that the Pullman Company should absorb our company, the Central Transportation Company, and by this means Mr. Pullman, instead of being confined to the West, obtained control of the rights on the great Pennsylvania trunk line to the Atlantic seaboard. This placed his company beyond all possible rivals. Mr. Pullman was one of the ablest men of affairs I have ever known, and I am indebted to him, among other things, for one story which carried a moral.

Mr. Pullman, like every other man, had his difficulties and disappointments, and did not hit the mark every time. No one does. Indeed, I do not know anyone but himself who could have surmounted the difficulties surrounding the business of running sleeping-cars in a satisfactory manner and still retained some rights which the railway companies were bound to respect. Railway companies should, of course, operate their own sleeping cars. On one occasion when we were comparing notes he told me that he always found comfort in this story. An old man in a Western county having suffered from all the ills that flesh is heir to, and a great many more than it usually encounters, and being commiserated by his neighbors, replied:

"Yes, my friends, all that you say is true. I have had a long, long life full of troubles, but there is one curious fact about them — nine tenths of them never happened."

True indeed; most of the troubles of humanity are imaginary and should be laughed out of court. It is folly to cross a bridge until you come to it, or to bid the Devil good-morning until you meet him — perfect folly. All is well until the stroke falls, and even then nine times out of ten it is not so bad as anticipated. A wise man is the confirmed optimist.

Success in these various negotiations had brought me into some notice in New York, and my next large operation was in connection with the Union Pacific Railway in 1871. One of its directors came to me saying that they must raise in some way a sum of six hundred thousand dollars (equal to many millions to-day) to carry them through a crisis; and some friends who knew me and were on the executive committee of that road had suggested that I might be able to obtain the money and at the same time get for the Pennsylvania Railroad Company virtual control of that important Western line. I believe Mr. Pullman came with the director, or perhaps it was Mr. Pullman himself who first came to me on the subject.

I took up the matter, and it occurred to me that if the directors of the Union Pacific Railway would be willing to elect to its board of directors a few such men as the Pennsylvania Railroad would nominate, the traffic to be thus obtained for the Pennsylvania would justify that company in helping the Union Pacific. I went to Philadelphia and laid the subject before President Thomson. I suggested that if the Pennsylvania Railroad Company would trust me with securities upon which the Union Pacific could borrow money in New York, we could control the Union Pacific in the interests of the Pennsylvania. Among many marks of Mr. Thomson's confidence this was up to that time the greatest. He was much more conservative when handling the money of the railroad company than his own, but the prize offered was too great to be missed. Even if the six hundred thousand dollars had been lost, it would not have been a losing investment for his company, and there was little danger of this because we were ready to hand over to him the securities which we obtained in return for the loan to the Union Pacific.

My interview with Mr. Thomson took place at his house in Philadelphia, and as I rose to go he laid his hand upon my shoulder, saying:

"Remember, Andy, I look to you in this matter. It is you I trust, and I depend on your holding all the securities you obtain and seeing that the Pennsylvania Railroad is never in a position where it can lose a dollar."

I accepted the responsibility, and the result was a triumphant success. The Union Pacific Company was exceedingly anxious that Mr. Thomson himself should take the presidency, but this he said was out of the question. He nominated Mr. Thomas A. Scott, vice-president of the Pennsylvania Railroad, for the position. Mr. Scott, Mr. Pullman, and myself were accordingly elected directors of the Union Pacific Railway Company in 1871.

The securities obtained for the loan consisted of three millions of the shares of the Union Pacific, which were locked in my safe, with the option of taking them at a price. As was to be expected, the accession of the Pennsylvania Railroad party rendered the stock of the Union Pacific infinitely more valuable. The shares advanced enormously. At this time I undertook to negotiate bonds in London for a bridge to cross the Missouri at Omaha, and while I was absent upon this business Mr. Scott decided to sell our Union Pacific shares. I had left instructions with my secretary that Mr. Scott, as one of the partners in the venture, should have access to the vault, as it might be necessary in my absence that the securities should be within reach of some one; but the idea that these should be sold, or that our party should lose the splendid position we had acquired in connection with the Union Pacific, never entered my brain.

I returned to find that, instead of being a trusted colleague of the Union Pacific directors, I was regarded as having used them for speculative purposes. No quartet of men ever had a finer opportunity for identifying themselves with a great work than we had; and never was an opportunity more recklessly thrown away. Mr. Pullman was ignorant of the matter and as indignant as myself, and I believe that he at once re-invested his profits in the shares of the Union Pacific. I felt that much as I wished to do this and to repudiate what had been done, it would be unbecoming and perhaps ungrateful in me to separate myself so distinctly from my first of friends, Mr. Scott.

At the first opportunity we were ignominiously but deservedly expelled from the Union Pacific board. It was a bitter dose for a young man to swallow. And the transaction marked my first serious difference with a man who up to that time had the greatest influence with me, the kind and affectionate employer of my boyhood, Thomas A. Scott. Mr. Thomson regretted the matter, but, as he said, having paid no attention to it and having left the whole control of it in the hands of Mr. Scott and myself, he presumed that I had thought best to sell out. For a time I feared I had lost a valued friend in Levi P. Morton, of Morton, Bliss & Co., who was interested in Union Pacific, but at last he found out that I was innocent.

The negotiations concerning two and a half millions of bonds for the construction of the Omaha Bridge were successful, and as these bonds had been purchased by persons connected with the Union Pacific before I had anything to do with the company, it was for them and not for the Union Pacific Company that the negotiations were conducted. This was not explained to me by the director who talked with me before I left for London. Unfortunately, when I returned to New York I found that the entire proceeds of the bonds, including my profit, had been appropriated by the parties to pay their own debts, and I was thus beaten out of a handsome sum, and had to credit to profit and loss my expenses and time. I had never before been cheated and found it out so positively and so clearly. I saw that I was still young and had a good deal to learn. Many men can be trusted, but a few need watching.

CHAPTER XII
Business Negotiations

COMPLETE success attended a negotiation which I conducted about this time for Colonel William Phillips, president of the Allegheny Valley Railway at Pittsburgh. One day the Colonel entered my New York office and told me that he needed money badly, but that he could get no house in America to entertain the idea of purchasing five millions of bonds of his company although they were to be guaranteed by the Pennsylvania Railroad Company. The old gentleman felt sure that he was being driven from pillar to post by the bankers because they had agreed among themselves to purchase the bonds only upon their own terms. He asked ninety cents on the dollar for them, but this the bankers considered preposterously high. Those were the days when Western railway bonds were often sold to the bankers at eighty cents on the dollar.

Colonel Phillips said he had come to see whether I could not suggest some way out of his difficulty. He had pressing need for two hundred and fifty thousand dollars, and this Mr. Thomson, of the Pennsylvania Railroad, could not give him. The Allegheny bonds were seven per cents, but they were payable, not in gold, but in currency, in America. They were therefore wholly unsuited for the foreign market. But I knew that the Pennsylvania Railroad Company had a large amount of Philadelphia and Erie Railroad six per cent gold bonds in its treasury. It would be a most desirable exchange on its part, I thought, to give these bonds for the seven per cent Allegheny bonds which bore its guarantee.

I telegraphed Mr. Thomson, asking if the Pennsylvania Railroad Company would take two hundred and fifty thousand dollars at interest and lend it to the Allegheny Railway Company. Mr. Thomson replied, "Certainly." Colonel Phillips was happy. He agreed, in consideration of my services, to give me a sixty-days option to take his five millions of bonds at the desired ninety cents on the dollar. I laid the matter before Mr. Thomson and suggested an exchange, which that company was only too glad to make, as it saved one per cent interest on the bonds. I sailed at once for London with the control of five millions of first mortgage Philadelphia and Erie Bonds, guaranteed by the Pennsylvania Railroad Company — a magnificent security for which I wanted a high price. And here comes in one of the greatest of the hits and misses of my financial life.

I wrote the Barings from Queenstown that I had for sale a security which even their house might unhesitatingly consider. On my arrival in London I found at the hotel a note from them requesting me to call. I did so the next morning, and before I had left their banking house I had closed an agreement by which they were to bring out this loan, and that until they sold the bonds at par, less their two and a half per cent commission, they would advance the Pennsylvania Railroad Company four millions of dollars at five per cent interest. The sale left me a clear profit of more than half a million dollars.

The papers were ordered to be drawn up, but as I was leaving Mr. Russell Sturgis said they had just heard that Mr. Baring himself was coming up to town in the morning. They had arranged to hold a "court," and as it would be fitting to lay the transaction before him as a matter of courtesy they would postpone the signing of the papers until the morrow. If I would call at two o'clock the transaction would be closed.

Never shall I forget the oppressed feeling which overcame me as I stepped out and proceeded to the telegraph office to wire President Thomson. Something told me that I ought not to do so. I would wait till to-morrow when I had the contract in my pocket. I walked from the banking house to the Langham Hotel — four long miles. When I reached there I found a messenger waiting breathless to hand me a sealed note from the Barings. Bismarck had locked up a hundred millions in Magdeburg. The financial world was panic-stricken, and the Barings begged to say that under the circumstances they could not propose to Mr. Baring to go on with the matter. There was as much chance that I should be struck by lightning on my way home as that an arrangement agreed to by the Barings should be broken. And yet it was. It was too great a blow to produce anything like irritation or indignation. I was meek enough to be quite resigned, and merely congratulated myself that I had not telegraphed Mr. Thomson.

I decided not to return to the Barings, and although J. S. Morgan & Co. had been bringing out a great many American securities I subsequently sold the bonds to them at a reduced price as compared with that agreed to by the Barings. I thought it best not to go to Morgan & Co. at first, because I had understood from Colonel Phillips that the bonds had been unsuccessfully offered by him to their house in America and I supposed that the Morgans in London might consider themselves connected with the negotiations through their house in New York. But in all subsequent negotiations I made it a rule to give the first offer to Junius S. Morgan, who seldom permitted me to leave his banking house without taking what I had to offer. If he could not buy for his own house, he placed me in communication with a friendly house that did, he taking an interest in the issue. It is a great satisfaction to reflect that I never negotiated a security which did not to the end command a premium. Of course in this case I made a mistake in not returning to the Barings, giving them time and letting the panic subside, which it soon did. When one party to a bargain becomes excited, the other should keep cool and patient.

As an incident of my financial operations I remember saying to Mr. Morgan one day:

"Mr. Morgan, I will give you an idea and help you to carry it forward if you will give me one quarter of all the money you make by acting upon it."

He laughingly said: "That seems fair, and as I have the option to act upon it, or not, certainly we ought to be willing to pay you a quarter of the profit."

I called attention to the fact that the Allegheny Valley Railroad bonds which I had exchanged for the Philadelphia and Erie bonds bore the guarantee of the Pennsylvania Railroad Company, and that that great company was always in need of money for essential extensions. A price might be offered for these bonds which might tempt the company to sell them, and that at the moment there appeared to be such a demand for American securities that no doubt they could be floated. I would write a prospectus which I thought would float the bonds. After examining the matter with his usual care he decided that he would act upon my suggestion.

Mr. Thomson was then in Paris and I ran over there to see him. Knowing that the Pennsylvania Railroad had need for money I told him that I had recommended these securities to Mr. Morgan and if he would give me a price for them I would see if I could not sell them. He named a price which was then very high, but less than the price which these bonds have since reached. Mr. Morgan purchased part of them with the right to buy others, and in this way the whole nine or ten millions of Allegheny bonds were marketed and the Pennsylvania Railroad Company placed in funds.

The sale of the bonds had not gone very far when the panic of 1873 was upon us. One of the sources of revenue which I then had was Mr. Pierpont Morgan. He said to me one day:

"My father has cabled to ask whether you wish to sell out your interest in that idea you gave him."

I said: "Yes, I do. In these days I will sell anything for money."

"Well," he said, "what would you take?"

I said I believed that a statement recently rendered to me showed that there were already fifty thousand dollars to my credit, and I would take sixty thousand. Next morning when I called Mr. Morgan handed me checks for seventy thousand dollars.

"Mr. Carnegie," he said, "you were mistaken. You sold out for ten thousand dollars less than the statement showed to your credit, and the additional ten makes seventy."

The payments were in two checks, one for sixty thousand dollars and the other for the additional ten thousand. I handed him back the ten-thousand-dollar check, saying:

"Well, that is something worthy of you. Will you please accept these ten thousand with my best wishes?"

"No, thank you," he said, "I cannot do that."

Such acts, showing a nice sense of honorable understanding as against mere legal rights, are not so uncommon in business as the uninitiated might believe. And, after that, it is not to be wondered at if I determined that so far as lay in my power neither Morgan, father or son, nor their house, should suffer through me. They had in me henceforth a firm friend.

A great business is seldom if ever built up, except on lines of the strictest integrity. A reputation for "cuteness" and sharp dealing is fatal in great affairs. Not the letter of the law, but the spirit, must be the rule. The standard of commercial morality is now very high. A mistake made by anyone in favor of the firm is corrected as promptly as if the error were in favor of the other party. It is essential to permanent success that a house should obtain a reputation for being governed by what is fair rather than what is merely legal. A rule which we adopted and adhered to has given greater returns than one would believe possible, namely: always give the other party the benefit of the doubt. This, of course, does not apply to the speculative class. An entirely different atmosphere pervades that world. Men are only gamblers there. Stock gambling and honorable business are incompatible. In recent years it must be admitted that the old-fashioned "banker," like Junius S. Morgan of London, has become rare.

Soon after being deposed as president of the Union Pacific, Mr. Scott[1] resolved upon the construction of

[1] Colonel Thomas A. Scott left the Union Pacific in 1872, the same year he became president of the Texas Pacific, and in 1874 president of the Pennsylvania.

the Texas Pacific Railway. He telegraphed me one day in New York to meet him at Philadelphia without fail. I met him there with several other friends, among them Mr. J. N. McCullough, vice-president of the Pennsylvania Railroad Company at Pittsburgh. A large loan for the Texas Pacific had fallen due in London and its renewal was agreed to by Morgan & Co., provided I would join the other parties to the loan. I declined. I was then asked whether I would bring them all to ruin by refusing to stand by my friends. It was one of the most trying moments of my whole life. Yet I was not tempted for a moment to entertain the idea of involving myself. The question of what was my duty came first and prevented that. All my capital was in manufacturing and every dollar of it was required. I was the capitalist (then a modest one, indeed) of our concern. All depended upon me. My brother with his wife and family, Mr. Phipps and his family, Mr. Kloman and his family, all rose up before me and claimed protection.

I told Mr. Scott that I had done my best to prevent him from beginning to construct a great railway before he had secured the necessary capital. I had insisted that thousands of miles of railway lines could not be constructed by means of temporary loans. Besides, I had paid two hundred and fifty thousand dollars cash for an interest in it, which he told me upon my return from Europe he had reserved for me, although I had never approved the scheme. But nothing in the world would ever induce me to be guilty of endorsing the paper of that construction company or of any other concern than our own firm.

I knew that it would be impossible for me to pay the Morgan loan in sixty days, or even to pay my proportion of it. Besides, it was not that loan by itself, but the half-dozen other loans that would be required thereafter that had to be considered. This marked another step in the total business separation which had to come between Mr. Scott and myself. It gave more pain than all the financial trials to which I had been subjected up to that time.

It was not long after this meeting that the disaster came and the country was startled by the failure of those whom it had regarded as its strongest men. I fear Mr. Scott's premature death[1] can measurably be attributed to the humiliation which he had to bear. He was a sensitive rather than a proud man, and his seemingly impending failure cut him to the quick. Mr. McManus and Mr. Baird, partners in the enterprise, also soon passed away. These two men were manufacturers like myself and in no position to engage in railway construction.

The business man has no rock more dangerous to encounter in his career than this very one of endorsing commercial paper. It can easily be avoided if he asks himself two questions: Have I surplus means for all possible requirements which will enable me to pay without inconvenience the utmost sum for which I am liable under this endorsement? Secondly: Am I willing to lose this sum for the friend for whom I endorse? If these two questions can be answered in the affirmative he may be permitted to oblige his friend, but not otherwise, if he be a wise man. And if he can answer the first question in the affirmative it will be well for him to consider whether it would not be better then and there to pay the entire sum for which his name is asked. I am sure it would be. A man's means are a trust to be

---

[1] Died May 21, 1881.

sacredly held for his own creditors as long as he has debts and obligations.

Notwithstanding my refusal to endorse the Morgan renewal, I was invited to accompany the parties to New York next morning in their special car for the purpose of consultation. This I was only too glad to do. Anthony Drexel was also called in to accompany us. During the journey Mr. McCullough remarked that he had been looking around the car and had made up his mind that there was only one sensible man in it; the rest had all been "fools." Here was "Andy" who had paid for his shares and did not owe a dollar or have any responsibility in the matter, and that was the position they all ought to have been in.

Mr. Drexel said he would like me to explain how I had been able to steer clear of these unfortunate troubles. I answered: by strict adherence to what I believed to be my duty never to put my name to anything which I knew I could not pay at maturity; or, to recall the familiar saying of a Western friend, never to go in where you couldn't wade. This water was altogether too deep for me.

Regard for this rule has kept not only myself but my partners out of trouble. Indeed, we had gone so far in our partnership agreement as to prevent ourselves from endorsing or committing ourselves in any way beyond trifling sums, except for the firm. This I also gave as a reason why I could not endorse.

During the period which these events cover I had made repeated journeys to Europe to negotiate various securities, and in all I sold some thirty millions of dollars worth. This was at a time when the Atlantic cable had not yet made New York a part of London financially considered, and when London bankers would lend their balances to Paris, Vienna, or Berlin for a shadow of difference in the rate of interest rather than to the United States at a higher rate. The Republic was considered less safe than the Continent by these good people. My brother and Mr. Phipps conducted the iron business so successfully that I could leave for weeks at a time without anxiety. There was danger lest I should drift away from the manufacturing to the financial and banking business. My successes abroad brought me tempting opportunities, but my preference was always for manufacturing. I wished to make something tangible and sell it and I continued to invest my profits in extending the works at Pittsburgh.

The small shops put up originally for the Keystone Bridge Company had been leased for other purposes and ten acres of ground had been secured in Lawrenceville on which new and extensive shops were erected. Repeated additions to the Union Iron Mills had made them the leading mills in the United States for all sorts of structural shapes. Business was promising and all the surplus earnings I was making in other fields were required to expand the iron business. I had become interested, with my friends of the Pennsylvania Railroad Company, in building some railways in the Western States, but gradually withdrew from all such enterprises and made up my mind to go entirely contrary to the adage not to put all one's eggs in one basket. I determined that the proper policy was "to put all good eggs in one basket and then watch that basket."

I believe the true road to preeminent success in any line is to make yourself master in that line. I have no faith in the policy of scattering one's resources, and in my experience I have rarely if ever met a man who achieved preeminence in money-making — certainly never one in manufacturing — who was interested in many concerns. The men who have succeeded are men who have chosen one line and stuck to it. It is surprising how few men appreciate the enormous dividends derivable from investment in their own business. There is scarcely a manufacturer in the world who has not in his works some machinery that should be thrown out and replaced by improved appliances; or who does not for the want of additional machinery or new methods lose more than sufficient to pay the largest dividend obtainable by investment beyond his own domain. And yet most business men whom I have known invest in bank shares and in faraway enterprises, while the true gold mine lies right in their own factories.

I have tried always to hold fast to this important fact. It has been with me a cardinal doctrine that I could manage my own capital better than any other person, much better than any board of directors. The losses men encounter during a business life which seriously embarrass them are rarely in their own business, but in enterprises of which the investor is not master. My advice to young men would be not only to concentrate their whole time and attention on the one business in life in which they engage, but to put every dollar of their capital into it. If there be any business that will not bear extension, the true policy is to invest the surplus in first-class securities which will yield a moderate but certain revenue if some other growing business cannot be found. As for myself my decision was taken early. I would concentrate upon the manufacture of iron and steel and be master in that.

My visits to Britain gave me excellent opportunities to renew and make acquaintance with those prominent in the iron and steel business — Bessemer in the front,

Sir Lothian Bell, Sir Bernard Samuelson, Sir Windsor Richards, Edward Martin, Bingley, Evans, and the whole host of captains in that industry. My election to the council, and finally to the presidency of the British Iron and Steel Institute soon followed, I being the first president who was not a British subject. That honor was highly appreciated, although at first declined, because I feared that I could not give sufficient time to its duties, owing to my residence in America.

As we had been compelled to engage in the manufacture of wrought-iron in order to make bridges and other structures, so now we thought it desirable to manufacture our own pig iron. And this led to the erection of the Lucy Furnace in the year 1870 — a venture which would have been postponed had we fully appreciated its magnitude. We heard from time to time the ominous predictions made by our older brethren in the manufacturing business with regard to the rapid growth and extension of our young concern, but we were not deterred. We thought we had sufficient capital and credit to justify the building of one blast furnace.

The estimates made of its cost, however, did not cover more than half the expenditure. It was an experiment with us. Mr. Kloman knew nothing about blast-furnace operations. But even without exact knowledge no serious blunder was made. The yield of the Lucy Furnace (named after my bright sister-in-law) exceeded our most sanguine expectations and the then unprecedented output of a hundred tons per day was made from one blast furnace, for one week — an output that the world had never heard of before. We held the record and many visitors came to marvel at the marvel.

It was not, however, all smooth sailing with our iron business. Years of panic came at intervals. We had passed safely through the fall in values following the war, when iron from nine cents per pound dropped to three. Many failures occurred and our financial manager had his time fully occupied in providing funds to meet emergencies. Among many wrecks our firm stood with credit unimpaired. But the manufacture of pig iron gave us more anxiety than any other department of our business so far. The greatest service rendered us in this branch of manufacturing was by Mr. Whitwell, of the celebrated Whitwell Brothers of England, whose blast-furnace stoves were so generally used. Mr. Whitwell was one of the best-known of the visitors who came to marvel at the Lucy Furnace, and I laid the difficulty we then were experiencing before him. He said immediately:

"That comes from the angle of the bell being wrong."

He explained how it should be changed. Our Mr. Kloman was slow to believe this, but I urged that a small glass-model furnace and two bells be made, one as the Lucy was and the other as Mr. Whitwell advised it should be. This was done, and upon my next visit experiments were made with each, the result being just as Mr. Whitwell had foretold. Our bell distributed the large pieces to the sides of the furnace, leaving the center a dense mass through which the blast could only partially penetrate. The Whitwell bell threw the pieces to the center leaving the circumference dense. This made all the difference in the world. The Lucy's troubles were over.

What a kind, big, broad man was Mr. Whitwell, with no narrow jealousy, no withholding his knowledge! We had in some departments learned new things and were able to be of service to his firm in return. At all events, after that everything we had was open to the Whitwells.

[To-day, as I write, I rejoice that one of the two still is with us and that our friendship is still warm. He was my predecessor in the presidency of the British Iron and Steel Institute.]

CHAPTER XIII
The Age of Steel

L OOKING back to-day it seems incredible that only forty years ago (1870) chemistry in the United States was an almost unknown agent in connection with the manufacture of pig iron. It was the agency, above all others, most needful in the manufacture of iron and steel. The blast-furnace manager of that day was usually a rude bully, generally a foreigner, who in addition to his other acquirements was able to knock down a man now and then as a lesson to the other unruly spirits under him. He was supposed to diagnose the condition of the furnace by instinct, to possess some almost supernatural power of divination, like his congener in the country districts who was reputed to be able to locate an oil well or water supply by means of a hazel rod. He was a veritable quack doctor who applied whatever remedies occurred to him for the troubles of his patient.

The Lucy Furnace was out of one trouble and into another, owing to the great variety of ores, limestone, and coke which were then supplied with little or no regard to their component parts. This state of affairs became intolerable to us. We finally decided to dispense with the rule-of-thumb-and-intuition manager, and to place a young man in charge of the furnace. We had a young shipping clerk, Henry M. Curry, who had distinguished himself, and it was resolved to make him manager.

Mr. Phipps had the Lucy Furnace under his special charge. His daily visits to it saved us from failure there. Not that the furnace was not doing as well as other furnaces in the West as to money-making, but being so much larger than other furnaces its variations entailed much more serious results. I am afraid my partner had something to answer for in his Sunday morning visits to the Lucy Furnace when his good father and sister left the house for more devotional duties. But even if he had gone with them his real earnest prayer could not but have had reference at times to the precarious condition of the Lucy Furnace then absorbing his thoughts.

The next step taken was to find a chemist as Mr. Curry's assistant and guide. We found the man in a learned German, Dr. Fricke, and great secrets did the doctor open up to us. Ironstone from mines that had a high reputation was now found to contain ten, fifteen, and even twenty per cent less iron than it had been credited with. Mines that hitherto had a poor reputation we found to be now yielding superior ore. The good was bad and the bad was good, and everything was topsy-turvy. Nine tenths of all the uncertainties of pig-iron making were dispelled under the burning sun of chemical knowledge.

At a most critical period when it was necessary for the credit of the firm that the blast furnace should make its best product, it had been stopped because an exceedingly rich and pure ore had been substituted for an inferior ore — an ore which did not yield more than two thirds of the quantity of iron of the other. The furnace had met with disaster because too much lime had been used to flux this exceptionally pure ironstone. The very superiority of the materials had involved us in serious losses.

What fools we had been! But then there was this consolation: we were not as great fools as our competitors. It was years after we had taken chemistry to guide us that it was said by the proprietors of some other furnaces that they could not afford to employ a chemist. Had they known the truth then, they would have known that they could not afford to be without one. Looking back it seems pardonable to record that we were the first to employ a chemist at blast furnaces — something our competitors pronounced extravagant.

The Lucy Furnace became the most profitable branch of our business, because we had almost the entire monopoly of scientific management. Having discovered the secret, it was not long (1872) before we decided to erect an additional furnace. This was done with great economy as compared with our first experiment. The mines which had no reputation and the products of which many firms would not permit to be used in their blast furnaces found a purchaser in us. Those mines which were able to obtain an enormous price for their products, owing to a reputation for quality, we quietly ignored. A curious illustration of this was the celebrated Pilot Knob mine in Missouri. Its product was, so to speak, under a cloud. A small portion of it only could be used, it was said, without obstructing the furnace. Chemistry told us that it was low in phosphorus, but very high in silicon. There was no better ore and scarcely any as rich, if it were properly fluxed. We therefore bought heavily of this and received the thanks of the proprietors for rendering their property valuable.

It is hardly believable that for several years we were able to dispose of the highly phosphoric cinder from the puddling furnaces at a higher price than we had to pay for the pure cinder from the heating furnaces of our competitors — a cinder which was richer in iron than the puddled cinder and much freer from phosphorus. Upon some occasion a blast furnace had attempted to smelt the flue cinder, and from its greater purity the furnace did not work well with a mixture intended for an impurer article; hence for years it was thrown over the banks of the river at Pittsburgh by our competitors as worthless. In some cases we were even able to exchange a poor article for a good one and obtain a bonus.

But it is still more unbelievable that a prejudice, equally unfounded, existed against putting into the blast furnaces the roll-scale from the mills which was pure oxide of iron. This reminds me of my dear friend and fellow-Dunfermline townsman, Mr. Chisholm, of Cleveland. We had many pranks together. One day, when I was visiting his works at Cleveland, I saw men wheeling this valuable roll-scale into the yard. I asked Mr. Chisholm where they were going with it, and he said:

"To throw it over the bank. Our managers have always complained that they had bad luck when they attempted to remelt it in the blast furnace."

I said nothing, but upon my return to Pittsburgh I set about having a joke at his expense. We had then a young man in our service named Du Puy, whose father was known as the inventor of a direct process in iron-making with which he was then experimenting in Pittsburgh. I recommended our people to send Du Puy to Cleveland to contract for all the roll-scale of my friend's establishment. He did so, buying it for fifty cents per ton and having it shipped to him direct. This continued for some time. I expected always to hear of the joke being discovered. The premature death of Mr. Chisholm occurred before I could apprise him of it. His successors soon, however, followed our example.

I had not failed to notice the growth of the Bessemer process. If this proved successful I knew that iron was

destined to give place to steel; that the Iron Age would
pass away and the Steel Age take its place. My friend,
John A. Wright, president of the Freedom Iron Works at
Lewiston, Pennsylvania, had visited England purposely
to investigate the new process. He was one of our best
and most experienced manufacturers, and his decision
was so strongly in its favor that he induced his company to erect Bessemer works. He was quite right, but
just a little in advance of his time. The capital required
was greater than he estimated. More than this, it was
not to be expected that a process which was even then
in somewhat of an experimental stage in Britain could
be transplanted to the new country and operated successfully from the start. The experiment was certain to
be long and costly, and for this my friend had not made
sufficient allowance.

At a later date, when the process had become established in England, capitalists began to erect the present
Pennsylvania Steel Works at Harrisburg. These also had
to pass through an experimental stage and at a critical
moment would probably have been wrecked but for the
timely assistance of the Pennsylvania Railroad Company.
It required a broad and able man like President Thomson, of the Pennsylvania Railroad, to recommend to his
board of directors that so large a sum as six hundred
thousand dollars should be advanced to a manufacturing
concern on his road, that steel rails might be secured for
the line. The result fully justified his action.

The question of a substitute for iron rails upon the
Pennsylvania Railroad and other leading lines had become a very serious one. Upon certain curves at Pittsburgh, on the road connecting the Pennsylvania with
the Fort Wayne, I had seen new iron rails placed every

six weeks or two months. Before the Bessemer process was known I had called President Thomson's attention to the efforts of Mr. Dodds in England, who had carbonized the heads of iron rails with good results. I went to England and obtained control of the Dodds patents and recommended President Thomson to appropriate twenty thousand dollars for experiments at Pittsburgh, which he did. We built a furnace on our grounds at the upper mill and treated several hundred tons of rails for the Pennsylvania Railroad Company and with remarkably good results as compared with iron rails. These were the first hard-headed rails used in America. We placed them on some of the sharpest curves and their superior service far more than compensated for the advance made by Mr. Thomson. Had the Bessemer process not been successfully developed, I verily believe that we should ultimately have been able to improve the Dodds process sufficiently to make its adoption general. But there was nothing to be compared with the solid steel article which the Bessemer process produced.

Our friends of the Cambria Iron Company at Johnstown, near Pittsburgh — the principal manufacturers of rails in America — decided to erect a Bessemer plant. In England I had seen it demonstrated, at least to my satisfaction, that the process could be made a grand success without undue expenditure of capital or great risk. Mr. William Coleman, who was ever alive to new methods, arrived at the same conclusion. It was agreed we should enter upon the manufacture of steel rails at Pittsburgh. He became a partner and also my dear friend Mr. David McCandless, who had so kindly offered aid to my mother at my father's death. The latter was not forgotten. Mr. John Scott and Mr. David A. Stewart, and others joined me; Mr. Edgar Thompson and Mr. Thomas Scott, president and vice-president of the Pennsylvania Railroad, also became stockholders, anxious to encourage the development of steel. The steel-rail company was organized January 1, 1873.

The question of location was the first to engage our serious attention. I could not reconcile myself to any location that was proposed, and finally went to Pittsburgh to consult with my partners about it. The subject was constantly in my mind and in bed Sunday morning the site suddenly appeared to me. I rose and called to my brother:

"Tom, you and Mr. Coleman are right about the location; right at Braddock's, between the Pennsylvania, the Baltimore and Ohio, and the river, is the best situation in America; and let's call the works after our dear friend Edgar Thomson. Let us go over to Mr. Coleman's and drive out to Braddock's."

We did so that day, and the next morning Mr. Coleman was at work trying to secure the property. Mr. McKinney, the owner, had a high idea of the value of his farm. What we had expected to purchase for five or six hundred dollars an acre cost us two thousand. But since then we have been compelled to add to our original purchase at a cost of five thousand dollars per acre.

There, on the very field of Braddock's defeat, we began the erection of our steel-rail mills. In excavating for the foundations many relics of the battle were found — bayonets, swords, and the like. It was there that the then provost of Dunfermline, Sir Arthur Halkett, and his son were slain. How did they come to be there will very naturally be asked. It must not be forgotten that, in those days, the provosts of the cities of Britain were members of the aristocracy — the great men of the district who condescended to enjoy the honor of the position without performing the duties. No one in trade was considered good enough for the provostship. We have remnants of this aristocratic notion throughout Britain to-day. There is scarcely any life assurance or railway company, or in some cases manufacturing company but must have at its head, to enjoy the honors of the presidency, some titled person totally ignorant of the duties of the position. So it was that Sir Arthur Halkett, as a gentleman, was Provost of Dunfermline, but by calling he followed the profession of arms and was killed on this spot. It was a coincidence that what had been the field of death to two native-born citizens of Dunfermline should be turned into an industrial hive by two others.

Another curious fact has recently been discovered. Mr. John Morley's address, in 1904 on Founder's Day at the Carnegie Institute, Pittsburgh, referred to the capture of Fort Duquesne by General Forbes and his writing Prime Minister Pitt that he had rechristened it "Pittsburgh" for him. This General Forbes was then Laird of Pittencrieff and was born in the Glen which I purchased in 1902 and presented to Dunfermline for a public park. So that two Dunfermline men have been Lairds of Pittencrieff whose chief work was in Pittsburgh. One named Pittsburgh and the other labored for its development.

In naming the steel mills as we did the desire was to honor my friend Edgar Thomson, but when I asked permission to use his name his reply was significant. He said that as far as American steel rails were concerned, he did not feel that he wished to connect his name with them, for they had proved to be far from creditable. Uncertainty was, of course, inseparable from the experimental stage; but, when I assured him that it was now possible to make steel rails in America as good in every particular as the foreign article, and that we intended to obtain for our rails the reputation enjoyed by the Keystone bridges and the Kloman axles, he consented.

He was very anxious to have us purchase land upon the Pennsylvania Railroad, as his first thought was always for that company. This would have given the Pennsylvania a monopoly of our traffic. When he visited Pittsburgh a few months later and Mr. Robert Pitcairn, my successor as superintendent of the Pittsburgh Division of the Pennsylvania, pointed out to him the situation of the new works at Braddock's Station, which gave us not only a connection with his own line, but also with the rival Baltimore and Ohio line, and with a rival in one respect greater than either — the Ohio River — he said, with a twinkle of his eye to Robert, as Robert told me:

"Andy should have located his works a few miles farther east." But Mr. Thomson knew the good and sufficient reasons which determined the selection of the unrivaled site.

The works were well advanced when the financial panic of September, 1873, came upon us. I then entered upon the most anxious period of my business life. All was going well when one morning in our summer cottage, in the Allegheny Mountains at Cresson, a telegram came announcing the failure of Jay Cooke & Co. Almost every hour after brought news of some fresh disaster. House after house failed. The question every morning was which would go next. Every failure depleted the resources of other concerns. Loss after loss ensued, until a total paralysis of business set in. Every weak spot was discovered and houses that otherwise would have been strong were borne down largely because our country lacked a proper banking system.

We had not much reason to be anxious about our debts. Not what we had to pay of our own debts could give us much trouble, but rather what we might have to pay for our debtors. It was not our bills payable but our bills receivable which required attention, for we soon had to begin meeting both. Even our own banks had to beg us not to draw upon our balances. One incident will shed some light upon the currency situation. One of our pay-days was approaching. One hundred thousand dollars in small notes were absolutely necessary, and to obtain these we paid a premium of twenty-four hundred dollars in New York and had them expressed to Pittsburgh. It was impossible to borrow money, even upon the best collaterals; but by selling securities, which I had in reserve, considerable sums were realized — the company undertaking to replace them later.

It happened that some of the railway companies whose lines centered in Pittsburgh owed us large sums for material furnished — the Fort Wayne road being the largest debtor. I remember calling upon Mr. Thaw, the vice-president of the Fort Wayne, and telling him we must have our money. He replied:

"You ought to have your money, but we are not paying anything these days that is not protestable."

"Very good," I said, "your freight bills are in that category and we shall follow your excellent example. Now I am going to order that we do not pay you one dollar for freight."

"Well, if you do that," he said, "we will stop your freight."

I said we would risk that. The railway company could not proceed to that extremity. And as a matter of fact we ran for some time without paying the freight bills. It was simply impossible for the manufacturers of Pittsburgh to pay their accruing liabilities when their customers stopped payment. The banks were forced to renew maturing paper. They behaved splendidly to us, as they always have done, and we steered safely through. But in a critical period like this there was one thought uppermost with me, to gather more capital and keep it in our business so that come what would we should never again be called upon to endure such nights and days of racking anxiety.

Speaking for myself in this great crisis, I was at first the most excited and anxious of the partners. I could scarcely control myself. But when I finally saw the strength of our financial position I became philosophically cool and found myself quite prepared, if necessary, to enter the directors' rooms of the various banks with which we dealt, and lay our entire position before their boards. I felt that this could result in nothing discreditable to us. No one interested in our business had lived extravagantly. Our manner of life had been the very reverse of this. No money had been withdrawn from the business to build costly homes, and, above all, not one of us had made speculative ventures upon the stock exchange, or invested in any other enterprises than those connected with the main business. Neither had we exchanged endorsements with others. Besides this we could show a prosperous business that was making money every year.

I was thus enabled to laugh away the fears of my partners, but none of them rejoiced more than I did that the necessity for opening our lips to anybody about our finances did not arise. Mr. Coleman, good friend and true, with plentiful means and splendid credit, did not fail to volunteer to give us his endorsements. In this we stood alone; William Coleman's name, a tower of strength, was for us only. How the grand old man comes before me as I write. His patriotism knew no bounds. Once when visiting his mills, stopped for the Fourth of July, as they always were, he found a corps of men at work repairing the boilers. He called the manager to him and asked what this meant. He ordered all work suspended.

"Work on the Fourth of July!" he exclaimed, "when there's plenty of Sundays for repairs!" He was furious.

When the cyclone of 1873 struck us we at once began to reef sail in every quarter. Very reluctantly did we decide that the construction of the new steel works must cease for a time. Several prominent persons, who had invested in them, became unable to meet their payments and I was compelled to take over their interests, repaying the full cost to all. In that way control of the company came into my hands.

The first outburst of the storm had affected the financial world connected with the Stock Exchange. It was some time before it reached the commercial and manufacturing world. But the situation grew worse and worse and finally led to the crash which involved my friends in the Texas Pacific enterprise, of which I have already spoken. This was to me the severest blow of all. People could, with difficulty, believe that occupying such intimate relations as I did with the Texas groups, I could by any possibility have kept myself clear of their financial obligations.

Mr. Schoenberger, president of the Exchange Bank at Pittsburgh, with which we conducted a large business, was in New York when the news reached him of the embarrassment of Mr. Scott and Mr. Thomson. He hastened to Pittsburgh, and at a meeting of his board next morning said it was simply impossible that I was not involved with them. He suggested that the bank should refuse to discount more of our bills receivable. He was alarmed to find that the amount of these bearing our endorsement and under discount, was so large. Prompt action on my part was necessary to prevent serious trouble. I took the first train for Pittsburgh, and was able to announce there to all concerned that, although I was a shareholder in the Texas enterprise, my interest was paid for. My name was not upon one dollar of their paper or of any other outstanding paper. I stood clear and clean without a financial obligation or property which I did not own and which was not fully paid for. My only obligations were those connected with our business; and I was prepared to pledge for it every dollar I owned, and to endorse every obligation the firm had outstanding.

Up to this time I had the reputation in business of being a bold, fearless, and perhaps a somewhat reckless young man. Our operations had been extensive, our growth rapid and, although still young, I had been handling millions. My own career was thought by the elderly ones of Pittsburgh to have been rather more brilliant than substantial. I know of an experienced one who declared that if "Andrew Carnegie's brains did not carry him through his luck would." But I think nothing could be farther from the truth than the estimate thus suggested. I am sure that any competent judge would be surprised to find how little I ever risked for myself or my partners. When I did big things, some large corporation like the Pennsylvania Railroad Company was behind me and the responsible party. My supply of Scotch caution never has been small; but I was apparently something of a dare-devil now and then to the manufacturing fathers of Pittsburgh. They were old and I was young, which made all the difference.

The fright which Pittsburgh financial institutions had with regard to myself and our enterprises rapidly gave place to perhaps somewhat unreasoning confidence. Our credit became unassailable, and thereafter in times of financial pressure the offerings of money to us increased rather than diminished, just as the deposits of the old Bank of Pittsburgh were never so great as when the deposits of other banks ran low. It was the only bank in America which redeemed its circulation in gold, disdaining to take refuge under the law and pay its obligations in greenbacks. It had few notes, and I doubt not the decision paid as an advertisement.

In addition to the embarrassment of my friends Mr. Scott, Mr. Thomson, and others, there came upon us later an even severer trial in the discovery that our partner, Mr. Andrew Kloman, had been led by a party of speculative people into the Escanaba Iron Company. He was assured that the concern was to be made a stock company, but before this was done his colleagues had succeeded in creating an enormous amount of liabilities — about seven hundred thousand dollars. There was nothing but bankruptcy as a means of reinstating Mr. Kloman.

This gave us more of a shock than all that had preceded, because Mr. Kloman, being a partner, had no right to invest in another iron company, or in any other company involving personal debt, without informing his partners. There is one imperative rule for men in business — no secrets from partners. Disregard of this rule involved not only Mr. Kloman himself, but our company, in peril, coming, as it did, atop of the difficulties of my Texas Pacific friends with whom I had been intimately associated. The question for a time was whether there was anything really sound. Where could we find bedrock upon which we could stand?

Had Mr. Kloman been a business man it would have been impossible ever to allow him to be a partner with us again after this discovery. He was not such, however, but the ablest of practical mechanics with some business ability. Mr. Kloman's ambition had been to be in the office, where he was worse than useless, rather than in the mill devising and running new machinery, where he was without a peer. We had some difficulty in placing him in his proper position and keeping him there, which may have led him to seek an outlet elsewhere. He was perhaps flattered by men who were well known in the community; and in this case he was led by persons who knew how to reach him by extolling his wonderful business abilities in addition to his mechanical genius — abilities which his own partners, as already suggested, but faintly recognized.

After Mr. Kloman had passed through the bankruptcy court and was again free, we offered him a ten per cent interest in our business, charging for it only the actual capital invested, with nothing whatever for good-will. This we were to carry for him until the profits paid for it. We were to charge interest only on the cost, and he was to assume no responsibility. The offer was accompanied by the condition that he should not enter into any other business or endorse for others, but give his whole time and attention to the mechanical and not the business management of the mills. Could he have been persuaded to accept this, he would have been a multimillionaire; but his pride, and more particularly that of his family, perhaps, would not permit this. He would go into business on his own account, and notwithstanding the most urgent appeals on my part, and that of my colleagues, he persisted in the determination to start a new rival concern with his sons as business managers. The result was failure and premature death.

How foolish we are not to recognize what we are best fitted for and can perform, not only with ease but with pleasure, as masters of the craft. More than one able man I have known has persisted in blundering in an office when he had gained talent for the mill, and has worn himself out, oppressed with cares and anxieties, his life a continual round of misery, and the result at last failure. I never regretted parting with any man so much as with Mr. Kloman. His was a good heart, a great mechanical brain, and had he been left to himself I believe he would have been glad to remain with us. Offers of capital from others — offers which failed when needed — turned his head, and the great mechanic soon proved the poor man of affairs.[1]

[1] Long after the circumstances here recited, Mr. Isidor Straus called upon Mr. Henry Phipps and asked him if two statements which had been publicly made about Mr. Carnegie and his partners in the steel company were true. Mr. Phipps replied they were not. Then said Mr. Straus:

"Mr. Phipps, you owe it to yourself and also to Mr. Carnegie to say so publicly."

This Mr. Phipps did in the *New York Herald*, January 30, 1904, in the following handsome manner and without Mr. Carnegie's knowledge:

Question: "In a recent publication mention was made of Mr. Carnegie's not having treated Mr. Miller, Mr. Kloman, and yourself properly during your early partnership, and at its termination. Can you tell me anything about this?"

Answer: "Mr. Miller has already spoken for himself in this matter, and I can say that the treatment received from Mr. Carnegie during our partnership, so far as I was concerned, was always fair and liberal.

"My association with Mr. Kloman in business goes back forty-three years. Everything in connection with Mr. Carnegie's partnership with Mr. Kloman was of a pleasant nature.

"At a much more recent date, when the firm of Carnegie, Kloman and Company was formed, the partners were Andrew Carnegie, Thomas M. Carnegie, Andrew Kloman, and myself. The Carnegies held the controlling interest.

"After the partnership agreement was signed, Mr. Kloman said to me that the Carnegies, owning the larger interest, might be too enterprising in making improvements, which might lead us into serious trouble; and he thought that they should consent to an article in the partnership agreement requiring the consent of three partners to make effective any vote for improvements. I told him that we could not exact what he asked, as their larger interest assured them control, but I would speak to them. When the subject was broached, Mr. Carnegie promptly said that if he could not carry Mr. Kloman or myself with his brother in any improvements he would not wish them made. Other matters were arranged by courtesy during our partnership in the same manner."

Question: "What you have told me suggests the question: Why did Mr. Kloman leave the firm?"

Answer: "During the great depression which followed the panic of 1873, Mr. Kloman, through an unfortunate partnership in the Escanaba Furnace Company, lost his means, and his interest in our firm had to be disposed of. We bought it at book value at a time when manufacturing properties were selling at ruinous prices, often as low as one third or one half their cost.

"After the settlement had been made with the creditors of the Escanaba Company, Mr. Kloman was offered an interest by Mr. Carnegie of $100,000 in our firm, to be paid only from future profits. This Mr. Kloman declined, as he did not feel like taking an interest which formerly had been much larger. Mr. Carnegie gave him $40,000 from the firm to make a new start. This amount was invested in a rival concern, which soon closed.

"I knew of no disagreement during this early period with Mr. Carnegie, and their relations continued pleasant as long as Mr. Kloman lived. Harmony always marked their intercourse, and they had the kindliest feeling one for the other."

CHAPTER XIV
Partners, Books, and Travel

WHEN Mr. Kloman had severed his connection with us there was no hesitation in placing William Borntraeger in charge of the mills. It has always been with especial pleasure that I have pointed to the career of William. He came direct from Germany — a young man who could not speak English, but being distantly connected with Mr. Kloman was employed in the mills, at first in a minor capacity. He promptly learned English and became a shipping clerk at six dollars per week. He had not a particle of mechanical knowledge, and yet such was his unflagging zeal and industry for the interests of his employer that he soon became marked for being everywhere about the mill, knowing everything, and attending to everything.

William was a character. He never got over his German idioms and his inverted English made his remarks very effective. Under his superintendence the Union Iron Mills became a most profitable branch of our business. He had overworked himself after a few years' application and we decided to give him a trip to Europe. He came to New York by way of Washington. When he called upon me in New York he expressed himself as more anxious to return to Pittsburgh than to revisit Germany. In ascending the Washington Monument he had seen the Carnegie beams in the stairway and also at other points in public buildings, and as he expressed it:

"It yust make me so broud dat I want to go right back and see dat everyting is going right at de mill."

Early hours in the morning and late in the dark hours

at night William was in the mills. His life was there. He was among the first of the young men we admitted to partnership, and the poor German lad at his death was in receipt of an income, as I remember, of about $50,000 a year, every cent of which was deserved. Stories about him are many. At a dinner of our partners to celebrate the year's business, short speeches were in order from everyone. William summed up his speech thus:

"What we haf to do, shentlemens, is to get brices up and costs down and efery man *stand on his own bottom.*" There was loud, prolonged, and repeated laughter.

Captain Evans ("Fighting Bob") was at one time government inspector at our mills. He was a severe one. William was sorely troubled at times and finally offended the Captain, who complained of his behavior. We tried to get William to realize the importance of pleasing a government official. William's reply was:

"But he gomes in and smokes my cigars" (bold Captain! William reveled in one-cent Wheeling tobies) "and then he goes and contems my iron. What does you tinks of a man like dat? But I apologize and dreat him right tomorrow."

The Captain was assured William had agreed to make due amends, but he laughingly told us afterward that William's apology was:

"Vell, Captain, I hope you vas all right dis morning. I haf noting against you, Captain," holding out his hand, which the Captain finally took and all was well.

William once sold to our neighbor, the pioneer steelmaker of Pittsburgh, James Park, a large lot of old rails which we could not use. Mr. Park found them of a very bad quality. He made claims for damages and William was told that he must go with Mr. Phipps to meet Mr. Parks and settle. Mr. Phipps went into Mr. Park's office, while William took a look around the works in search of the condemned material, which was nowhere to be seen. Well did William know where to look. He finally entered the office, and before Mr. Park had time to say a word William began:

"Mr. Park, I was glad to hear dat de old rails what I sell you don't suit for steel. I will buy dem all from you back, five dollars ton profit for you." Well did William know that they had all been used. Mr. Park was nonplussed, and the affair ended. William had triumphed.

Upon one of my visits to Pittsburgh William told me he had something "particular" he wished to tell me — something he couldn't tell anyone else. This was upon his return from the trip to Germany. There he had been asked to visit for a few days a former schoolfellow, who had risen to be a professor:

"Well, Mr. Carnegie, his sister who kept his house was very kind to me, and ven I got to Hamburg I tought I sent her yust a little present. She write me a letter, then I write her a letter. She write me and I write her, and den I ask her would she marry me. She was very educated, but she write yes. Den I ask her to come to New York, and I meet her dere, but, Mr. Carnegie, dem people don't know noting about business and de mills. Her bruder write me dey want me to go dere again and marry her in Chairmany, and I can go away not again from de mills. I tought I yust ask you aboud it."

"Of course you can go again. Quite right, William, you should go. I think the better of her people for feeling so. You go over at once and bring her home. I'll arrange it." Then, when parting, I said: "William, I suppose your sweetheart is a beautiful, tall, 'peaches-and-cream' kind of German young lady."

"Vell, Mr. Carnegie, she is a leetle stout. If *I had the*

rolling of her I give her yust one more pass." All William's illustrations were founded on mill practice. [I find myself bursting into fits of laughter this morning (June, 1912) as I re-read this story. But I did this also when reading that "Every man must stand on his own bottom."]

Mr. Phipps had been head of the commercial department of the mills, but when our business was enlarged, he was required for the steel business. Another young man, William L. Abbott, took his place. Mr. Abbott's history is somewhat akin to Borntraeger's. He came to us as a clerk upon a small salary and was soon assigned to the front in charge of the business of the iron mills. He was no less successful than was William. He became a partner with an interest equal to William's, and finally was promoted to the presidency of the company.

Mr. Curry had distinguished himself by this time in his management of the Lucy Furnaces, and he took his place among the partners, sharing equally with the others. There is no way of making a business successful than can vie with the policy of promoting those who render exceptional service. We finally converted the firm of Carnegie, McCandless & Co. into the Edgar Thomson Steel Company, and included my brother and Mr. Phipps, both of whom had declined at first to go into the steel business with their too enterprising senior. But when I showed them the earnings for the first year and told them if they did not get into steel they would find themselves in the wrong boat, they both reconsidered and came with us. It was fortunate for them as for us.

My experience has been that no partnership of new men gathered promiscuously from various fields can prove a good working organization as at first constituted. Changes are required. Our Edgar Thomson Steel Company was no exception to this rule. Even before we began to make rails, Mr. Coleman became dissatisfied with the management of a railway official who had come to us with a great and deserved reputation for method and ability. I had, therefore, to take over Mr. Coleman's interest. It was not long, however, before we found that his judgment was correct. The new man had been a railway auditor, and was excellent in accounts, but it was unjust to expect him, or any other office man, to be able to step into manufacturing and be successful from the start. He had neither the knowledge nor the training for this new work. This does not mean that he was not a splendid auditor. It was our own blunder in expecting the impossible.

The mills were at last about ready to begin[1] and an organization the auditor proposed was laid before me for approval. I found he had divided the works into two departments and had given control of one to Mr. Stevenson, a Scotsman who afterwards made a fine record as a manufacturer, and control of the other to a Mr. Jones. Nothing, I am certain, ever affected the success of the steel company more than the decision which I gave upon that proposal. Upon no account could two men be in the same works with equal authority. An army with two commanders-in-chief, a ship with two captains, could not fare more disastrously than a manufacturing concern with two men in command upon the same ground, even though in two different departments. I said:

"This will not do. I do not know Mr. Stevenson, nor do I know Mr. Jones, but one or the other must be made captain and he alone must report to you."

---

[1] The steel-rail mills were ready and rails were rolled in 1874.

The decision fell upon Mr. Jones and in this way we obtained "The Captain," who afterward made his name famous wherever the manufacture of Bessemer steel is known.

The Captain was then quite young, spare and active, bearing traces of his Welsh descent even in his stature, for he was quite short. He came to us as a two-dollar-a-day mechanic from the neighboring works at Johnstown. We soon saw that he was a character. Every movement told it. He had volunteered as a private during the Civil War and carried himself so finely that he became captain of a company which was never known to flinch. Much of the success of the Edgar Thomson Works belongs to this man.

In later years he declined an interest in the firm which would have made him a millionaire. I told him one day that some of the young men who had been given an interest were now making much more than he was and we had voted to make him a partner. This entailed no financial responsibility, as we always provided that the cost of the interest given was payable only out of profits.

"No," he said, "I don't want to have my thoughts running on business. I have enough trouble looking after these works. Just give me a h—l of a salary if you think I'm worth it."

"All right, Captain, the salary of the President of the United States is yours."

"That's the talk," said the little Welshman.[1]

[1] The story is told that when Mr. Carnegie was selecting his younger partners he one day sent for a young Scotsman, Alexander R. Peacock, and asked him rather abruptly:

"Peacock, what would you give to be made a millionaire?"

"A liberal discount for cash, sir," was the answer.

He was a partner owning a two per cent interest when the Carnegie Steel Company was merged into the United States Steel Corporation.

Our competitors in steel were at first disposed to ignore us. Knowing the difficulties they had in starting their own steel works, they could not believe we would be ready to deliver rails for another year, and declined to recognize us as competitors. The price of steel rails when we began was about seventy dollars per ton. We sent our agent through the country with instructions to take orders at the best prices he could obtain; and before our competitors knew it, we had obtained a large number — quite sufficient to justify us in making a start.

So perfect was the machinery, so admirable the plans, so skillful were the men selected by Captain Jones, and so great a manager was he himself, that our success was phenomenal. I think I place a unique statement on record when I say that the result of the first month's operations left a margin of profit of $11,000. It is also remarkable that so perfect was our system of accounts that we knew the exact amount of the profit. We had learned from experience in our iron works what exact accounting meant. There is nothing more profitable than clerks to check up each transfer of material from one department to another in process of manufacture.

The new venture in steel having started off so promisingly, I began to think of taking a holiday, and my long-cherished purpose of going around the world came to the front. Mr. J. W. Vandevort ("Vandy") and I accordingly set out in the autumn of 1878. I took with me several pads suitable for penciling and began to make a few notes day by day, not with any intention of publishing a book; but thinking, perhaps, I might print a few copies of my notes for private circulation. The sensation which one has when he first sees his remarks in the form of a printed book is great. When the package came from the printers I re-read the book trying to decide whether it was worth while to send copies to my friends. I came to the conclusion that upon the whole it was best to do so and await the verdict.

The writer of a book designed for his friends has no reason to anticipate an unkind reception, but there is always some danger of its being damned with faint praise. The responses in my case, however, exceeded expectations, and were of such a character as to satisfy me that the writers really had enjoyed the book, or meant at least a part of what they said about it. Every author is prone to believe sweet words. Among the first that came were in a letter from Anthony Drexel, Philadelphia's great banker, complaining that I had robbed him of several hours of sleep. Having begun the book he could not lay it down and retired at two o'clock in the morning after finishing. Several similar letters were received. I remember Mr. Huntington, president of the Central Pacific Railway, meeting me one morning and saying he was going to pay me a great compliment.

"What is it?" I asked.

"Oh, I read your book from end to end."

"Well," I said, "that is not such a great compliment. Others of our mutual friends have done that."

"Oh, yes, but probably none of your friends are like me. I have not read a book for years except my ledger, and I did not intend to read yours, but when I began it I could not lay it down. My ledger is the only book I have gone through for five years."

I was not disposed to credit all that my friends said, but others who had obtained the book from them were pleased with it and I lived for some months under intoxicating, but I trust not periously pernicious, flattery. Several editions of the book were printed to meet the request for copies. Some notices of it and extracts got into the papers, and finally Charles Scribner's Sons asked to publish it for the market. So "Round the World"[1] came before the public and I was at last "an author."

A new horizon was opened up to me by this voyage. It quite changed my intellectual outlook. Spencer and Darwin were then high in the zenith, and I had become deeply interested in their work. I began to view the various phases of human life from the standpoint of the evolutionist. In China I read Confucius; in India, Buddha and the sacred books of the Hindoos; among the Parsees, in Bombay, I studied Zoroaster. The result of my journey was to bring a certain mental peace. Where there had been chaos there was now order. My mind was at rest. I had a philosophy at last. The words of Christ "The Kingdom of Heaven is within you," had a new meaning for me. Not in the past or in the future, but now and here is Heaven within us. All our duties lie in this world and in the present, and trying impatiently to peer into that which lies beyond is as vain as fruitless.

All the remnants of theology in which I had been born and bred, all the impressions that Swedenborg had made upon me, now ceased to influence me or to occupy my thoughts. I found that no nation had all the truth in the revelation it regards as divine, and no tribe is so low as to be left without some truth; that every people has had its great teacher; Buddha for one; Confucius for another; Zoroaster for a third; Christ for a fourth. The teachings of all these I found ethically akin so that I could say with Matthew Arnold, one I was so proud to call friend:

---

[1] *Round the World,* by Andrew Carnegie. New York and London, 1884.

"Children of men! the unseen Power, whose eye
  For ever doth accompany mankind
  Hath looked on no religion scornfully
      That men did ever find.

Which has not taught weak wills how much they can?
Which has not fall'n in the dry heart like rain?
Which has not cried to sunk, self-weary man,
      Thou must be born again."

"The Light of Asia," by Edwin Arnold, came out at this time and gave me greater delight than any similar poetical work I had recently read. I had just been in India and the book took me there again. My appreciation of it reached the author's ears and later having made his acquaintance in London, he presented me with the original manuscript of the book. It is one of my most precious treasures. Every person who can, even at a sacrifice, make the voyage around the world should do so. All other travel compared to it seems incomplete, gives us merely vague impressions of parts of the whole. When the circle has been completed, you feel on your return that you have seen (of course only in the mass) all there is to be seen. The parts fit into one symmetrical whole and you see humanity wherever it is placed working out a destiny tending to one definite end.

The world traveler who gives careful study to the bibles of the various religions of the East will be well repaid. The conclusion reached will be that the inhabitants of each country consider their own religion the best of all. They rejoice that their lot has been cast where it is, and are disposed to pity the less fortunate condemned to live beyond their sacred limits. The masses of all nations are usually happy, each mass certain that:

"East or West
Home is best."

Two illustrations of this from our "Round the World" trip may be noted:

Visiting the tapioca workers in the woods near Singapore, we found them busily engaged, the children running about stark naked, the parents clothed in the usual loose rags. Our party attracted great attention. We asked our guide to tell the people that we came from a country where the water in such a pond as that before us would become solid at this season of the year and we could walk upon it, and that sometimes it would be so hard that horses and wagons crossed wide rivers on the ice. They wondered and asked why we didn't come and live among them. They really were very happy.

Again:

On the way to the North Cape we visited a reindeer camp of the Laplanders. A sailor from the ship was deputed to go with the party. I walked homeward with him, and as we approached the fiord looking down and over to the opposite shore we saw a few straggling huts and one two-story house under construction. "What is that new building for?" we asked.

"That is to be the home of a man born in Tromso who has made a great deal of money and has now come back to spend his days there. He is very rich."

"You told me you had travelled all over the world. You have seen London, New York, Calcutta, Melbourne, and other places. If you made a fortune like that man what place would you make your home in old age?" His eye glistened as he said:

"Ah, there's no place like Tromso." This is in the arctic circle, six months of night, but he had been born in Tromso. Home, sweet, sweet home!

Among the conditions of life or the laws of Nature, some of which seem to us faulty, some apparently un-just and merciless, there are many that amaze us by their beauty and sweetness. Love of home, regardless of its character or location, certainly is one of these. And what a pleasure it is to find that, instead of the

Supreme Being confining revelation to one race or nation, every race has the message best adapted for it in its present stage of development. The Unknown Power has neglected none.

CHAPTER XV
Coaching Trip and Marriage

THE Freedom of my native town (Dunfermline) was conferred upon me July 12, 1877, the first Freedom and the greatest honor I ever received. I was overwhelmed. Only two signatures upon the roll came between mine and Sir Walter Scott's, who had been made a Burgess. My parents had seen him one day sketching Dunfermline Abbey and often told me about his appearance. My speech in reply to the Freedom was the subject of much concern. I spoke to my Uncle Bailie Morrison, telling him I just felt like saying so and so, as this really was in my heart. He was an orator himself and he spoke words of wisdom to me then.

"Just say that, Andra; nothing like saying just what you really feel."

It was a lesson in public speaking which I took to heart. There is one rule I might suggest for youthful orators. When you stand up before an audience reflect that there are before you only men and women. You should speak to them as you speak to other men and women in daily intercourse. If you are not trying to be something different from yourself, there is no more occasion for embarrassment than if you were talking in your office to a party of your own people — none whatever. It is trying to be other than one's self that unmans one. Be your own natural self and go ahead. I once asked Colonel Ingersoll, the most effective public speaker I ever heard, to what he attributed his power. "Avoid elocutionists like snakes," he said, "and be yourself."

I spoke again at Dunfermline, July 27, 1881, when my mother laid the foundation stone there of the first free library building I ever gave. My father was one of five weavers who founded the earliest library in the town by opening their own books to their neighbors. Dunfermline named the building I gave "Carnegie Library." The architect asked for my coat of arms. I informed him I had none, but suggested that above the door there might be carved a rising sun shedding its rays with the motto: "Let there be light." This he adopted.

We had come up to Dunfermline with a coaching party. When walking through England in the year 1867 with George Lauder and Harry Phipps I had formed the idea of coaching from Brighton to Inverness with a party of my dearest friends. The time had come for the long-promised trip, and in the spring of 1881 we sailed from New York, a party of eleven, to enjoy one of the happiest excursions of my life. It was one of the holidays from business that kept me young and happy — worth all the medicine in the world.

All the notes I made of the coaching trip were a few lines a day in twopenny pass-books bought before we started. As with "Round the World," I thought that I might some day write a magazine article, or give some account of my excursion for those who accompanied me; but one wintry day I decided that it was scarcely worth while to go down to the New York office, three miles distant, and the question was how I should occupy the spare time. I thought of the coaching trip, and decided to write a few lines just to see how I should get on. The narrative flowed freely, and before the day was over I had written between three and four thousand words. I took up the pleasing task every stormy day when it was unnecessary for me to visit the office, and in exactly twenty sittings I had finished a book. I handed the notes to Scribner's people and asked them to print a few hundred copies for private circulation. The volume pleased my friends, as "Round the World" had done. Mr. Champlin one day told me that Mr. Scribner had read the book and would like very much to publish it for general circulation upon his own account, subject to a royalty.

The vain author is easily persuaded that what he has done is meritorious, and I consented. [Every year this still nets me a small sum in royalties. And thirty years have gone by, 1912.] The letters I received upon the publication[1] of it were so numerous and some so gushing that my people saved them and they are now bound together in scrapbook form, to which additions are made from time to time. The number of invalids who have been pleased to write me, stating that the book had brightened their lives, has been gratifying. Its reception in Britain was cordial; the "Spectator" gave it a favorable review. But any merit that the book has comes, I am sure, from the total absence of effort on my part to make an impression. I wrote for my friends; and what one does easily, one does well. I reveled in the writing of the book, as I had in the journey itself.

The year 1886 ended in deep gloom for me. My life as a happy careless young man, with every want looked after, was over. I was left alone in the world. My mother and brother passed away in November, within a few days of each other, while I lay in bed under a severe attack of typhoid fever, unable to move and, perhaps

[1] Published privately in 1882 under the title *Our Coaching Trip, Brighton to Inverness*. Published by the Scribners in 1883 under the title of *An American Four-in-Hand in Britain*.

fortunately, unable to feel the full weight of the catastrophe, being myself face to face with death.

I was the first stricken, upon returning from a visit in the East to our cottage at Cresson Springs on top of the Alleghanies where my mother and I spent our happy summers. I had been quite unwell for a day or two before leaving New York. A physician being summoned, my trouble was pronounced typhoid fever. Professor Dennis was called from New York and he corroborated the diagnosis. An attendant physician and trained nurse were provided at once. Soon after my mother broke down and my brother in Pittsburgh also was reported ill.

I was despaired of, I was so low, and then my whole nature seemed to change. I became reconciled, indulged in pleasing meditations, was without the slightest pain. My mother's and brother's serious condition had not been revealed to me, and when I was informed that both had left me forever it seemed only natural that I should follow them. We had never been separated; why should we be now? But it was decreed otherwise.

I recovered slowly and the future began to occupy my thoughts. There was only one ray of hope and comfort in it. Toward that my thoughts always turned. For several years I had known Miss Louise Whitfield. Her mother permitted her to ride with me in the Central Park. We were both very fond of riding. Other young ladies were on my list. I had fine horses and often rode in the Park and around New York with one or the other of the circle. In the end the others all faded into ordinary beings. Miss Whitfield remained alone as the perfect one beyond any I had met. Finally I began to find and admit to myself that she stood the supreme test I had applied to several fair ones in my time. She alone did so of all I had ever known. I could recommend young men to apply this test before offering themselves. If they can honestly believe the following lines, as I did, then all is well:

> "Full many a lady
> I've eyed with best regard: for several virtues
> Have I liked several women, never any
> With so full soul, but some defect in her
> Did quarrel with the noblest grace she owed,
> And put it to the foil; but you, O you,
> So perfect and so peerless are created
> Of every creature's best."[1]

In my soul I could echo those very words. To-day, after twenty years of life with her, if I could find stronger words I could truthfully use them.

My advances met with indifferent success. She was not without other and younger admirers. My wealth and future plans were against me. I was rich and had everything and she felt she could be of little use or benefit to me. Her ideal was to be the real helpmeet of a young, struggling man to whom she could and would be indispensable, as her mother had been to her father. The care of her own family had largely fallen upon her after her father's death when she was twenty-one. She was now twenty-eight; her views of life were formed. At times she seemed more favorable and we corresponded. Once, however, she returned my letters saying she felt she must put aside all thought of accepting me.

Professor and Mrs. Dennis took me from Cresson to their own home in New York, as soon as I could be removed, and I lay there some time under the former's personal supervision. Miss Whitfield called to see me, for I had written her the first words from Cresson I was

---

[1] Ferdinand to Miranda in *The Tempest*.

DUNFERMLINE ABBEY

ANDREW CARNEGIE'S BIRTHPLACE

ANDREW CARNEGIE AT SIXTEEN
WITH HIS BROTHER THOMAS

ANDREW CARNEGIE'S MOTHER

ROBERT PITCAIRN

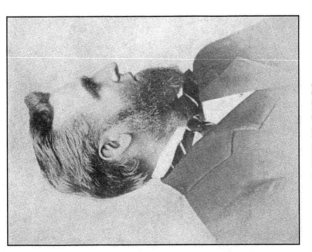

DAVID McCARGO

HENRY PHIPPS

COLONEL JAMES ANDERSON

JOHN EDGAR THOMSON

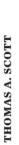

THOMAS A. SCOTT

GEORGE LAUDER

THOMAS MORRISON CARNEGIE

JOHN PIERPONT MORGAN

JUNIUS SPENCER MORGAN

AN AMERICAN FOUR-IN-HAND IN BRITAIN

MRS. ANDREW CARNEGIE

ANDREW CARNEGIE
(ABOUT 1878)

CHARLES M. SCHWAB

MARGARET CARNEGIE AT FIFTEEN

THE CARNEGIE INSTITUTE AT PITTSBURGH

MATTHEW ARNOLD

ANDREW CARNEGIE AND VISCOUNT BRYCE

VISCOUNT MORLEY OF BLACKBURN

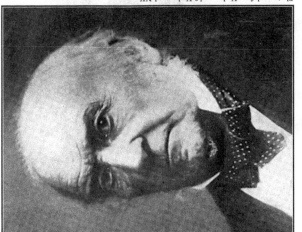

WILLIAM E. GLADSTONE

THE CARNEGIE FAMILY AT SKIBO

MR. CARNEGIE WITH VISCOUNT MORLEY

JAMES G. BLAINE

HERBERT SPENCER AT SEVENTY-EIGHT

ANDREW CARNEGIE AT SKIBO
(1914)

SKIBO CASTLE

able to write. She saw now that I needed her. I was left alone in the world. Now she could be in every sense the "helpmeet." Both her heart and head were now willing and the day was fixed. We were married in New York April 22, 1887, and sailed for our honeymoon which was passed on the Isle of Wight.

Her delight was intense in finding the wild flowers. She had read of Wandering Willie, Heartsease, Forget-me-nots, the Primrose, Wild Thyme, and the whole list of homely names that had been to her only names till now. Everything charmed her. Uncle Lauder and one of my cousins came down from Scotland and visited us, and then we soon followed to the residence at Kilgraston they had selected for us in which to spend the summer. Scotland captured her. There was no doubt about that. Her girlish reading had been of Scotland — Scott's novels and "Scottish Chiefs" being her favorites. She soon became more Scotch than I. All this was fulfilling my fondest dreams.

We spent some days in Dunfermline and enjoyed them much. The haunts and incidents of my boyhood were visited and recited to her by all and sundry. She got nothing but flattering accounts of her husband which gave me a good start with her.

I was presented with the Freedom of Edinburgh as we passed northward — Lord Rosebery making the speech. The crowd in Edinburgh was great. I addressed the working-men in the largest hall and received a present from them as did Mrs. Carnegie also — a brooch she values highly. She heard and saw the pipers in all their glory and begged there should be one at our home — a piper to walk around and waken us in the morning and also to play us in to dinner. American as she is to the core, and Connecticut Puritan at that, she declared that if condemned to live upon a lonely island and allowed to choose only one musical instrument, it would be the pipes. The piper was secured quickly enough. One called and presented credentials from Cluny McPherson. We engaged him and were preceded by him playing the pipes as we entered our Kilgraston house.

We enjoyed Kilgraston, although Mrs. Carnegie still longed for a wilder and more Highland home. Matthew Arnold visited us, as did Mr. and Mrs. Blaine, Senator and Mrs. Eugene Hale, and many friends.[1] Mrs. Carnegie would have my relatives up from Dunfermline, especially the older uncles and aunties. She charmed everyone. They expressed their surprise to me that she ever married me, but I told them I was equally surprised. The match had evidently been predestined.

We took our piper with us when we returned to New York, and also our housekeeper and some of the servants. Mrs. Nicoll remains with us still and is now, after twenty years' faithful service, as a member of the family. George Irvine, our butler, came to us a year later and is also as one of us. Maggie Anderson, one of the

---

[1] John Hay, writing to his friend Henry Adams under date of London, August 25, 1887, has the following to say about the party at Kilgraston: "After that we went to Andy Carnegie in Perthshire, who is keeping his honeymoon, having just married a pretty girl. . . . The house is thronged with visitors — sixteen when we came away — we merely stayed three days: the others were there for a fortnight. Among them were your friends Blaine and Hale of Maine. Carnegie likes it so well he is going to do it every summer and is looking at all the great estates in the County with a view of renting or purchasing. We went with him one day to Dupplin Castle, where I saw the most beautiful trees I ever beheld in my wandering life. The old Earl of —— is miserably poor — not able to buy a bottle of seltzer — with an estate worth millions in the hands of his creditors, and sure to be sold one of these days to some enterprising Yankee or British Buttonmaker. I wish you or Carnegie would buy it. I would visit you frequently." (Thayer, *Life and Letters of John Hay*, vol. II, p. 74.)

servants, is the same. They are devoted people, of high character and true loyalty.[1]

The next year we were offered and took Cluny Castle. Our piper was just the man to tell us all about it. He had been born and bred there and perhaps influenced our selection of that residence where we spent several summers.

On March 30, 1897, there came to us our daughter. As I first gazed upon her Mrs. Carnegie said,

"Her name is Margaret after your mother. Now one request I have to make."

"What is it, Lou?"

"We must get a summer home since this little one has been given us. We cannot rent one and be obliged to go in and go out at a certain date. It should be our home."

"Yes," I agreed.

"I make only one condition."

"What is that?" I asked.

"It must be in the Highlands of Scotland."

"Bless you," was my reply. "That suits me. You know I have to keep out of the sun's rays, and where can we do that so surely as among the heather? I'll be a committee of one to inquire and report."

Skibo Castle was the result.

It is now twenty years since Mrs. Carnegie entered and changed my life, a few months after the passing of my mother and only brother left me alone in the world. My life has been made so happy by her that I cannot imagine myself living without her guardianship. I thought I knew her when she stood Ferdinand's test,[2] but it was only the surface of her qualities I had seen

---

[1] "No man is a true gentleman who does not inspire the affection and devotion of his servants." (*Problems of To-day*, by Andrew Carnegie. New York, 1908, p. 59.)

[2] The reference is to the quotation from *The Tempest* on page 214.

and felt. Of their purity, holiness, wisdom, I had not sounded the depth. In every emergency of our active, changing, and in later years somewhat public life, in all her relations with others, including my family and her own, she has proved the diplomat and peace-maker. Peace and goodwill attend her footsteps wherever her blessed influence extends. In the rare instances demanding heroic action it is she who first realizes this and plays the part.

The Peace-Maker has never had a quarrel in all her life, not even with a schoolmate, and there does not live a soul upon the earth who has met her who has the slightest cause to complain of neglect. Not that she does not welcome the best and gently avoid the undesirable — none is more fastidious than she — but neither rank, wealth, nor social position affects her one iota. She is incapable of acting or speaking rudely; all is in perfect good taste. Still, she never lowers the standard. Her intimates are only of the best. She is always thinking how she can do good to those around her — planning for this one and that in case of need and making such judicious arrangements or presents as surprise those cooperating with her.

I cannot imagine myself going through these twenty years without her. Nor can I endure the thought of living after her. In the course of nature I have not that to meet; but then the thought of what will be cast upon her, a woman left alone with so much requiring attention and needing a man to decide, gives me intense pain and I sometimes wish I had this to endure for her. But then she will have our blessed daughter in her life and perhaps that will keep her patient. Besides, Margaret needs her more than she does her father.

Why, oh, why, are we compelled to leave the heaven

we have found on earth and go we know not where! For I
can say with Jessica:

> "It is very meet
> The Lord Bassanio live an upright life;
> For, having such a blessing in his lady,
> He finds the joys of heaven here on earth."

CHAPTER XVI
Mills and the Men

THE one vital lesson in iron and steel that I learned in Britain was the necessity for owning raw materials and finishing the completed article ready for its purpose. Having solved the steel-rail problem at the Edgar Thomson Works, we soon proceeded to the next step. The difficulties and uncertainties of obtaining regular supplies of pig iron compelled us to begin the erection of blast furnaces. Three of these were built, one, however, being a reconstructed blast furnace purchased from the Escanaba Iron Company, with which Mr. Kloman had been connected. As is usual in such cases, the furnace cost us as much as a new one, and it never was as good. There is nothing so unsatisfactory as purchases of inferior plants.

But although this purchase was a mistake, directly considered, it proved, at a subsequent date, a source of great profit because it gave us a furnace small enough for the manufacture of spiegel and, at a later date, of ferro-manganese. We were the second firm in the United States to manufacture our own spiegel, and the first, and for years the only, firm in America that made ferro-manganese. We had been dependent upon foreigners for a supply of this indispensable article, paying as high as eighty dollars a ton for it. The manager of our blast furnaces, Mr. Julian Kennedy, is entitled to the credit of suggesting that with the ores within reach we could make ferro-manganese in our small furnace. The experiment was worth trying and the result was a great success. We were able to supply the entire American demand and prices fell from eighty to fifty dollars per ton as a consequence.

While testing the ores of Virginia we found that these were being quietly purchased by Europeans for ferromanganese, the owners of the mine being led to believe that they were used for other purposes. Our Mr. Phipps at once set about purchasing that mine. He obtained an option from the owners, who had neither capital nor skill to work it efficiently. A high price was paid to them for their interests, and (with one of them, Mr. Davis, a very able young man) we became the owners, but not until a thorough investigation of the mine had proved that there was enough of manganese ore in sight to repay us. All this was done with speed; not a day was lost when the discovery was made. And here lies the great advantage of a partnership over a corporation. The president of the latter would have had to consult a board of directors and wait several weeks and perhaps months for their decision. By that time the mine would probably have become the property of others.

We continued to develop our blast-furnace plant, every new one being a great improvement upon the preceding, until at last we thought we had arrived at a standard furnace. Minor improvements would no doubt be made, but so far as we could see we had a perfect plant and our capacity was then fifty thousand tons per month of pig iron.

The blast-furnace department was no sooner added than another step was seen to be essential to our independence and success. The supply of superior coke was a fixed quantity — the Connellsville field being defined. We found that we could not get on without a supply of the fuel essential to the smelting of pig iron; and a very thorough investigation of the question led us to the conclusion that the Frick Coke Company had not only the best coal and coke property, but that it had in Mr. Frick himself a man with a positive genius for its management. He had proved his ability by starting as a poor railway clerk and succeeding. In 1882 we purchased one half of the stock of this company, and by subsequent purchases from other holders we became owners of the great bulk of the shares.

There now remained to be acquired only the supply of ironstone. If we could obtain this we should be in the position occupied by only two or three of the European concerns. We thought at one time we had succeeded in discovering in Pennsylvania this last remaining link in the chain. We were misled, however, in our investment in the Tyrone region, and lost considerable sums as the result of our attempts to mine and use the ores of that section. They promised well at the edges of the mines, where the action of the weather for ages had washed away impurities and enriched the ore, but when we penetrated a small distance they proved too "lean" to work.

Our chemist, Mr. Prousser, was then sent to a Pennsylvania furnace among the hills which we had leased, with instructions to analyze all the materials brought to him from the district, and to encourage people to bring him specimens of minerals. A striking example of the awe inspired by the chemist in those days was that only with great difficulty could he obtain a man or a boy to assist him in the laboratory. He was suspected of illicit intercourse with the Powers of Evil when he undertook to tell by his suspicious-looking apparatus what a stone contained. I believe that at last we had to send him a man from our office at Pittsburgh.

One day he sent us a report of analyses of ore remarkable for the absence of phosphorus. It was really an ore suitable for making Bessemer steel. Such a discovery attracted our attention at once. The owner of the property was Moses Thompson, a rich farmer, proprietor of seven thousand acres of the most beautiful agricultural land in Center County, Pennsylvania. An appointment was made to meet him upon the ground from which the ore had been obtained. We found the mine had been worked for a charcoal blast furnace fifty or sixty years before, but it had not borne a good reputation then, the reason no doubt being that its product was so much purer than other ores that the same amount of flux used caused trouble in smelting. It was so good it was good for nothing in those days of old.

We finally obtained the right to take the mine over at any time within six months, and we therefore began the work of examination, which every purchaser of mineral property should make most carefully. We ran lines across the hillside fifty feet apart, with cross-lines at distances of a hundred feet apart, and at each point of intersection we put a shaft down through the ore. I believe there were eighty such shafts in all and the ore was analyzed at every few feet of depth so that before we paid, over the hundred thousand dollars asked we knew exactly what there was of ore. The result hoped for was more than realized. Through the ability of my cousin and partner, Mr. Lauder, the cost of mining and washing was reduced to a low figure, and the Scotia ore made good all the losses we had incurred in the other mines, paid for itself, and left a profit besides. In this case, at least, we snatched victory from the jaws of defeat. We trod upon sure ground with the chemist as our guide. It will be seen that we were determined to get raw materials and were active in the pursuit.

We had lost and won, but the escapes in business affairs are sometimes very narrow. Driving with Mr. Phipps from the mills one day we passed the National Trust Company office on Penn Street, Pittsburgh. I noticed the large gilt letters across the window, "Stockholders individually liable." That very morning in looking over a statement of our affairs I had noticed twenty shares "National Trust Company" on the list of assets. I said to Harry:

"If this is the concern we own shares in, won't you please sell them before you return to the office this afternoon?"

He saw no need for haste. It would be done in good time.

"No, Harry, oblige me by doing it instantly."

He did so and had it transferred. Fortunate, indeed, was this, for in a short time the bank failed with an enormous deficit. My cousin, Mr. Morris, was among the ruined shareholders. Many others met the same fate. Times were panicky, and had we been individually liable for all the debts of the National Trust Company our credit would inevitably have been seriously imperiled. It was a narrow escape. And with only twenty shares (two thousand dollars' worth of stock), taken to oblige friends who wished our name on their list of shareholders! The lesson was not lost. The sound rule in business is that you may give money freely when you have a surplus, but your name never — neither as endorser nor as member of a corporation with individual liability. A trifling investment of a few thousand dollars, a mere trifle — yes, but a trifle possessed of deadly explosive power.

The rapid substitution of steel for iron in the immediate future had become obvious to us. Even in our

Keystone Bridge Works, steel was being used more and more in place of iron. King Iron was about to be deposed by the new King Steel, and we were becoming more and more dependent upon it. We had about concluded in 1886 to build alongside of the Edgar Thomson Mills new works for the manufacture of miscellaneous shapes of steel when it was suggested to us that the five or six leading manufacturers of Pittsburgh, who had combined to build steel mills at Homestead, were willing to sell their mills to us.

These works had been built originally by a syndicate of manufacturers, with the view of obtaining the necessary supplies of steel which they required in their various concerns, but the steel-rail business, being then in one of its booms, they had been tempted to change plans and construct a steel-rail mill. They had been able to make rails as long as prices remained high, but, as the mills had not been specially designed for this purpose, they were without the indispensable blast furnaces for the supply of pig iron, and had no coke lands for the supply of fuel. They were in no condition to compete with us.

It was advantageous for us to purchase these works. I felt there was only one way we could deal with their owners, and that was to propose a consolidation with Carnegie Brothers & Co. We offered to do so on equal terms, every dollar they had invested to rank against our dollars. Upon this basis the negotiation was promptly concluded. We, however, gave to all parties the option to take cash, and most fortunately for us, all elected to do so except Mr. George Singer, who continued with us to his and our entire satisfaction. Mr. Singer told us afterwards that his associates had been greatly exercised as to how they could meet the proposition I was to lay before them. They were much afraid of being over-reached but when I proposed equality all around, dollar for dollar, they were speechless.

This purchase led to the reconstruction of all our firms. The new firm of Carnegie, Phipps & Co. was organized in 1886 to run the Homestead Mills. The firm of Wilson, Walker & Co. was embraced in the firm of Carnegie, Phipps & Co., Mr. Walker being elected chairman. My brother was chairman of Carnegie Brothers & Co. and at the head of all. A further extension of our business was the establishing of the Hartman Steel Works at Beaver Falls, designed to work into a hundred various forms the product of the Homestead Mills. So now we made almost everything in steel from a wire nail up to a twenty-inch steel girder, and it was then not thought probable that we should enter into any new field.

It may be interesting here to note the progress of our works during the decade 1888 to 1897. In 1888 we had twenty millions of dollars invested; in 1897 more than double or over forty-five millions. The 600,000 tons of pig iron we made per annum in 1888 was trebled; we made nearly 2,000,000. Our product of iron and steel was in 1888, say, 2000 tons per day; it grew to exceed 6000 tons. Our coke works then embraced about 5000 ovens; they were trebled in number, and our capacity, then 6000 tons, became 18,000 tons per day. Our Frick Coke Company in 1897 had 42,000 acres of coal land, more than two thirds of the true Connellsville vein. Ten years hence increased production may be found to have been equally rapid. It may be accepted as an axiom that a manufacturing concern in a growing country like ours begins to decay when it stops extending.

To make a ton of steel one and a half tons of iron

stone has to be mined, transported by rail a hundred miles to the Lakes, carried by boat hundreds of miles, transferred to cars, transported by rail one hundred and fifty miles to Pittsburgh; one and a half tons of coal must be mined and manufactured into coke and carried fifty-odd miles by rail; and one ton of limestone mined and carried one hundred and fifty miles to Pittsburgh. How then could steel be manufactured and sold without loss at three pounds for two cents? This, I confess, seemed to me incredible, and little less than miraculous, but it was so.

America is soon to change from being the dearest steel manufacturing country to the cheapest. Already the shipyards of Belfast are our customers. This is but the beginning. Under present conditions America can produce steel as cheaply as any other land, notwithstanding its higher-priced labor. There is no labor so cheap as the dearest in the mechanical field, provided it is free, contented, zealous, and reaping reward as it renders service. And here America leads.

One great advantage which America will have in competing in the markets of the world is that her manufacturers will have the best home market. Upon this they can depend for a return upon capital, and the surplus product can be exported with advantage, even when the prices received for it do not more than cover actual cost, provided the exports be charged with their proportion of all expenses. The nation that has the best home market, especially if products are standardized, as ours are, can soon outsell the foreign producer. The phrase I used in Britain in this connection was: "The Law of the Surplus." It afterward came into general use in commercial discussions.

CHAPTER XVII
The Homestead Strike

WHILE upon the subject of our manufacturing interests, I may record that on July 1, 1892, during
my absence in the Highlands of Scotland, there occurred
the one really serious quarrel with our workmen in our
whole history. For twenty-six years I had been actively in
charge of the relations between ourselves and our men,
and it was the pride of my life to think how delightfully satisfactory these had been and were. I hope I fully deserved
what my chief partner, Mr. Phipps, said in his letter to the
"New York Herald," January 30, 1904, in reply to one who
had declared I had remained abroad during the Homestead strike, instead of flying back to support my partners.
It was to the effect that "I was always disposed to yield to
the demands of the men, however unreasonable"; hence
one or two of my partners did not wish me to return.[1]
Taking no account of the reward that comes from feel-

[1] The full statement of Mr. Phipps is as follows:

Question: "It was stated that Mr. Carnegie acted in a cowardly manner in
not returning to America from Scotland and being present when the strike
was in progress at Homestead."

Answer: "When Mr. Carnegie heard of the trouble at Homestead he immediately wired that he would take the first ship for America, but his partners begged him not to appear, as they were of the opinion that the welfare
of the Company required that he should not be in this country at the time.
They knew of his extreme disposition to always grant the demands of labor,
however unreasonable.

"I have never known of anyone interested in the business to make any
complaint about Mr. Carnegie's absence at that time, but all the partners
rejoiced that they were permitted to manage the affair in their own way."
(Henry Phipps in the *New York Herald*, January 30, 1904.)

ing that you and your employees are friends and judging only from economical results, I believe that higher wages to men who respect their employers and are happy and contented are a good investment, yielding, indeed, big dividends.

The manufacture of steel was revolutionized by the Bessemer open-hearth and basic inventions. The machinery hitherto employed had become obsolete, and our firm, recognizing this, spent several millions at Homestead reconstructing and enlarging the works. The new machinery made about sixty per cent more steel than the old. Two hundred and eighteen tonnage men (that is, men who were paid by the ton of steel produced) were working under a three years' contract, part of the last year being with the new machinery. Thus their earnings had increased almost sixty per cent before the end of the contract.

The firm offered to divide this sixty per cent with them in the new scale to be made thereafter. That is to say, the earnings of the men would have been thirty per cent greater than under the old scale and the other thirty per cent would have gone to the firm to recompense it for its outlay. The work of the men would not have been much harder than it had been hitherto, as the improved machinery did the work. This was not only fair and liberal, it was generous, and under ordinary circumstances would have been accepted by the men with thanks. But the firm was then engaged in making armor for the United States Government, which we had declined twice to manufacture and which was urgently needed. It had also the contract to furnish material for the Chicago Exhibition. Some of the leaders of the men, knowing these conditions, insisted upon demanding the whole sixty per cent, thinking the firm would be compelled to give it. The firm could not agree, nor should it have agreed to such an attempt as this to take it by the throat and say, "Stand and deliver." It very rightly declined. Had I been at home nothing would have induced me to yield to this unfair attempt to extort.

Up to this point all had been right enough. The policy I had pursued in cases of difference with our men was that of patiently waiting, reasoning with them, and showing them that their demands were unfair; but never attempting to employ new men in their places — never. The superintendent of Homestead, however, was assured by the three thousand men who were not concerned in the dispute that they could run the works, and were anxious to rid themselves of the two hundred and eighteen men who had banded themselves into a union and into which they had hitherto refused to admit those in other departments — only the "heaters" and "rollers" of steel being eligible.

My partners were misled by this superintendent, who was himself misled. He had not had great experience in such affairs, having recently been promoted from a subordinate position. The unjust demands of the few union men, and the opinion of the three thousand non-union men that they were unjust, very naturally led him into thinking there would be no trouble and that the workmen would do as they had promised. There were many men among the three thousand who could take, and wished to take, the places of the two hundred and eighteen — at least so it was reported to me.

It is easy to look back and say that the vital step of opening the works should never have been taken. All the firm had to do was to say to the men: "There is a labor dispute here and you must settle it between yourselves. The firm has made you a most liberal offer. The works will run when the dispute is adjusted, and not till then. Meanwhile your places remain open to you." Or, it might have been well if the superintendent had said to the three thousand men, "All right, if you will come and run the works without protection," thus throwing upon them the responsibility of protecting themselves — three thousand men as against two hundred and eighteen. Instead of this it was thought advisable (as an additional precaution by the state officials, I understand) to have the sheriff with guards to protect the thousands against the hundreds. The leaders of the latter were violent and aggressive men; they had guns and pistols, and, as was soon proved, were able to intimidate the thousands.

I quote what I once laid down in writing as our rule: "My idea is that the Company should be known as determined to let the men at any works stop work; that it will confer freely with them and wait patiently until they decide to return to work, never thinking of trying new men — never." The best men as men, and the best workmen, are not walking the streets looking for work. Only the inferior class as a rule is idle. The kind of men we desired are rarely allowed to lose their jobs, even in dull times. It is impossible to get new men to run successfully the complicated machinery of a modern steel plant. The attempt to put in new men converted the thousands of old men who desired to work, into lukewarm supporters of our policy, for workmen can always be relied upon to resent the employment of new men. Who can blame them?

If I had been at home, however, I might have been persuaded to open the works, as the superintendent desired, to test whether our old men would go to work as they had promised. But it should be noted that the works were not opened at first by my partners for new men. On the contrary, it was, as I was informed upon my return, at the wish of the thousands of our old men that they were opened. This is a vital point. My partners were in no way blamable for making the trial so recommended by the superintendent. Our rule never to employ new men, but to wait for the old to return, had not been violated so far. In regard to the second opening of the works, after the strikers had shot the sheriff's officers, it is also easy to look back and say, "How much better had the works been closed until the old men voted to return"; but the Governor of Pennsylvania, with eight thousand troops, had meanwhile taken charge of the situation.

I was traveling in the Highlands of Scotland when the trouble arose, and did not hear of it until two days after. Nothing I have ever had to meet in all my life, before or since, wounded me so deeply. No pangs remain of any wound received in my business career save that of Homestead. It was so unnecessary. The men were outrageously wrong. The strikers, with the new machinery, would have made from four to nine dollars a day under the new scale — thirty per cent more than they were making with the old machinery. While in Scotland I received the following cable from the officers of the union of our workmen:

"Kind master, tell us what you wish us to do and we shall do it for you."

This was most touching, but, alas, too late. The mischief was done, the works were in the hands of the Governor; it was too late.

I received, while abroad, numerous kind messages from friends conversant with the circumstances, who imagined my unhappiness. The following from Mr. Gladstone was greatly appreciated:

MY DEAR MR. CARNEGIE,

My wife has long ago offered her thanks, with my own, for your most kind congratulations. But I do not forget that you have been suffering yourself from anxieties, and have been exposed to imputations in connection with your gallant efforts to direct rich men into a course of action more enlightened than that which they usually follow. I wish I could relieve you from these imputations of journalists, too often rash, conceited or censorious, rancorous, ill-natured. I wish to do the little, the very little, that is in my power, which is simply to say how sure I am that no one who knows you will be prompted by the unfortunate occurrences across the water (of which manifestly we cannot know the exact merits) to qualify in the slightest degree either his confidence in your generous views or his admiration of the good and great work you have already done.

Wealth is at present like a monster threatening to swallow up the moral life of man; you by precept and by example have been teaching him to disgorge. I for one thank you.

Believe me.

Very faithfully yours

(Signed)   W. E. GLADSTONE

I insert this as giving proof, if proof were needed, of Mr. Gladstone's large, sympathetic nature, alive and sensitive to everything transpiring of a nature to arouse sympathy — Neapolitans, Greeks, and Bulgarians one day, or a stricken friend the next.

The general public, of course, did not know that I was in Scotland and knew nothing of the initial trouble at Homestead. Workmen had been killed at the Carnegie Works, of which I was the controlling owner. That was sufficient to make my name a by-word for years. But at last some satisfaction came. Senator Hanna was

president of the National Civic Federation, a body composed of capitalists and workmen which exerted a benign
influence over both employers and employed, and the
Honorable Oscar Straus, who was then vice-president,
invited me to dine at his house and meet the officials of
the Federation. Before the date appointed Mark Hanna,
its president, my lifelong friend and former agent at
Cleveland, had suddenly passed away. I attended the dinner. At its close Mr. Straus arose and said that the question of a successor to Mr. Hanna had been considered,
and he had to report that every labor organization heard
from had favored me for the position. There were present several of the labor leaders who, one after another,
arose and corroborated Mr. Straus.

I do not remember so complete a surprise and, I shall
confess, one so grateful to me. That I deserved well from
labor I felt. I knew myself to be warmly sympathetic
with the working-man, and also that I had the regard of
our own workmen; but throughout the country it was
naturally the reverse, owing to the Homestead riot. The
Carnegie Works meant to the public Mr. Carnegie's war
upon labor's just earnings.

I arose to explain to the officials at the Straus dinner
that I could not possibly accept the great honor, because
I had to escape the heat of summer and the head of
the Federation must be on hand at all seasons ready to
grapple with an outbreak, should one occur. My embarrassment was great, but I managed to let all understand that this was felt to be the most welcome tribute I could have received — a balm to the hurt mind. I
closed by saying that if elected to my lamented friend's
place upon the Executive Committee I should esteem
it an honor to serve. To this position I was elected by
unanimous vote. I was thus relieved from the feeling that I

was considered responsible by labor generally, for the Homestead riot and the killing of workmen.

I owe this vindication to Mr. Oscar Straus, who had read my articles and speeches of early days upon labor questions, and who had quoted these frequently to workmen. The two labor leaders of the Amalgamated Union, White and Schaeffer from Pittsburgh, who were at this dinner, were also able and anxious to enlighten their fellow-workmen members of the Board as to my record with labor, and did not fail to do so.

A mass meeting of the workmen and their wives was afterwards held in the Library Hall at Pittsburgh to greet me, and I addressed them from both my head and my heart. The one sentence I remember, and always shall, was to the effect that capital, labor, and employer were a three-legged stool, none before or after the others, all equally indispensable. Then came the cordial hand-shaking and all was well. Having thus rejoined hands and hearts with our employees and their wives, I felt that a great weight had been effectually lifted, but I had had a terrible experience although thousands of miles from the scene.

An incident flowing from the Homestead trouble is told by my friend, Professor John C. Van Dyke, of Rutgers College:

In the spring of 1900, I went up from Guaymas, on the Gulf of California, to the ranch of a friend at La Noria Verde, thinking to have a week's shooting in the mountains of Sonora. The ranch was far enough removed from civilization, and I had expected meeting there only a few Mexicans and many Yaqui Indians, but much to my surprise I found an English-speaking man, who proved to be an American. I did not have long to wait in order to find out what brought him there, for he was very lonesome and disposed to talk. His name was McLuckie, and up to 1892 he had been a skilled mechanic in the employ of the Carnegie Steel Works at Homestead. He was what was called a "top hand," received large wages, was married, and at that time had a home and considerable property. In addition, he had been honored by his fellow-townsmen and had been made burgomaster of Homestead.

When the strike of 1892 came McLuckie naturally sided with the strikers, and in his capacity as burgomaster gave the order to arrest the Pinkerton detectives who had come to Homestead by steamer to protect the works and preserve order. He believed he was fully justified in doing this. As he explained it to me, the detectives were an armed force invading his bailiwick, and he had a right to arrest and disarm them. The order led to bloodshed, and the conflict was begun in real earnest.

The story of the strike is, of course, well known to all. The strikers were finally defeated. As for McLuckie, he was indicted for murder, riot, treason, and I know not what other offenses. He was compelled to flee from the State, was wounded, starved, pursued by the officers of the law, and obliged to go into hiding until the storm blew over. Then he found that he was blacklisted by all the steel men in the United States and could not get employment anywhere. His money was gone, and, as a final blow, his wife died and his home was broken up. After many vicissitudes he resolved to go to Mexico, and at the time I met him he was trying to get employment in the mines about fifteen miles from La Noria Verde. But he was too good a mechanic for the Mexicans, who required in mining the cheapest kind of unskilled peon labor. He could get nothing to do and had no money. He was literally down to his last copper. Naturally, as he told the story of his misfortunes, I felt very sorry for him, especially as he was a most intelligent person and did no unnecessary whining about his troubles.

I do not think I told him at the time that I knew Mr. Carnegie and had been with him at Cluny in Scotland shortly after the Homestead strike, nor that I knew from Mr. Carnegie the other side of the story. But McLuckie was rather careful not to blame Mr. Carnegie, saying to me several times that if "Andy" had been there the trouble would never have arisen. He seemed to think "the boys" could get on very well with "Andy" but not so well with some of his partners.

I was at the ranch for a week and saw a good deal of McLuckie in the evenings. When I left there, I went directly to Tucson, Arizona, and from there I had occasion to write to Mr. Carnegie, and in the letter I told him about meeting with McLuckie. I added that I felt very sorry for the man and thought he had been treated rather badly. Mr. Carnegie answered at once, and on the margin of the letter wrote in lead pencil: "Give McLuckie all the money he wants, but don't mention my name." I wrote to McLuckie immediately, offering him what money he needed, mentioning no sum, but giving him to understand that it would be sufficient to put him on his feet again. He declined it. He said he would fight it out and make his own way, which was the right-enough American spirit. I could not help but admire it in him.

As I remember now, I spoke about him later to a friend, Mr. J. A. Naugle, the general manager of the Sonora Railway. At any rate, McLuckie got a job with the railway at driving wells, and made a great success of it. A year later, or perhaps it was in the autumn of the same year, I again met him at Guaymas, where he was superintending some repairs on his machinery at the railway shops. He was much changed for the better, seemed happy, and to add to his contentment, had taken unto himself a Mexican wife. And now that his sky was cleared, I was anxious to tell him the truth about my offer that he might not think unjustly of those who had been compelled to fight him. So before I left him, I said,

"McLuckie, I want you to know now that the money I offered you was not mine. That was Andrew Carnegie's money. It was his offer, made through me."

McLuckie was fairly stunned, and all he could say was:

"Well, that was damned white of Andy, wasn't it?"

I would rather risk that verdict of McLuckie's as a passport to Paradise than all the theological dogmas invented by man. I knew McLuckie well as a good fellow. It was said his property in Homestead was worth thirty thousand dollars. He was under arrest for the shooting of the police officers because he was the burgomaster, and also the chairman of the Men's Committee of Homestead. He had to fly, leaving all behind him.

After this story got into print, the following skit appeared in the newspapers because I had declared I'd rather have McLuckie's few words on my tombstone than any other inscription, for it indicated I had been kind to one of our workmen:

"JUST BY THE WAY"

SANDY ON ANDY

Oh! hae ye heared what Andy's spiered to hae upo' his tomb,
When a' his gowd is gie'n awa an' Death has sealed his doom!
Nae Scriptur' line wi' tribute fine that dealers aye keep handy,
But juist this irreleegious screed — "That's damned white of
      Andy!"

The gude Scot laughs at epitaphs that are but meant to flatter,
But never ane was sae profane, an' that's nae laughin' matter.
Yet, gin he gies his siller all awa, mon, he's a dandy,
An' we'll admit his right to it, for "That's damned white of Andy!"

There's not to be a "big, big D," an' then a dash thereafter,
For Andy would na spoil the word by trying to make it safter;
He's not the lad to juggle terms, or soothing speech to bandy.
A blunt, straightforward mon is he — an' "That's damned white of
      Andy!"

Sae when he's deid, we'll gie good heed, an' write it as he askit;
We'll carve it on his headstone an' we'll stamp it on his casket:
"Wha dees rich, dees disgraced," says he, an' sure's my name is
      Sandy,
'T wull be nae rich man that he'll dee — an' "That's damned white
      of Andy !"[1]

[1] Mr. Carnegie was very fond of this story because, being human, he was fond of applause and, being a Robert Burns radical, he preferred the applause of Labor to that of Rank. That one of his men thought he had acted

"white" pleased him beyond measure. He stopped short with that tribute and never asked, never knew, why or how the story happened to be told. Perhaps this is the time and place to tell the story of the story.

Sometime in 1901 over a dinner table in New York, I heard a statement regarding Mr. Carnegie that he never gave anything without the requirement that his name be attached to the gift. The remark came from a prominent man who should have known he was talking nonsense. It rather angered me. I denied the statement, saying that I, personally, had given away money for Mr. Carnegie that only he and I knew about, and that he had given many thousands in this way through others. By way of illustration I told the story about McLuckie. A Pittsburgh man at the table carried the story back to Pittsburgh, told it there, and it finally got into the newspapers. Of course the argument of the story, namely, that Mr. Carnegie sometimes gave without publicity, was lost sight of and only the refrain, "It was damned white of Andy," remained. Mr. Carnegie never knew that there was an argument. He liked the refrain. Some years afterward at Skibo (1906), when he was writing this Autobiography, he asked me if I would not write out the story for him. I did so. I am now glad of the chance to write an explanatory note about it. . . . *John C. Van Dyke.*

CHAPTER XVIII
Problems of Labor

I SHOULD like to record here some of the labor disputes I have had to deal with, as these may point a moral to both capital and labor.

The workers at the blast furnaces in our steel-rail works once sent in a "round-robin" stating that unless the firm gave them an advance of wages by Monday afternoon at four o'clock they would leave the furnaces. Now, the scale upon which these men had agreed to work did not lapse until the end of the year, several months off. I felt if men would break an agreement there was no use in making a second agreement with them, but nevertheless I took the night train from New York and was at the works early in the morning.

I asked the superintendent to call together the three committees which governed the works — not only the blast-furnace committee that was alone involved, but the mill and the converting works committees as well. They appeared and, of course, were received by me with great courtesy, not because it was good policy to be courteous, but because I have always enjoyed meeting our men. I am bound to say that the more I know of working-men the higher I rate their virtues. But it is with them as Barrie says with women: "Dootless the Lord made a' things weel, but he left some michty queer kinks in women." They have their prejudices and "red rags," which have to be respected, for the main root of trouble is ignorance, not hostility. The committee sat in a semicircle before me, all with their hats off, of course, as mine was also; and really there was the appearance of a model assembly.

Addressing the chairman of the mill committee, I said:

"Mr. Mackay" (he was an old gentleman and wore spectacles), "have we an agreement with you covering the remainder of the year?"

Taking the spectacles off slowly, and holding them in his hand, he said:

"Yes, sir, you have, Mr. Carnegie, and you haven't got enough money to make us break it either."

"There spoke the true American workman," I said. "I am proud of you."

"Mr. Johnson" (who was chairman of the rail converters' committee), "have we a similar agreement with you?"

Mr. Johnson was a small, spare man; he spoke very deliberately:

"Mr. Carnegie, when an agreement is presented to me to sign, I read it carefully, and if it don't suit me, I don't sign it, and if it does suit me, I do sign it, and when I sign it I keep it."

"There again speaks the self-respecting American workman," I said.

Turning now to the chairman of the blast-furnaces committee, an Irishman named Kelly, I addressed the same question to him:

"Mr. Kelly, have we an agreement with you covering the remainder of this year?"

Mr. Kelly answered that he couldn't say exactly. There was a paper sent round and he signed it, but didn't read it over carefully, and didn't understand just what was in it. At this moment our superintendent, Captain Jones, excellent manager, but impulsive, exclaimed abruptly:

"Now, Mr. Kelly, you know I read that over twice and discussed it with you!"

"Order, order, Captain! Mr. Kelly is entitled to give his explanation. I sign many a paper that I do not read — documents our lawyers and partners present to me to sign. Mr. Kelly states that he signed this document under such circumstances and his statement must be received. But, Mr. Kelly, I have always found that the best way is to carry out the provisions of the agreement one signs carelessly and resolve to be more careful next time. Would it not be better for you to continue four months longer under this agreement, and then, when you sign the next one, see that you understand it?"

There was no answer to this, and I arose and said:

"Gentlemen of the Blast-Furnace Committee, you have threatened our firm that you will break your agreement and that you will leave these blast furnaces (which means disaster) unless you get a favorable answer to your threat by four o'clock to-day. It is not yet three, but your answer is ready. You may leave the blast furnaces. The grass will grow around them before we yield to your threat. The worst day that labor has ever seen in this world is that day in which it dishonors itself by breaking its agreement. You have your answer."

The committee filed out slowly and there was silence among the partners. A stranger who was coming in on business met the committee in the passage and he reported:

"As I came in, a man wearing spectacles pushed up alongside of an Irishman he called Kelly, and he said: 'You fellows might just as well understand it now as later. There's to be no d——d monkeying round these works.'"

That meant business. Later we heard from one of our

clerks what took place at the furnaces. Kelly and his committee marched down to them. Of course, the men were waiting and watching for the committee and a crowd had gathered. When the furnaces were reached, Kelly called out to them:

"Get to work, you spalpeens, what are you doing here? Begorra, the little boss just hit from the shoulder. He won't fight, but he says he has sat down, and begorra, we all know he'll be a skeleton afore he rises. Get to work, ye spalpeens."

The Irish and Scotch-Irish are queer, but the easiest and best fellows to get on with, if you only know how. That man Kelly was my stanch friend and admirer ever afterward, and he was before that one of our most violent men. My experience is that you can always rely upon the great body of working-men to do what is right, provided they have not taken up a position and promised their leaders to stand by them. But their loyalty to their leaders even when mistaken, is something to make us proud of them. Anything can be done with men who have this feeling of loyalty within them. They only need to be treated fairly.

The way a strike was once broken at our steel-rail mills is interesting. Here again, I am sorry to say, one hundred and thirty-four men in one department had bound themselves under secret oath to demand increased wages at the end of the year, several months away. The new year proved very unfavorable for business, and other iron and steel manufacturers throughout the country had effected reductions in wages. Nevertheless, these men, having secretly sworn months previously that they would not work unless they got increased wages, thought themselves bound to insist upon their demands. We could not advance wages when our competitors were reducing them, and the works were stopped in consequence. Every department of the works was brought to a stand by these strikers. The blast furnaces were abandoned a day or two before the time agreed upon, and we were greatly troubled in consequence.

I went to Pittsburgh and was surprised to find the furnaces had been banked, contrary to agreement. I was to meet the men in the morning upon arrival at Pittsburgh, but a message was sent to me from the works stating that the men had "left the furnaces and would meet me to-morrow." Here was a nice reception! My reply was:

"No they won't. Tell them I shall not be here to-morrow. Anybody can stop work; the trick is to start it again. Some fine day these men will want the works started and will be looking around for somebody who can start them, and I will tell them then just what I do now: that the works will never start except upon a sliding scale based upon the prices we get for our products. That scale will last three years and it will not be submitted by the men. They have submitted many scales to us. It is our turn now, and we are going to submit a scale to them.

"Now," I said to my partners, "I am going back to New York in the afternoon. Nothing more is to be done."

A short time after my message was received by the men they asked if they could come in and see me that afternoon before I left.

I answered: "Certainly!"

They came in and I said to them:

"Gentlemen, your chairman here, Mr. Bennett, assured you that I would make my appearance and settle with you in some way or other, as I always have settled.

That is true. And he told you that I would not fight, which is also true. He is a true prophet. But he told you something else in which he was slightly mistaken. He said I *could* not fight. Gentlemen," looking Mr. Bennett straight in the eye and closing and raising my fist, "he forgot that I was Scotch. But I will tell you something; I will never fight you. I know better than to fight labor. I will not fight, but I can beat any committee that was ever made at sitting down, and I have sat down. These works will never start until the men vote by a two-thirds majority to start them, and then, as I told you this morning, they will start on our sliding scale. I have nothing more to say."

They retired. It was about two weeks afterwards that one of the house servants came to my library in New York with a card, and I found upon it the names of two of our workmen, and also the name of a reverend gentleman. The men said they were from the works at Pittsburgh and would like to see me.

"Ask if either of these gentlemen belongs to the blast-furnace workers who banked the furnaces contrary to agreement."

The man returned and said "No." I replied: "In that case go down and tell them that I shall be pleased to have them come up."

Of course they were received with genuine warmth and cordiality and we sat and talked about New York, for some time, this being their first visit.

"Mr. Carnegie, we really came to talk about the trouble at the works," the minister said at last.

"Oh, indeed!" I answered. "Have the men voted?"

"No," he said.

My rejoinder was:

"You will have to excuse me from entering upon that

subject; I said I never would discuss it until they voted by a two-thirds majority to start the mills. Gentlemen, you have never seen New York. Let me take you out and show you Fifth Avenue and the Park, and we shall come back here to lunch at half-past one."

This we did, talking about everything except the one thing that they wished to talk about. We had a good time, and I know they enjoyed their lunch. There is one great difference between the American working-man and the foreigner. The American is a man; he sits down at lunch with people as if he were (as he generally is) a gentleman born. It is splendid.

They returned to Pittsburgh, not another word having been said about the works. But the men soon voted (there were very few votes against starting) and I went again to Pittsburgh. I laid before the committee the scale under which they were to work. It was a sliding scale based on the price of the product. Such a scale really makes capital and labor partners, sharing prosperous and disastrous times together. Of course it has a minimum, so that the men are always sure of living wages. As the men had seen these scales, it was unnecessary to go over them. The chairman said:

"Mr. Carnegie, we will agree to everything. And now," he said hesitatingly, "we have one favor to ask of you, and we hope you will not refuse it."

"Well, gentlemen, if it be reasonable I shall surely grant it."

"Well, it is this: That you permit the officers of the union to sign these papers for the men."

"Why, certainly, gentlemen! With the greatest pleasure! And then I have a small favor to ask of you, which I hope you will not refuse, as I have granted yours. Just to please me, after the officers have signed, let every workman sign also for himself. You see, Mr. Bennett, this scale lasts for three years, and some man, or body of men, might dispute whether your president of the union had authority to bind them for so long, but if we have his signature also, there cannot be any misunderstanding."

There was a pause; then one man at his side whispered to Mr. Bennett (but I heard him perfectly):

"By golly, the jig's up!"

So it was, but it was not by direct attack, but by a flank movement. Had I not allowed the union officers to sign, they would have had a grievance and an excuse for war. As it was, having allowed them to do so, how could they refuse so simple a request as mine, that each free and independent American citizen should also sign for himself. My recollection is that as a matter of fact the officers of the union never signed, but they may have done so. Why should they, if every man's signature was required? Besides this, the workmen, knowing that the union could do nothing for them when the scale was adopted, neglected to pay dues and the union was deserted. We never heard of it again. [That was in 1889, now twenty-seven years ago. The scale has never been changed. The men would not change it if they could; it works for their benefit, as I told them it would.]

Of all my services rendered to labor the introduction of the sliding scale is chief. It is the solution of the capital and labor problem, because it really makes them partners — alike in prosperity and adversity. There was a yearly scale in operation in the Pittsburgh district in the early years, but it is not a good plan because men and employers at once begin preparing for a struggle which is almost certain to come. It is far better for both employers and employed to set no date for an agreed-upon scale to end. It should be subject to six months' or a year's notice on either side, and in that way might and probably would run on for years.

To show upon what trifles a contest between capital and labor may turn, let me tell of two instances which were amicably settled by mere incidents of seemingly little consequence. Once when I went out to meet a men's committee, which had in our opinion made unfair demands, I was informed that they were influenced by a man who secretly owned a drinking saloon, although working in the mills. He was a great bully. The sober, quiet workmen were afraid of him, and the drinking men were his debtors. He was the real instigator of the movement.

We met in the usual friendly fashion. I was glad to see the men, many of whom I had long known and could call by name. When we sat down at the table the leader's seat was at one end and mine at the other. We therefore faced each other. After I had laid our proposition before the meeting, I saw the leader pick up his hat from the floor and slowly put it on his head, intimating that he was about to depart. Here was my chance.

"Sir, you are in the presence of gentlemen! Please be so good as to take your hat off or leave the room!"

My eyes were kept full upon him. There was a silence that could be felt. The great bully hesitated, but I knew whatever he did, he was beaten. If he left it was because he had treated the meeting discourteously by keeping his hat on, he was no gentleman; if he remained and took off his hat, he had been crushed by the rebuke. I didn't care which course he took. He had only two and either of them was fatal. He had delivered himself into my hands. He very slowly took off the hat and put it on the floor. Not a word did he speak thereafter in that conference. I was told afterward that he had to leave the place. The men rejoiced in the episode and a settlement was harmoniously effected.

When the three years' scale was proposed to the men, a committee of sixteen was chosen by them to confer with us. Little progress was made at first, and I announced my engagements compelled me to return the next day to New York. Inquiry was made as to whether we would meet a committee of thirty-two, as the men wished others added to the committee — a sure sign of division in their ranks. Of course we agreed. The committee came from the works to meet me at the office in Pittsburgh. The proceedings were opened by one of our best men, Billy Edwards (I remember him well; he rose to high position afterwards), who thought that the total offered was fair, but that the scale was not equable. Some departments were all right, others were not fairly dealt with. Most of the men were naturally of this opinion, but when they came to indicate the underpaid, there was a difference, as was to be expected. No two men in the different departments could agree. Billy began:

"Mr. Carnegie, we agree that the total sum per ton to be paid is fair, but we think it is not properly distributed among us. Now Mr. Carnegie, you take my job — "

"Order, order!" I cried. "None of that, Billy. Mr. Carnegie 'takes no man's job.' Taking another's job is an unpardonable offense among high-classed workmen."

There was loud laughter, followed by applause, and then more laughter. I laughed with them. We had scored on Billy. Of course the dispute was soon settled. It is not solely, often it is not chiefly, a matter of dollars with workmen. Appreciation, kind treatment, a fair deal — these are often the potent forces with the American workmen.

Employers can do so many desirable things for their men at little cost. At one meeting when I asked what we could do for them, I remember this same Billy Edwards rose and said that most of the men had to run in debt to the storekeepers because they were paid monthly. Well I remember his words:

"I have a good woman for wife who manages well. We go into Pittsburgh every fourth Saturday afternoon and buy our supplies wholesale for the next month and save one third. Not many of your men can do this. Shopkeepers here charge so much. And another thing, they charge very high for coal. If you paid your men every two weeks, instead of monthly, it would be as good for the careful men as a raise in wages of ten per cent or more."

"Mr. Edwards, that shall be done," I replied.

It involved increased labor and a few more clerks, but that was a small matter. The remark about high prices charged set me to thinking why the men could not open a cooperative store. This was also arranged — the firm agreeing to pay the rent of the building, but insisting that the men themselves take the stock and manage it. Out of that came the Braddock's Cooperative Society, a valuable institution for many reasons, not the least of them that it taught the men that business had its difficulties.

The coal trouble was cured effectively by our agreeing that the company sell all its men coal at the net cost price to us (about half of what had been charged by coal dealers, so I was told) and arranging to deliver it at the men's houses — the buyer paying only actual cost of cartage.

There was another matter. We found that the men's savings caused them anxiety, for little faith have the prudent, saving men in banks and, unfortunately, our Government at that time did not follow the British in having post-office deposit banks. We offered to take the actual savings of each workman, up to two thousand dollars, and pay six per cent interest upon them, to encourage thrift. Their money was kept separate from the business, in a trust fund, and lent to such as wished to build homes for themselves. I consider this one of the best things that can be done for the saving workman.

It was such concessions as these that proved the most profitable investments ever made by the company, even from an economical standpoint. It pays to go beyond the letter of the bond with your men. Two of my partners, as Mr. Phipps has put it, "knew my extreme disposition to always grant the demands of labor, however unreasonable," but looking back upon my failing in this respect, I wish it had been greater — much greater. No expenditure returned such dividends as the friendship of our workmen.

We soon had a body of workmen, I truly believe, wholly unequaled — the best workmen and the best men ever drawn together. Quarrels and strikes became things of the past. Had the Homestead men been our own old men, instead of men we had to pick up, it is scarcely possible that the trouble there in 1892 could have arisen. The scale at the steel-rail mills, introduced in 1889, has been running up to the present time (1914), and I think there never has been a labor grievance at the works since. The men, as I have already stated, dissolved their old union because there was no use paying dues to a union when the men themselves had a three years' contract. Although their labor union is dissolved another and a better one has taken its place — a cordial union between the employers and their men, the best union of all for both parties.

It is for the interest of the employer that his men shall make good earnings and have steady work. The sliding scale enables the company to meet the market; and sometimes to take orders and keep the works running, which is the main thing for the working-men. High wages are well enough, but they are not to be compared with steady employment. The Edgar Thomson Mills are, in my opinion, the ideal works in respect to the relations of capital and labor. I am told the men in our day, and even to this day (1914) prefer two to three turns, but three turns are sure to come. Labor's hours are to be shortened as we progress. Eight hours will be the rule — eight for work, eight for sleep, and eight for rest and recreation.

There have been many incidents in my business life proving that labor troubles are not solely founded upon wages. I believe the best preventive of quarrels to be recognition of, and sincere interest in, the men, satisfying them that you really care for them and that you rejoice in their success. This I can sincerely say — that I always enjoyed my conferences with our workmen, which were not always in regard to wages, and that the better I knew the men the more I liked them. They have usually two virtues to the employer's one, and they are certainly more generous to each other.

Labor is usually helpless against capital. The employer, perhaps, decides to shut up the shops; he ceases to make profits for a short time. There is no change in his habits, food, clothing, pleasures — no agonizing fear of want. Contrast this with his workman whose lessening means of subsistence torment him. He has few comforts, scarcely the necessities for his wife and children in health, and for the sick little ones no proper treatment. It is not capital we need to guard, but helpless labor. If I returned to business to-morrow, fear of labor troubles would not enter my mind, but tenderness for poor and sometimes misguided though well-meaning laborers would fill my heart and soften it; and thereby soften theirs.

Upon my return to Pittsburgh in 1892, after the Homestead trouble, I went to the works and met many of the old men who had not been concerned in the riot. They expressed the opinion that if I had been at home the strike would never have happened. I told them that the company had offered generous terms and beyond its offer I should not have gone; that before their cable reached me in Scotland, the Governor of the State had appeared on the scene with troops and wished the law vindicated; that the question had then passed out of my partners' hands. I added:

"You were badly advised. My partners' offer should have been accepted. It was very generous. I don't know that I would have offered so much."

To this one of the rollers said to me:

"Oh, Mr. Carnegie, it wasn't a question of dollars. The boys would have let you kick 'em, but they wouldn't let that other man stroke their hair."

So much does sentiment count for in the practical affairs of life, even with the laboring classes. This is not generally believed by those who do not know them, but I am certain that disputes about wages do not account for one half the disagreements between capital and labor. There is lack of due appreciation and of kind treatment of employees upon the part of the employers.

Suits had been entered against many of the strikers,

but upon my return these were promptly dismissed. All the old men who remained, and had not been guilty of violence, were taken back. I had cabled from Scotland urging that Mr. Schwab be sent back to Homestead. He had been only recently promoted to the Edgar Thomson Works. He went back, and "Charlie," as he was affectionately called, soon restored order, peace, and harmony. Had he remained at the Homestead Works, in all probability no serious trouble would have arisen. "Charlie" liked his workmen and they liked him; but there still remained at Homestead an unsatisfactory element in the men who had previously been discarded from our various works for good reasons and had found employment at the new works before we purchased them.

CHAPTER XIX

The "Gospel of Wealth"

AFTER my book, "The Gospel of Wealth,"[1] was published, it was inevitable that I should live up to its teachings by ceasing to struggle for more wealth. I resolved to stop accumulating and begin the infinitely more serious and difficult task of wise distribution. Our profits had reached forty millions of dollars per year and the prospect of increased earnings before us was amazing. Our successors, the United States Steel Corporation, soon after the purchase, netted sixty millions in one year. Had our company continued in business and adhered to our plans of extension, we figured that seventy millions in that year might have been earned.

Steel had ascended the throne and was driving away all inferior material. It was clearly seen that there was a great future ahead; but so far as I was concerned I knew the task of distribution before me would tax me in my old age to the utmost. As usual, Shakespeare had placed his talismanic touch upon the thought and framed the sentence —

"So distribution should undo excess,
And each man have enough."

At this juncture — that is March, 1901 — Mr. Schwab

[1] *The Gospel of Wealth* (Century Company, New York, 1900) contains various magazine articles written between 1886 and 1899 and published in the *Youth's Companion*, the *Century Magazine*, the *North American Review*, the *Forum*, the *Contemporary Review*, the *Fortnightly Review*, the *Nineteenth Century*, and the *Scottish Leader*. Gladstone asked that the article in the *North American Review* be printed in England. It was published in the *Pall Mall Budget* and christened the "Gospel of Wealth." Gladstone, Cardinal Manning, Rev. Hugh Price, and Rev. Dr. Herman Adler answered it, and Mr. Carnegie replied to them.

told me Mr. Morgan had said to him he should really like to know if I wished to retire from business; if so he thought he could arrange it. He also said he had consulted our partners and that they were disposed to sell, being attracted by the terms Mr. Morgan had offered. I told Mr. Schwab that if my partners were desirous to sell I would concur, and we finally sold.

There had been so much deception by speculators buying old iron and steel mills and foisting them upon innocent purchasers at inflated values — hundred-dollar shares in some cases selling for a trifle — that I declined to take anything for the common stock. Had I done so, it would have given me just about one hundred millions more of five per cent bonds, which Mr. Morgan said afterwards I could have obtained. Such was the prosperity and such the money value of our steel business. Events proved I should have been quite justified in asking the additional sum named, for the common stock has paid five per cent continuously since.[1] But I had enough, as has been proved, to keep me busier than ever before, trying to distribute it.

My first distribution was to the men in the mills. The following letters and papers will explain the gift:

New York, N.Y., March 12, 1901

I make this first use of surplus wealth, four millions of first mortgage 5% Bonds, upon retiring from business, as an ac-

[1] The Carnegie Steel Company was bought by Mr. Morgan at Mr. Carnegie's own price. There was some talk at the time of his holding out for a higher price than he received, but testifying before a committee of the House of Representatives in January, 1912, Mr. Carnegie said: "I considered what was fair: and that is the option Morgan got. Schwab went down and arranged it. I never saw Morgan on the subject or any man connected with him. Never a word passed between him and me. I gave my memorandum and Morgan saw it was eminently fair. I have been told many times since by insiders that I should have asked $100,000,000 more and could have got it easily. Once for all, I want to put a stop to all this talk about Mr. Carnegie 'forcing high prices for anything.'"

knowledgment of the deep debt which I owe to the workmen who have contributed so greatly to my success. It is designed to relieve those who may suffer from accidents, and provide small pensions for those needing help in old age.

In addition I give one million dollars of such bonds, the proceeds thereof to be used to maintain the libraries and halls I have built for our workmen.

In return, the Homestead workmen presented the following address:

Munhall, Pa., Feb'y 23, 1903

MR. ANDREW CARNEGIE
   New York, N. Y.

DEAR SIR:

We, the employees of the Homestead Steel Works, desire by this means to express to you through our Committee our great appreciation of your benevolence in establishing the "Andrew Carnegie Relief Fund," the first annual report of its operation having been placed before us during the past month.

The interest which you have always shown in your workmen has won for you an appreciation which cannot be expressed by mere words. Of the many channels through which you have sought to do good, we believe that the "Andrew Carnegie Relief Fund" stands first. We have personal knowledge of cares lightened and of hope and strength renewed in homes where human prospects seemed dark and discouraging.

Respectfully yours

Committee {
HARRY F. ROSE, *Roller*
JOHN BELL, JR., *Blacksmith*
J. A. HORTON, *Timekeeper*
WALTER A. GREIG, *Electric Foreman*
HARRY CUSACK, *Yardmaster*

The Lucy Furnace men presented me with a beautiful silver plate and inscribed upon it the following address:

Andrew Carnegie Relief Fund

Lucy Furnaces

Whereas, Mr. Andrew Carnegie, in his munificent philanthropy, has endowed the "Andrew Carnegie Relief Fund" for the benefit of employees of the Carnegie Company, Therefore be it

Resolved, that the employees of the Lucy Furnaces, in special meeting assembled, do convey to Mr. Andrew Carnegie their sincere thanks for and appreciation of his unexcelled and bounteous endowment, and furthermore be it

Resolved, that it is their earnest wish and prayer that his life may be long spared to enjoy the fruits of his works.

Committee

James Scott, *Chairman*
Louis A. Hutchinson, *Secretary*
James Daly
R. C. Taylor
John V. Ward
Frederick Voelker
John M. Veigh

I sailed soon for Europe, and as usual some of my partners did not fail to accompany me to the steamer and bade me good-bye. But, oh! the difference to me! Say what we would, do what we would, the solemn change had come. This I could not fail to realize. The wrench was indeed severe and there was pain in the good-bye which was also a farewell.

Upon my return to New York some months later, I felt myself entirely out of place, but was much cheered by seeing several of "the boys" on the pier to welcome me — the same dear friends, but so different. I had lost my partners, but not my friends. This was something; it was much. Still a vacancy was left. I had now to take up my self-appointed task of wisely disposing of surplus wealth. That would keep me deeply interested.

One day my eyes happened to see a line in that most

valuable paper, the "Scottish American," in which I had found many gems. This was the line:

"The gods send thread for a web begun."

It seemed almost as if it had been sent directly to me. This sank into my heart, and I resolved to begin at once my first web. True enough, the gods sent thread in the proper form. Dr. J. S. Billings, of the New York Public Libraries, came as their agent, and of dollars, five and a quarter millions went at one stroke for sixty-eight branch libraries, promised for New York City. Twenty more libraries for Brooklyn followed.

My father, as I have stated, had been one of the five pioneers in Dunfermline who combined and gave access to their few books to their less fortunate neighbors. I had followed in his footsteps by giving my native town a library — its foundation stone laid by my mother — so that this public library was really my first gift. It was followed by giving a public library and hall to Allegheny City — our first home in America. President Harrison kindly accompanied me from Washington and opened these buildings. Soon after this, Pittsburgh asked for a library, which was given. This developed, in due course, into a group of buildings embracing a museum, a picture gallery, technical schools, and the Margaret Morrison School for Young Women. This group of buildings I opened to the public November 5, 1895. In Pittsburgh I had made my fortune and in the twenty-four millions already spent on this group,[1] she gets back only a small part of what she gave, and to which she is richly entitled.

The second large gift was to found the Carnegie Institution of Washington. The 28th of January, 1902,

---

[1] The total gifts to the Carnegie Institute at Pittsburgh amounted to about twenty-eight million dollars.

I gave ten million dollars in five per cent bonds, to which there has been added sufficient to make the total cash value twenty-five millions of dollars, the additions being made upon record of results obtained. I naturally wished to consult President Roosevelt upon the matter, and if possible to induce the Secretary of State, Mr. John Hay, to serve as chairman, which he readily agreed to do. With him were associated as directors my old friend Abram S. Hewitt, Dr. Billings, William E. Dodge, Elihu Root, Colonel Higginson, D. O. Mills, Dr. S. Weir Mitchell, and others.

When I showed President Roosevelt the list of the distinguished men who had agreed to serve, he remarked: "You could not duplicate it." He strongly favored the foundation, which was incorporated by an act of Congress April 28, 1904, as follows:

To encourage in the broadest and most liberal manner investigations, research and discovery, and the application of knowledge to the improvement of mankind; and, in particular, to conduct, endow and assist investigation in any department of science, literature or art, and to this end to cooperate with governments, universities, colleges, technical schools, learned societies, and individuals.

I was indebted to Dr. Billings as my guide, in selecting Dr. Daniel C. Gilman as the first president. He passed away some years later. Dr. Billings then recommended the present highly successful president, Dr. Robert S. Woodward. Long may he continue to guide the affairs of the Institution! The history of its achievements is so well known through its publications that details here are unnecessary. I may, however, refer to two of its undertakings that are somewhat unique. It is doing a world-wide service with the wood-and-bronze yacht, "Carnegie," which is voyaging around the world correcting the errors of the earlier surveys. Many of these ocean surveys have been found misleading, owing to variations of the compass. Bronze being non-magnetic, while iron and steel are highly so, previous observations have proved liable to error. A notable instance is that of the stranding of a Cunard steamship near the Azores. Captain Peters, of the "Carnegie," thought it advisable to test this case and found that the captain of the ill-fated steamer was sailing on the course laid down upon the admiralty map, and was not to blame. The original observation was wrong. The error caused by variation was promptly corrected.

This is only one of numerous corrections reported to the nations who go down to the sea in ships. Their thanks are our ample reward. In the deed of the gift I expressed the hope that our young Republic might some day be able to repay, at least in some degree, the great debt it owes to the older lands. Nothing gives me deeper satisfaction than the knowledge that it has to some extent already begun to do so.

With the unique service rendered by the wandering "Carnegie," we may rank that of the fixed observatory upon Mount Wilson, California, at an altitude of 5886 feet. Professor Hale is in charge of it. He attended the gathering of leading astronomers in Rome one year, and such were his revelations there that these savants resolved their next meeting should be on top of Mount Wilson. And so it was.

There is but one Mount Wilson. From a depth seventy-two feet down in the earth photographs have been taken of new stars. On the first of these plates many new worlds — I believe sixteen — were discovered. On the second I think it was sixty new worlds which had come into our ken, and on the third plate there were estimated to be more than a hundred — several of them said to be twenty times the size of our sun. Some of them were so distant as to require eight years for their light to reach us, which inclines us to bow our heads whispering to ourselves, "All we know is as nothing to the unknown." When the monster new glass, three times larger than any existing, is in operation, what revelations are to come! I am assured if a race inhabits the moon they will be clearly seen.

The third delightful task was founding the Hero Fund, in which my whole heart was concerned. I had heard of a serious accident in a coal pit near Pittsburgh, and how the former superintendent, Mr. Taylor, although then engaged in other pursuits, had instantly driven to the scene, hoping to be of use in the crisis. Rallying volunteers, who responded eagerly, he led them down the pit to rescue those below. Alas, alas, he the heroic leader lost his own life.

I could not get the thought of this out of my mind. My dear, dear friend, Mr. Richard Watson Gilder, had sent me the following true and beautiful poem, and I re-read it the morning after the accident, and resolved then to establish the Hero Fund.

IN THE TIME OF PEACE

'T was said: "When roll of drum and battle's roar
Shall cease upon the earth, O, then no more

The deed — the race — of heroes in the land."
But scarce that word was breathed when one small hand

Lifted victorious o'er a giant wrong
That had its victims crushed through ages long;

Some woman set her pale and quivering face
Firm as a rock against a man's disgrace;

A little child suffered in silence lest
His savage pain should wound a mother's breast;

Some quiet scholar flung his gauntlet down
And risked, in Truth's great name, the synod's frown;

A civic hero, in the calm realm of laws,
Did that which suddenly drew a world's applause;

And one to the pest his lithe young body gave
That he a thousand thousand lives might save.

Hence arose the five-million-dollar fund to reward heroes, or to support the families of heroes, who perish in the effort to serve or save their fellows, and to supplement what employers or others do in contributing to the support of the families of those left destitute through accidents. This fund, established April 15, 1904, has proved from every point of view a decided success. I cherish a fatherly regard for it since no one suggested it to me. As far as I know, it never had been thought of; hence it is emphatically "my ain bairn." Later I extended it to my native land, Great Britain, with headquarters at Dunfermline—the Trustees of the Carnegie Dunfermline Trust undertaking its administration, and splendidly have they succeeded. In due time it was extended to France, Germany, Italy, Belgium, Holland, Norway, Sweden, Switzerland, and Denmark.

Regarding its workings in Germany, I received a letter from David Jayne Hill, our American Ambassador at Berlin, from which I quote:

My main object in writing now is to tell you how pleased His Majesty is with the working of the German Hero Fund. He is enthusiastic about it and spoke in most complimentary terms of your discernment, as well as your generosity in founding it. He did not believe it would fill so important a place as it is doing. He told me of several cases that are really touching, and which would otherwise have been wholly unprovided for. One was that of a young man who saved a boy from drowning and just as they were about to lift him out of the water, after passing up the child into a boat, his heart failed, and he sank. He left a lovely young wife and a little boy. She has already been helped by the Hero Fund to establish a little business from which she can make a living, and the education of the boy, who is very bright, will be looked after. This is but one example.

Valentini (Chief of the Civil Cabinet), who was somewhat skeptical at first regarding the need of such a fund, is now glowing with enthusiasm about it, and he tells me the whole Commission, which is composed of carefully chosen men, is earnestly devoted to the work of making the very best and wisest use of their means and has devoted much time to their decisions.

They have corresponded with the English and French Commission, arranged to exchange reports, and made plans to keep in touch with one another in their work. They were deeply interested in the American report and have learned much from it.

King Edward of Britain was deeply impressed by the provisions of the fund, and wrote me an autograph letter of appreciation of this and other gifts to my native land, which I deeply value, and hence insert.

Windsor Castle, November 21, 1908

DEAR MR. CARNEGIE:

I have for some time past been anxious to express to you my sense of your generosity for the great public objects which you have presented to this country, the land of your birth.

Scarcely less admirable than the gifts themselves is the great care and thought you have taken in guarding against their misuse.

I am anxious to tell you how warmly I recognize your most generous benefactions and the great services they are likely to confer upon the country.

As a mark of recognition, I hope you will accept the portrait of myself which I am sending to you.

Believe me, dear Mr. Carnegie,

Sincerely yours
EDWARD R. & I.

Some of the newspapers in America were doubtful of the merits of the Hero Fund and the first annual report was criticized, but all this has passed away and the action of the fund is now warmly extolled. It has conquered, and long will it be before the trust is allowed to perish! The heroes of the barbarian past wounded or killed their fellows; the heroes of our civilized day serve or save theirs. Such the difference between physical and moral courage, between barbarism and civilization. Those who belong to the first class are soon to pass away, for we are finally to regard men who slay each other as we now do cannibals who eat each other; but those in the latter class will not die as long as man exists upon the earth, for such heroism as they display is god-like.

The Hero Fund will prove chiefly a pension fund. Already it has many pensioners, heroes or the widows or children of heroes. A strange misconception arose at first about it. Many thought that its purpose was to stimulate heroic action, that heroes were to be induced to play their parts for the sake of reward. This never entered my mind. It is absurd. True heroes think not of reward. They are inspired and think only of their fellows endangered; never of themselves. The fund is intended to pension or provide in the most suitable manner for the hero should he be disabled, or for those dependent upon him should he perish in his attempt to save others. It has made a fine start and will grow in popularity year after year as its aims and services are better understood. To-day we have in America 1430 hero pensioners or their families on our list.

I found the president for the Hero Fund in a Carnegie veteran, one of the original boys, Charlie Taylor. No salary for Charlie — not a cent would he ever take. He loves the work so much that I believe he would pay highly for permission to live with it. He is the right man in the right place. He has charge also, with Mr. Wilmot's able assistance, of the pensions for Carnegie workmen (Carnegie Relief Fund[1]); also the pensions for railway employees of my old division. Three relief funds and all of them benefiting others.

I got my revenge one day upon Charlie, who was always urging me to do for others. He is a graduate of Lehigh University and one of her most loyal sons. Lehigh wished a building and Charlie was her chief advocate. I said nothing, but wrote President Drinker offering the funds for the building conditioned upon my naming it. He agreed, and I called it "Taylor Hall." When Charlie discovered this, he came and protested that it would make him ridiculous, that he had only been a modest graduate, and was not entitled to have his name publicly honored, and so on. I enjoyed his plight immensely, waiting until he had finished, and then said that it would probably make him somewhat ridiculous if I insisted upon "Taylor Hall," but he ought to be willing to sacrifice himself somewhat for Lehigh. If he wasn't consumed with vanity he would not care much how his name was used if it helped his Alma Mater. Taylor was not much of a name anyhow. It was his insufferable vanity that made such a fuss. He should conquer it. He could make his decision. He could sacrifice the name of Taylor or sacrifice Lehigh, just as he

---

[1] This fund is now managed separately.

liked, but: "No Taylor, no Hall." I had him! Visitors who may look upon that structure in after days and wonder who Taylor was may rest assured that he was a loyal son of Lehigh, a working, not merely a preaching, apostle of the gospel of service to his fellow-men, and one of the best men that ever lived. Such is our Lord High Commissioner of Pensions.

CHAPTER XX
Educational and Pension Funds

THE fifteen-million-dollar pension fund for aged university professors (The Carnegie Foundation for the Advancement of Teaching), the fourth important gift, given in June, 1905, required the selection of twenty-five trustees from among the presidents of educational institutions in the United States. When twenty-four of these — President Harper, of Chicago University, being absent through illness — honored me by meeting at our house for organization, I obtained an important accession of those who were to become more intimate friends. Mr. Frank A. Vanderlip proved of great service at the start — his Washington experience being most valuable — and in our president, Dr. Henry S. Pritchett, we found the indispensable man.

This fund is very near and dear to me — knowing, as I do, many who are soon to become beneficiaries, and convinced as I am of their worth and the value of the service already rendered by them. Of all professions, that of teaching is probably the most unfairly, yes, most meanly paid, though it should rank with the highest. Educated men, devoting their lives to teaching the young, receive mere pittances. When I first took my seat as a trustee of Cornell University, I was shocked to find how small were the salaries of the professors, as a rule ranking below the salaries of some of our clerks. To save for old age with these men is impossible. Hence the universities without pension funds are compelled to retain men who are no longer able, should no longer be required, to perform their duties. Of the usefulness of the fund no doubt can be entertained.[1] The first list of beneficiaries published was conclusive upon this point, containing as it did several names of world-wide reputation, so great had been their contributions to the stock of human knowledge. Many of these beneficiaries and their widows have written me most affecting letters. These I can never destroy, for if I ever have a fit of melancholy, I know the cure lies in re-reading these letters.

My friend, Mr. Thomas Shaw (now Lord Shaw), of Dunfermline had written an article for one of the English reviews showing that many poor people in Scotland were unable to pay the fees required to give their children a university education, although some had deprived themselves of comforts in order to do so. After reading Mr. Shaw's article the idea came to me to give ten millions in five per cent bonds, one half of the £104,000 yearly revenue from it to be used to pay the fees of the deserving poor students and the other half to improve the universities.

The first meeting of the trustees of this fund (The Carnegie Trust for the Universities of Scotland) was held in the Edinburgh office of the Secretary of State for Scotland in 1902, Lord Balfour of Burleigh presiding. It was a notable body of men — Prime Minister Balfour, Sir Henry Campbell-Bannerman (afterwards Prime Minister), John Morley (now Viscount Morley), James Bryce (now Viscount Bryce), the Earl of Elgin, Lord Rosebery, Lord Reay, Mr. Shaw (now Lord Shaw), Dr. John Ross of Dunfermline, "the man-of-all-work" that makes for the happiness or instruction of his fellowman, and others. I explained that I had asked them to act because I could not entrust funds to the faculties of

---

[1] The total amount of this fund in 1919 was $29,250,000.

the Scottish universities after reading the report of a recent commission. Mr. Balfour promptly exclaimed: "Not a penny, not a penny!" The Earl of Elgin, who had been a member of the commission, fully concurred.

The details of the proposed fund being read, the Earl of Elgin was not sure about accepting a trust which was not strict and specific. He wished to know just what his duties were. I had given a majority of the trustees the right to change the objects of beneficence and modes of applying funds, should they in after days decide that the purposes and modes prescribed for education in Scotland had become unsuitable or unnecessary for the advanced times. Balfour of Burleigh agreed with the Earl and so did Prime Minister Balfour, who said he had never heard of a testator before who was willing to give such powers. He questioned the propriety of doing so.

"Well," I said, "Mr. Balfour, I have never known of a body of men capable of legislating for the generation ahead, and in some cases those who attempt to legislate even for their own generation are not thought to be eminently successful."

There was a ripple of laughter in which the Prime Minister himself heartily joined, and he then said:

"You are right, quite right; but you are, I think, the first great giver who has been wise enough to take this view."

I had proposed that a majority should have the power, but Lord Balfour suggested not less than two thirds. This was accepted by the Earl of Elgin and approved by all. I am very sure it is a wise provision, as after days will prove. It is incorporated in all my large gifts, and I rest assured that this feature will in future times prove valuable. The Earl of Elgin, of Dunfermline, did not hesitate to become Chairman of this trust. When I told Premier Balfour that I hoped Elgin could be induced to assume this duty, he said promptly, "You could not get a better man in Great Britain."

We are all entirely satisfied now upon that point. The query is: where could we get his equal?

It is an odd coincidence that there are only four living men who have been made Burgesses and received the Freedom of Dunfermline, and all are connected with the trust for the Universities of Scotland, Sir Henry Campbell-Bannerman, the Earl of Elgin, Dr. John Ross, and myself. But there is a lady in the circle to-day, the only one ever so greatly honored with the Freedom of Dunfermline, Mrs. Carnegie, whose devotion to the town, like my own, is intense.

My election to the Lord Rectorship of St. Andrews in 1902 proved a very important event in my life. It admitted me to the university world, to which I had been a stranger. Few incidents in my life have so deeply impressed me as the first meeting of the faculty, when I took my seat in the old chair occupied successively by so many distinguished Lord Rectors during the nearly five hundred years which have elapsed since St. Andrews was founded. I read the collection of rectorial speeches as a preparation for the one I was soon to make. The most remarkable paragraph I met with in any of them was Dean Stanley's advice to the students to "go to Burns for your theology." That a high dignitary of the Church and a favorite of Queen Victoria should venture to say this to the students of John Knox's University is most suggestive as showing how even theology improves with the years. The best rules of conduct are in Burns. First there is: "Thine own reproach alone do fear." I took it as a motto early in life. And secondly:

"The fear o' hell's a hangman's whip
To haud the wretch in order;
But where ye feel your honor grip,
Let that aye be your border."

John Stuart Mill's rectorial address to the St. Andrews students is remarkable. He evidently wished to give them of his best. The prominence he assigns to music as an aid to high living and pure refined enjoyment is notable. Such is my own experience.

An invitation given to the principals of the four Scotch universities and their wives or daughters to spend a week at Skibo resulted in much joy to Mrs. Carnegie and myself. The first meeting was attended by the Earl of Elgin, chairman of the Trust for the Universities of Scotland, and Lord Balfour of Burleigh, Secretary for Scotland, and Lady Balfour. After that "Principals' Week" each year became an established custom. They as well as we became friends, and thereby, they all agree, great good results to the universities. A spirit of cooperation is stimulated. Taking my hand upon leaving after the first yearly visit, Principal Lang said:

"It has taken the principals of the Scotch universities five hundred years to learn how to begin our sessions. Spending a week together is the solution."

One of the memorable results of the gathering at Skibo in 1906 was that Miss Agnes Irwin, Dean of Radcliffe College, and great-granddaughter of Benjamin Franklin, spent the principals' week with us and all were charmed with her. Franklin received his first doctor's degree from St. Andrews University, nearly one hundred and fifty years ago. The second centenary of his birth was finely celebrated in Philadelphia, and St. Andrews, with numerous other universities throughout the world, sent addresses. St. Andrews also sent a degree to the great-granddaughter. As Lord Rector, I was deputed to confer it and place the mantel upon her. This was done the first evening before a large audience, when more than two hundred addresses were presented.

The audience was deeply impressed, as well it might be. St. Andrews University, the first to confer the degree upon the great-grandfather, conferred the same degree upon the great-grandchild one hundred and forty-seven years later (and this upon her own merits as Dean of Radcliffe College); sent it across the Atlantic to be bestowed by the hands of its Lord Rector, the first who was not a British subject, but who was born one as Franklin was, and who became an American citizen as Franklin did; the ceremony performed in Philadelphia where Franklin rests, in the presence of a brilliant assembly met to honor his memory. It was all very beautiful, and I esteemed myself favored, indeed, to be the medium of such a graceful and appropriate ceremony. Principal Donaldson of St. Andrews was surely inspired when he thought of it!

My unanimous reelection by the students of St. Andrews, without a contest for a second term, was deeply appreciated. And I liked the Rector's nights, when the students claim him for themselves, no member of the faculty being invited. We always had a good time. After the first one, Principal Donaldson gave me the verdict of the Secretary as rendered to him: "Rector So-and-So talked *to* us, Rector Thus-and-So talked *at* us, both from the platform; Mr. Carnegie sat down in our circle and talked *with* us."

The question of aid to our own higher educational institutions often intruded itself upon me, but my belief was that our chief universities, such as Harvard and Columbia, with five to ten thousand students,[1] were large enough; that further growth was undesirable; that the smaller institutions (the colleges especially) were in greater need of help and that it would be a better use of surplus wealth to aid them. Accordingly, I afterwards confined myself to these and am satisfied that this was wise. At a later date we found Mr. Rockefeller's splendid educational fund, The General Education Board, and ourselves were working in this fruitful field without consultation, with sometimes undesirable results. Mr. Rockefeller wished me to join his board and this I did. Cooperation was soon found to be much to our mutual advantage, and we now work in unison.

In giving to colleges quite a number of my friends have been honored as was my partner Charlie Taylor. Conway Hall at Dickinson College, was named for Moncure D. Conway, whose Autobiography, recently published, is pronounced "literature" by the "Athenæum." It says: "These two volumes lie on the table glistening like gems 'midst the piles of autobiographical rubbish by which they are surrounded." That is rather suggestive for one who is adding to the pile.

The last chapter in Mr. Conway's Autobiography ends with the following paragraph:

Implore Peace, O my reader, from whom I now part. Implore peace not of deified thunder clouds but of every man, woman, child thou shalt meet. Do not merely offer the prayer, "Give peace in our time," but do thy part to answer it! Then, at least, though the world be at strife, there shall be peace in thee.

My friend has put his finger upon our deepest disgrace. It surely must soon be abolished between civilized nations.

---

[1] Columbia University in 1920 numbered all told some 25,000 students in the various departments.

The Stanton Chair of Economics at Kenyon College, Ohio, was founded in memory of Edwin M. Stanton, who kindly greeted me as a boy in Pittsburgh when I delivered telegrams to him, and was ever cordial to me in Washington, when I was an assistant to Secretary Scott. The Hanna Chair in Western Reserve University, Cleveland; the John Hay Library at Brown University; the second Elihu Root Fund for Hamilton, the Mrs. Cleveland Library for Wells, gave me pleasure to christen after these friends. I hope more are to follow, commemorating those I have known, liked, and honored. I also wished a General Dodge Library and Gayley Library to be erected from my gifts, but these friends had already obtained such honor from their respective Alma Maters.

My first gift to Hamilton College was to be named the Elihu Root Foundation, but that ablest of all our Secretaries of State, and in the opinion of President Roosevelt, "the wisest man he ever knew," took care, it seems, not to mention the fact to the college authorities. When I reproached him with this dereliction, he laughingly replied:

"Well, I promise not to cheat you the next gift you give us."

And by a second gift this lapse was repaired after all, but I took care not to entrust the matter directly to him. The Root Fund of Hamilton[1] is now established beyond his power to destroy. Root is a great man, and, as the greatest only are he is, in his simplicity, sublime. President Roosevelt declared he would crawl on his hands and knees from the White House to the Capitol if this would insure Root's nomination to the presidency with a prospect of success. He was considered

---

[1] It amounts to $250,000.

vulnerable because he had been counsel for corporations and was too little of the spouter and the demagogue, too much of the modest, retiring statesman to split the ears of the groundlings.[1] The party foolishly decided not to risk Root.

My connection with Hampton and Tuskegee Institutes, which promote the elevation of the colored race we formerly kept in slavery, has been a source of satisfaction and pleasure, and to know Booker Washington is a rare privilege. We should all take our hats off to the man who not only raised himself from slavery, but helped raise millions of his race to a higher stage of civilization. Mr. Washington called upon me a few days after my gift of six hundred thousand dollars was made to Tuskegee and asked if he might be allowed to make one suggestion. I said: "Certainly."

"You have kindly specified that a sum from that fund be set aside for the future support of myself and wife during our lives, and we are very grateful, but, Mr. Carnegie, the sum is far beyond our needs and will seem to my race a fortune. Some might feel that I was no longer a poor man giving my services without thought of saving money. Would you have any objection to changing that clause, striking out the sum, and substituting 'only suitable provision'? I'll trust

[1] At the Meeting in Memory of the Life and Work of Andrew Carnegie held on April 25, 1920, in the Engineering Societies Building in New York, Mr. Root made an address in the course of which, speaking of Mr. Carnegie, he said:

"He belonged to that great race of nation-builders who have made the development of America the wonder of the world. . . . He was the kindliest man I ever knew. Wealth had brought to him no hardening of the heart, nor made him forget the dreams of his youth. Kindly, affectionate, charitable in his judgments, unrestrained in his sympathies, noble in his impulses, I wish that all the people who think of him as a rich man giving away money he did not need could know of the hundreds of kindly things he did unknown to the world."

the trustees. Mrs. Washington and myself need very little."

I did so, and the deed now stands, but when Mr. Baldwin asked for the original letter to exchange it for the substitute, he told me that the noble soul objected. That document addressed to him was to be preserved forever, and handed down; but he would put it aside and let the substitute go on file.

This is an indication of the character of the leader of his race. No truer, more self-sacrificing hero ever lived: a man compounded of all the virtues. It makes one better just to know such pure and noble souls — human nature in its highest types is already divine here on earth. If it be asked which man of our age, or even of the past ages, has risen from the lowest to the highest, the answer must be Booker Washington. He rose from slavery to the leadership of his people — a modern Moses and Joshua combined, leading his people both onward and upward.

In connection with these institutions I came in contact with their officers and trustees — men like Principal Hollis B. Frissell of Hampton, Robert C. Ogden, George Foster Peabody, V. Everit Macy, George McAneny and William H. Baldwin — recently lost to us, alas! — men who labor for others. It was a blessing to know them intimately. The Cooper Union, the Mechanics and Tradesmen's Society, indeed every institution[1] in which I became interested, revealed many men and women devoting their time and thought, not to "miserable aims that end with self," but to high ideals which mean the relief and uplift of their less fortunate brethren.

[1] The universities, colleges, and educational institutions to which Mr. Carnegie gave either endowment funds or buildings number five hundred. All told his gifts to them amounted to $27,000,000.

My giving of organs to churches came very early in my career, I having presented to less than a hundred members of the Swedenborgian Church in Allegheny which my father favored, an organ, after declining to contribute to the building of a new church for so few. Applications from other churches soon began to pour in, from the grand Catholic Cathedral of Pittsburgh down to the small church in the country village, and I was kept busy. Every church seemed to need a better organ than it had, and as the full price for the new instrument was paid, what the old one brought was clear profit. Some ordered organs for very small churches which would almost split the rafters, as was the case with the first organ given the Swedenborgians; others had bought organs before applying but our check to cover the amount was welcome. Finally, however, a rigid system of giving was developed. A printed schedule requiring answers to many questions has now to be filled and returned before action is taken. The department is now perfectly systematized and works admirably because we graduate the gift according to the size of the church.

Charges were made in the rigid Scottish Highlands that I was demoralizing Christian worship by giving organs to churches. The very strict Presbyterians there still denounce as wicked an attempt "to worship God with a kist fu' o' whistles," instead of using the human God-given voice. After that I decided that I should require a partner in my sin, and therefore asked each congregation to pay one half of the desired new organ. Upon this basis the organ department still operates and continues to do a thriving business, the demand for improved organs still being great. Besides, many new churches are required for increasing populations and for these organs are essential.

I see no end to it. In requiring the congregation to pay one half the cost of better instruments, there is assurance of needed and reasonable expenditure. Believing from my own experience that it is salutary for the congregation to hear sacred music at intervals in the service and then slowly to disperse to the strains of the reverence-compelling organ after such sermons as often show us little of a Heavenly Father, I feel the money spent for organs is well spent. So we continue the organ department.[1]

Of all my work of a philanthropic character, my private pension fund gives me the highest and noblest return. No satisfaction equals that of feeling you have been permitted to place in comfortable circumstances, in their old age, people whom you have long known to be kind and good and in every way deserving, but who from no fault of their own, have not sufficient means to live respectably, free from solicitude as to their mere maintenance. Modest sums insure this freedom. It surprised me to find how numerous were those who needed some aid to make the difference between an old age of happiness and one of misery. Some such cases had arisen before my retirement from business, and I had sweet satisfaction from this source. Not one person have I ever placed upon the pension list[2] that did not fully deserve assistance. It is a real roll of honor and mutual affection. All are worthy. There is no publicity about it. No one knows who is embraced. Not a word is ever breathed to others.

This is my favorite and best answer to the question which will never down in my thoughts: "What good am

---

[1] The "organ department" up to 1919 had given 7689 organs to as many different churches at a cost of over six million dollars.

[2] This amounted to over $250,000 a year.

I doing in the world to deserve all my mercies?" Well, the dear friends of the pension list give me a satisfactory reply, and this always comes to me in need. I have had far beyond my just share of life's blessings; therefore I never ask the Unknown for anything. We are in the presence of universal law and should bow our heads in silence and obey the Judge within, asking nothing, fearing nothing, just doing our duty right along, seeking no reward here or hereafter.

It is, indeed, more blessed to give than to receive. These dear good friends would do for me and mine as I do for them were positions reversed. I am sure of this. Many precious acknowledgments have I received. Some venture to tell me they remember me every night in their prayers and ask for me every blessing. Often I cannot refrain from giving expression to my real feelings in return.

"Pray, don't," I say. "Don't ask anything more for me. I've got far beyond my just share already. Any fair committee sitting upon my case would take away more than half the blessings already bestowed." These are not mere words, I feel their truth.

The Railroad Pension Fund is of a similar nature. Many of the old boys of the Pittsburgh Division (or their widows) are taken care of by it. It began years ago and grew to its present proportions. It now benefits the worthy railroad men who served under me when I was superintendent on the Pennsylvania, or their widows, who need help. I was only a boy when I first went among these trainmen and got to know them by name. They were very kind to me. Most of the men beneficiaries of the fund I have known personally. They are dear friends.

Although the four-million-dollar fund I gave for

workmen in the mills (Steel Workers' Pensions) embraces hundreds that I never saw, there are still a sufficient number upon it that I do remember to give that fund also a strong hold upon me.

CHAPTER XXI
The Peace Palace and Pittencrieff

PEACE, at last as between English-speaking peoples,[1] must have been early in my thoughts. In 1869, when Britain launched the monster Monarch, then the largest warship known, there was, for some now-forgotten reason, talk of how she could easily compel tribute from our American cities one after the other. Nothing could resist her. I cabled John Bright, then in the British Cabinet (the cable had recently been opened):

"First and best service possible for Monarch, bringing home body Peabody."[2]

No signature was given. Strange to say, this was done, and thus the Monarch became the messenger of peace, not of destruction. Many years afterwards I met Mr. Bright at a small dinner party in Birmingham and told him I was his young anonymous correspondent. He was surprised that no signature was attached and said his heart was in the act. I am sure it was. He is entitled to all credit.

He was the friend of the Republic when she needed friends during the Civil War. He had always been my favorite living hero in public life as he had been my father's. Denounced as a wild radical at first, he kept

---

[1] "Let men say what they will, I say that as surely as the sun in the heavens once shone upon Britain and America united, so surely it is one morning to rise, shine upon, and greet again the Reunited States — the British-American Union." (Quoted in Alderson's *Andrew Carnegie, The Man and His Work*, p. 108. New York, 1909.)

[2] George Peabody, the American merchant and philanthropist, who died in London in 1869.

steadily on until the nation came to his point of view. Always for peace he would have avoided the Crimean War, in which Britain backed the wrong horse, as Lord Salisbury afterwards acknowledged. It was a great privilege that the Bright family accorded me, as a friend, to place a replica of the Manchester Bright statue in Parliament, in the stead of a poor one removed.

I became interested in the Peace Society of Great Britain upon one of my early visits and attended many of its meetings, and in later days I was especially drawn to the Parliamentary Union established by Mr. Cremer, the famous working-man's representative in Parliament. Few men living can be compared to Mr. Cremer. When he received the Nobel Prize of £8000 as the one who had done the most that year for peace, he promptly gave all but £1000, needed for pressing wants, to the Arbitration Committee. It was a noble sacrifice. What is money but dross to the true hero! Mr. Cremer is paid a few dollars a week by his trade to enable him to exist in London as their member of Parliament, and here was fortune thrown in his lap only to be devoted by him to the cause of peace. This is the heroic in its finest form.

I had the great pleasure of presenting the Committee to President Cleveland at Washington in 1887, who received the members cordially and assured them of his hearty cooperation. From that day the abolition of war grew in importance with me until it finally overshadowed all other issues. The surprising action of the first Hague Conference gave me intense joy. Called primarily to consider disarmament (which proved a dream), it created the commanding reality of a permanent tribunal to settle international disputes. I saw in this the greatest step toward peace that humanity had ever taken, and taken as if by inspiration, without much previous discussion. No wonder the sublime idea captivated the conference.

If Mr. Holls, whose death I so deeply deplored, were alive to-day and a delegate to the forthcoming second Conference with his chief, Andrew D. White, I feel that these two might possibly bring about the creation of the needed International Court for the abolition of war. He it was who started from The Hague at night for Germany, upon request of his chief, and saw the German Minister of Foreign Affairs, and the Emperor and finally prevailed upon them to approve of the High Court, and not to withdraw their delegates as threatened — a service for which Mr. Holls deserves to be enrolled among the greatest servants of mankind. Alas, death came to him while still in his prime.

The day that International Court is established will become one of the most memorable days in the world's history.[1] It will ring the knell of man killing man — the deepest and blackest of crimes. It should be celebrated in every land as I believe it will be some day, and that time, perchance, not so remote as expected. In that era not a few of those hitherto extolled as heroes will have found oblivion because they failed to promote peace and goodwill instead of war.

When Andrew D. White and Mr. Holls, upon their return from The Hague, suggested that I offer the funds needed for a Temple of Peace at The Hague, I informed them that I never could be so presumptuous; that if the

---

[1] "I submit that the only measure required to-day for the maintenance of world peace is an agreement between three or four of the leading Civilized Powers (and as many more as desire to join — the more the better) pledged to cooperate against disturbers of world peace, should such arise." (Andrew Carnegie, in address at unveiling of a bust of William Randall Cremer at the Peace Palace of The Hague, August 29, 1913.)

Government of the Netherlands informed me of its desire to have such a temple and hoped I would furnish the means, the request would be favorably considered. They demurred, saying this could hardly be expected from any government. Then I said I could never act in the matter.

Finally the Dutch Government did make application, through its Minister, Baron Gevers in Washington, and I rejoiced. Still, in writing him, I was careful to say that the drafts of his Government would be duly honored. I did not send the money. The Government drew upon me for it, and the draft for a million and a half is kept as a memento. It seems to me almost too much that any individual should be permitted to perform so noble a duty as that of providing means for this Temple of Peace — the most holy building in the world because it has the holiest end in view. I do not even except St. Peter's, or any building erected to the glory of God, whom, as Luther says, "we cannot serve or aid; He needs no help from us." This temple is to bring peace, which is so greatly needed among His erring creatures. "The highest worship of God is service to man." At least, I feel so with Luther and Franklin.

When in 1907 friends came and asked me to accept the presidency of the Peace Society of New York, which they had determined to organize, I declined, alleging that I was kept very busy with many affairs, which was true; but my conscience troubled me afterwards for declining. If I were not willing to sacrifice myself for the cause of peace what should I sacrifice for? What was I good for? Fortunately, in a few days, the Reverend Lyman Abbott, the Reverend Mr. Lynch, and some other notable laborers for good causes called to urge my reconsideration. I divined their errand and frankly told them they need not speak. My conscience had been tormenting me for declining and I would accept the presidency and do my duty. After that came the great national gathering (the following April) when for the first time in the history of Peace Society meetings, there attended delegates from thirty-five of the states of the Union, besides many foreigners of distinction.[1]

My first decoration then came unexpectedly. The French Government had made me Knight Commander of the Legion of Honor, and at the Peace Banquet in New York, over which I presided, Baron d'Estournelles de Constant appeared upon the stage and in a compelling speech invested me with the regalia amid the cheers of the company. It was a great honor, indeed, and appreciated by me because given for my services to the cause of International Peace. Such honors humble, they do not exalt; so let them come.[2] They serve also to remind me that I must strive harder than ever, and watch every act and word more closely, that I may reach just a little nearer the standard the givers — deluded souls — mistakenly assume in their speeches, that I have already attained.

.   .   .   .

No gift I have made or can ever make can possibly approach that of Pittencrieff Glen, Dunfermline. It is

---

[1] Mr. Carnegie does not mention the fact that in December, 1910, he gave to a board of trustees $10,000,000, the revenue of which was to be administered for "the abolition of international war, the foulest blot upon our civilization." This is known as the Carnegie Endowment for International Peace. The Honorable Elihu Root is president of the board of trustees.

[2] Mr. Carnegie received also the Grand Cross Order of Orange-Nassau from Holland, the Grand Cross Order of Danebrog from Denmark, a gold medal from twenty-one American Republics and had doctors' degrees from innumerable universities and colleges. He was also a member of many institutes, learned societies and clubs — over 190 in number.

saturated with childish sentiment — all of the purest and sweetest. I must tell that story:

Among my earliest recollections are the struggles of Dunfermline to obtain the rights of the town to part of the Abbey grounds and the Palace ruins. My Grandfather Morrison began the campaign, or, at least, was one of those who did. The struggle was continued by my Uncles Lauder and Morrison, the latter honored by being charged with having incited and led a band of men to tear down a certain wall. The citizens won a victory in the highest court and the then Laird ordered that thereafter "no Morrison be admitted to the Glen." I, being a Morrison like my brother-cousin, Dod, was debarred. The Lairds of Pittencrieff for generations had been at variance with the inhabitants.

The Glen is unique, as far as I know. It adjoins the Abbey and Palace grounds, and on the west and north it lies along two of the main streets of the town. Its area (between sixty and seventy acres) is finely sheltered, its high hills grandly wooded. It always meant paradise to the child of Dunfermline. It certainly did to me. When I heard of paradise, I translated the word into Pittencrieff Glen, believing it to be as near to paradise as anything I could think of. Happy were we if through an open lodge gate, or over the wall or under the iron grill over the burn, now and then we caught a glimpse inside.

Almost every Sunday Uncle Lauder took "Dod" and "Naig" for a walk around the Abbey to a part that overlooked the Glen — the busy crows fluttering around in the big trees below. Its Laird was to us children the embodiment of rank and wealth. The Queen, we knew, lived in Windsor Castle, but she didn't own Pittencrieff, not she! Hunt of Pittencrieff wouldn't exchange with her or with anyone. Of this we were sure, because certainly neither of us would. In all my childhood's — yes and in my early manhood's — air-castle building (which was not small), nothing comparable in grandeur approached Pittencrieff. My Uncle Lauder predicted many things for me when I became a man, but had he foretold that some day I should be rich enough, and so supremely fortunate as to become Laird of Pittencrieff, he might have turned my head. And then to be able to hand it over to Dunfermline as a public park — my paradise of childhood! Not for a crown would I barter that privilege.

When Dr. Ross whispered to me that Colonel Hunt might be induced to sell, my ears cocked themselves instantly. He wished an extortionate price, the doctor thought, and I heard nothing further for some time. When indisposed in London in the autumn of 1902, my mind ran upon the subject, and I intended to wire Dr. Ross to come up and see me. One morning, Mrs. Carnegie came into my room and asked me to guess who had arrived and I guessed Dr. Ross. Sure enough, there he was. We talked over Pittencrieff. I suggested that if our mutual friend and fellow-townsman, Mr. Shaw in Edinburgh (Lord Shaw of Dunfermline) ever met Colonel Hunt's agents he could intimate that their client might some day regret not closing with me as another purchaser equally anxious to buy might not be met with, and I might change my mind or pass away. Mr. Shaw told the doctor when he mentioned this that he had an appointment to meet with Hunt's lawyer on other business the next morning and would certainly say so.

I sailed shortly after for New York and received there one day a cable from Mr. Shaw stating that the Laird would accept forty-five thousand pounds. Should he close? I wired: "Yes, provided it is under Ross's conditions"; and on Christmas Eve, I received Shaw's reply: "Hail, Laird of Pittencrieff!" So I was the happy possessor of the grandest title on earth in my estimation. The King — well, he was only the King. He didn't own King Malcolm's tower nor St. Margaret's shrine, nor Pittencrieff Glen. Not he, poor man. I did, and I shall be glad to condescendingly show the King those treasures should he ever visit Dunfermline.

As the possessor of the Park and the Glen I had a chance to find out what, if anything, money could do for the good of the masses of a community, if placed in the hands of a body of public-spirited citizens. Dr. Ross was taken into my confidence so far as Pittencrieff Park was concerned, and with his advice certain men intended for a body of trustees were agreed upon and invited to Skibo to organize. They imagined it was in regard to transferring the Park to the town; not even to Dr. Ross was any other subject mentioned. When they heard that half a million sterling in bonds, bearing five per cent interest, was also to go to them for the benefit of Dunfermline, they were surprised.[1]

It is twelve years since the Glen was handed over to the trustees and certainly no public park was ever dearer to a people. The children's yearly gala day, the flower shows and the daily use of the Park by the people are surprising. The Glen now attracts people from neighboring towns. In numerous ways the trustees have succeeded finely in the direction indicated in the trust deed, namely:

To bring into the monotonous lives of the toiling masses of Dunfermline, more "of sweetness and light," to give to

[1] Additional gifts, made later, brought this gift up to $3,750,000.

them — especially the young — some charm, some happiness, some elevating conditions of life which residence elsewhere would have denied, that the child of my native town, looking back in after years, however far from home it may have roamed, will feel that simply by virtue of being such, life has been made happier and better. If this be the fruit of your labors, you will have succeeded; if not, you will have failed.

To this paragraph I owe the friendship of Earl Grey, formerly Governor-General of Canada. He wrote Dr. Ross: "I must know the man who wrote that document in the 'Times' this morning."

We met in London and became instantly sympathetic. He is a great soul who passes instantly into the heart and stays there. Lord Grey is also to-day a member (trustee) of the ten-million-dollar fund for the United Kingdom.[1]

---

[1] Mr. Carnegie refers to the gift of ten million dollars to the Carnegie United Kingdom Trust merely in connection with Earl Grey. His references to his gifts are casual, in that he refers only to the ones in which he happens for the moment to be interested. Those he mentions are merely a part of the whole. He gave to the Church Peace Union over $2,000,000, to the United Engineering Society $1,500,000, to the International Bureau of American Republics $850,000, and to a score or more of research, hospital, and educational boards sums ranging from $100,000 to $500,000. He gave to various towns and cities over twenty-eight hundred library buildings at a cost of over $60,000,000. The largest of his gifts he does not mention at all. This was made in 1911 to the Carnegie Corporation of New York and was $125,000,000. The Corporation is the residuary legatee under Mr. Carnegie's will and it is not yet known what further sum may come to it through that instrument. The object of the Corporation, as defined by Mr. Carnegie himself in a letter to the trustees, is:

"To promote the advancement and diffusion of knowledge and understanding among the people of the United States by aiding technical schools, institutions of higher learning, libraries, scientific research, hero funds, useful publications and by such other agencies and means as shall from time to time be found appropriate therefor."

The Carnegie benefactions, all told, amount to something over $350,000,000 — surely a huge sum to have been brought together and then distributed by one man.

Thus, Pittencrieff Glen is the most soul-satisfying public gift I ever made, or ever can make. It is poetic justice that the grandson of Thomas Morrison, radical leader in his day, nephew of Bailie Morrison, his son and successor, and above all son of my sainted father and my most heroic mother, should arise and dispossess the lairds, should become the agent for conveying the Glen and Park to the people of Dunfermline forever. It is a true romance, which no air-castle can quite equal or fiction conceive. The hand of destiny seems to hover over it, and I hear something whispering: "Not altogether in vain have you lived — not altogether in vain." This is the crowning mercy of my career! I set it apart from all my other public gifts. Truly the whirligig of time brings in some strange revenges.

It is now thirteen years since I ceased to accumulate wealth and began to distribute it. I could never have succeeded in either had I stopped with having enough to retire upon, but nothing to retire to. But there was the habit and the love of reading, writing and speaking upon occasion, and also the acquaintance and friendship of educated men which I had made before I gave up business. For some years after retiring I could not force myself to visit the works. This, alas, would recall so many who had gone before. Scarcely one of my early friends would remain to give me the hand-clasp of the days of old. Only one or two of these old men would call me "Andy."

Do not let it be thought, however, that my younger partners were forgotten, or that they have not played a very important part in sustaining me in the effort of reconciling myself to the new conditions. Far otherwise! The most soothing influence of all was their prompt organization of the Carnegie Veteran Association, to expire only when the last member dies. Our yearly dinner together, in our own home in New York, is a source of the greatest pleasure, — so great that it lasts from one year to the other. Some of the Veterans travel far to be present, and what occurs between us constitutes one of the dearest joys of my life. I carry with me the affection of "my boys." I am certain I do. There is no possible mistake about that because my heart goes out to them.

This I number among my many blessings and in many a brooding hour this fact comes to me, and I say to myself: "Rather this, minus fortune, than multi-millionairedom without it — yes, a thousand times, yes."

Many friends, great and good men and women, Mrs. Carnegie and I are favored to know, but not one whit shall these ever change our joint love for the "boys." For to my infinite delight her heart goes out to them as does mine. She it was who christened our new New York home with the first Veteran dinner. "The partners first" was her word. It was no mere idle form when they elected Mrs. Carnegie the first honorary member, and our daughter the second. Their place in our hearts is secure. Although I was the senior, still we were "boys together." Perfect trust and common aims, not for self only, but for each other, and deep affection, moulded us into a brotherhood. We were friends first and partners afterwards. Forty-three out of forty-five partners are thus bound together for life.

Another yearly event that brings forth many choice spirits is our Literary Dinner, at home, our dear friend Mr. Richard Watson Gilder, editor of the "Century," being the manager.[1] His devices and quotations from

---

[1] "Yesterday we had a busy day in Toronto. The grand event was a dinner at six o'clock where we all spoke, A. C. making a remarkable address. . . . I can't tell you how I am enjoying this. Not only seeing new places, but the talks

the writings of the guest of the year, placed upon the cards of the guests, are so appropriate, as to cause much hilarity. Then the speeches of the novitiates give zest to the occasion. John Morley was the guest of honor when with us in 1895 and a quotation from his works was upon the card at each plate.

One year Gilder appeared early in the evening of the dinner as he wished to seat the guests. This had been done, but he came to me saying it was well he had looked them over. He had found John Burroughs and Ernest Thompson Seton were side by side, and as they were then engaged in a heated controversy upon the habits of beasts and birds, in which both had gone too far in their criticisms, they were at daggers' points. Gilder said it would never do to seat them together. He had separated them. I said nothing, but slipped into the dining room unobserved and replaced the cards as before. Gilder's surprise was great when he saw the men next each other, but the result was just as I had expected. A reconciliation took place and they parted good friends. Moral: If you wish to play peace-maker, seat adversaries next each other where they must begin by being civil.

Burroughs and Seton both enjoyed the trap I set for them. True it is, we only hate those whom we do not

with our own party. It is, indeed, a liberal education. A. C. is truly a 'great' man; that is, a man of enormous faculty and a great imagination. I don't remember any friend who has such a range of poetical quotation, unless it is Stedman. (Not so much *range* as numerous quotations from Shakespeare, Burns, Byron, etc.) His views are truly large and prophetic. And, unless I am mistaken, he has a genuine ethical character. He is not perfect, but he is most interesting and remarkable; a true democrat; his benevolent actions having a root in principle and character. He is not accidentally the intimate friend of such high natures as Arnold and Morley." (*Letters of Richard Watson Gilder*, edited by his daughter Rosamond Gilder, p. 374. New York, 1916.)

know. It certainly is often the way to peace to invite your adversary to dinner and even beseech him to come, taking no refusal. Most quarrels become acute from the parties not seeing and communicating with each other and hearing too much of their disagreement from others. They do not fully understand the other's point of view and all that can be said for it. Wise is he who offers the hand of reconciliation should a difference with a friend arise. Unhappy he to the end of his days who refuses it. No possible gain atones for the loss of one who has been a friend even if that friend has become somewhat less dear to you than before. He is still one with whom you have been intimate, and as age comes on friends pass rapidly away and leave you.

He is the happy man who feels there is not a human being to whom he does not wish happiness, long life, and deserved success, not one in whose path he would cast an obstacle nor to whom he would not do a service if in his power. All this he can feel without being called upon to retain as a friend one who has proved unworthy beyond question by dishonorable conduct. For such there should be nothing felt but pity, infinite pity. And pity for your own loss also, for true friendship can only feed and grow upon the virtues.

> "When love begins to sicken and decay
> It useth an enforced ceremony."

The former geniality may be gone forever, but each can wish the other nothing but happiness.

None of my friends hailed my retirement from business more warmly than Mark Twain. I received from him the following note, at a time when the newspapers were talking much about my wealth.

DEAR SIR AND FRIEND:

You seem to be prosperous these days. Could you lend an admirer a dollar and a half to buy a hymn-book with? God will bless you if you do; I feel it, I know it. So will I. If there should be other applications this one not to count.

Yours
MARK

P.S. Don't send the hymn-book, send the money. I want to make the selection myself.

M.

When he was lying ill in New York I went to see him frequently, and we had great times together, for even lying in bed he was as bright as ever. One call was to say good-bye, before my sailing for Scotland. The Pension Fund for University Professors was announced in New York soon after I sailed. A letter about it from Mark, addressed to "Saint Andrew," reached me in Scotland, from which I quote the following:

You can take my halo. If you had told me what you had done when at my bedside you would have got it there and then. It is pure tin and paid "the duty" when it came down.

Those intimate with Mr. Clemens (Mark Twain) will certify that he was one of the charmers. Joe Jefferson is the only man who can be conceded his twin brother in manner and speech, their charm being of the same kind. "Uncle Remus" (Joel Chandler Harris) is another who has charm, and so has George W. Cable; yes, and Josh Billings also had it. Such people brighten the lives of their friends, regardless of themselves. They make sunshine wherever they go. In Rip Van Winkle's words: "All pretty much alike, dem fellers." Every one of them is unselfish and warm of heart.

The public only knows one side of Mr. Clemens — the amusing part. Little does it suspect that he was a man of strong convictions upon political and social questions and a moralist of no mean order. For instance, upon the capture of Aguinaldo by deception, his pen was the most trenchant of all. Junius was weak in comparison.

The gathering to celebrate his seventieth birthday was unique. The literary element was there in force, but Mark had not forgotten to ask to have placed near him the multi-millionaire, Mr. H. H. Rogers, one who had been his friend in need. Just like Mark. Without exception, the leading literary men dwelt in their speeches exclusively upon the guest's literary work. When my turn came, I referred to this and asked them to note that what our friend had done as a man would live as long as what he had written. Sir Walter Scott and he were linked indissolubly together. Our friend, like Scott, was ruined by the mistakes of partners, who had become hopelessly bankrupt. Two courses lay before him. One the smooth, easy, and short way — the legal path. Surrender all your property, go through bankruptcy, and start afresh. This was all he owed to creditors. The other path, long, thorny, and dreary, a life struggle, with everything sacrificed. There lay the two paths and this was his decision:

"Not what I owe to my creditors, but what I owe to myself is the issue."

There are times in most men's lives that test whether they be dross or pure gold. It is the decision made in the crisis which proves the man. Our friend entered the fiery furnace a man and emerged a hero. He paid his debts to the utmost farthing by lecturing around the world. "An amusing cuss, Mark Twain," is all very well as a popular verdict, but what of Mr. Clemens the man and the hero, for he is both and in the front rank, too, with Sir Walter.

He had a heroine in his wife. She it was who sustained him and traveled the world round with him as his guardian angel, and enabled him to conquer as Sir Walter did. This he never failed to tell to his intimates. Never in my life did three words leave so keen a pang as those uttered upon my first call after Mrs. Clemens passed away. I fortunately found him alone and while my hand was still in his, and before one word had been spoken by either, there came from him, with a stronger pressure of my hand, these words: "A ruined home, a ruined home." The silence was unbroken. I write this years after, but still I hear the words again and my heart responds.

One mercy, denied to our forefathers, comes to us of to-day. If the Judge within give us a verdict of acquittal as having lived this life well, we have no other Judge to fear.

> "To thine own self be true,
> And it must follow, as the night the day,
> Thou canst not then be false to any man."

Eternal punishment, because of a few years' shortcomings here on earth, would be the reverse of Godlike. Satan himself would recoil from it.

CHAPTER XXII
Matthew Arnold and Others

THE most charming man, John Morley and I agree, that we ever knew was Matthew Arnold. He had, indeed, "a charm" — that is the only word which expresses the effect of his presence and his conversation. Even his look and grave silences charmed.

He coached with us in 1880, I think, through Southern England — William Black and Edwin A. Abbey being of the party. Approaching a pretty village he asked me if the coach might stop there a few minutes. He explained that this was the resting-place of his godfather, Bishop Keble, and he should like to visit his grave. He continued:

"Ah, dear, dear Keble! I caused him much sorrow by my views upon theological subjects, which caused me sorrow also, but notwithstanding he was deeply grieved, dear friend as he was, he traveled to Oxford and voted for me for Professor of English Poetry."

We walked to the quiet churchyard together. Matthew Arnold in silent thought at the grave of Keble made upon me a lasting impression. Later the subject of his theological views was referred to. He said they had caused sorrow to his best friends.

"Mr. Gladstone once gave expression to his deep disappointment, or to something like displeasure, saying I ought to have been a bishop. No doubt my writings prevented my promotion, as well as grieved my friends, but I could not help it. I had to express my views."

I remember well the sadness of tone with which these

last words were spoken, and how very slowly. They came as from the deep. He had his message to deliver. Steadily has the age advanced to receive it. His teachings pass almost uncensured to-day. If ever there was a seriously religious man it was Matthew Arnold. No irreverent word ever escaped his lips. In this he and Gladstone were equally above reproach, and yet he had in one short sentence slain the supernatural. "The case against miracles is closed. They do not happen."

He and his daughter, now Mrs. Whitridge, were our guests when in New York in 1883, and also at our mountain home in the Alleghanies, so that I saw a great deal, but not enough, of him. My mother and myself drove him to the hall upon his first public appearance in New York. Never was there a finer audience gathered. The lecture was not a success, owing solely to his inability to speak well in public. He was not heard. When we returned home his first words were:

"Well, what have you all to say? Tell me! Will I do as a lecturer?"

I was so keenly interested in his success that I did not hesitate to tell him it would never do for him to go on unless he fitted himself for public speaking. He must get an elocutionist to give him lessons upon two or three points. I urged this so strongly that he consented to do so. After we all had our say, he turned to my mother, saying:

"Now, dear Mrs. Carnegie, they have all given me their opinions, but I wish to know what you have to say about my first night as a lecturer in America."

"Too ministerial, Mr. Arnold, too ministerial," was the reply slowly and softly delivered. And to the last Mr. Arnold would occasionally refer to that, saying he felt it hit the nail on the head. When he returned to New

York from his Western tour, he had so much improved that his voice completely filled the Brooklyn Academy of Music. He had taken a few lessons from a professor of elocution in Boston, as advised, and all went well thereafter.

He expressed a desire to hear the noted preacher, Mr. Beecher; and we started for Brooklyn one Sunday morning. Mr. Beecher had been apprised of our coming so that after the services he might remain to meet Mr. Arnold. When I presented Mr. Arnold he was greeted warmly. Mr. Beecher expressed his delight at meeting one in the flesh whom he had long known so well in the spirit, and, grasping his hand, he said:

"There is nothing you have written, Mr. Arnold, which I have not carefully read at least once and a great deal many times, and always with profit, always with profit!"

"Ah, then, I fear, Mr. Beecher," replied Arnold, "you may have found some references to yourself which would better have been omitted."

"Oh, no, no, those did me the most good of all," said the smiling Beecher, and they both laughed.

Mr. Beecher was never at a loss. After presenting Matthew Arnold to him, I had the pleasure of presenting the daughter of Colonel Ingersoll, saying, as I did so:

"Mr. Beecher, this is the first time Miss Ingersoll has ever been in a Christian church."

He held out both hands and grasped hers, and looking straight at her and speaking slowly, said:

"Well, well, you are the most beautiful heathen I ever saw." Those who remember Miss Ingersoll in her youth will not differ greatly with Mr. Beecher. Then:

"How's your father, Miss Ingersoll? I hope he's well.

Many times he and I have stood together on the platform, and wasn't it lucky for me we were on the same side!"

Beecher was, indeed, a great, broad, generous man, who absorbed what was good wherever found. Spencer's philosophy, Arnold's insight tempered with sound sense, Ingersoll's staunch support of high political ends were powers for good in the Republic. Mr. Beecher was great enough to appreciate and hail as helpful friends all of these men.

Arnold visited us in Scotland in 1887, and talking one day of sport he said he did not shoot, he could not kill anything that had wings and could soar in the clear blue sky; but, he added, he could not give up fishing — "the accessories are so delightful." He told of his happiness when a certain duke gave him a day's fishing twice or three times a year. I forget who the kind duke was, but there was something unsavory about him and mention was made of this. He was asked how he came to be upon intimate terms with such a man.

"Ah!" he said, "a duke is always a personage with us, always a personage, independent of brains or conduct. We are all snobs. Hundreds of years have made us so, all snobs. We can't help it. It is in the blood."

This was smilingly said, and I take it he made some mental reservations. He was no snob himself, but one who naturally "smiled at the claims of long descent," for generally the "descent" cannot be questioned.

He was interested, however, in men of rank and wealth, and I remember when in New York he wished particularly to meet Mr. Vanderbilt. I ventured to say he would not find him different from other men.

"No, but it is something to know the richest man in the world," he replied. "Certainly the man who makes his own wealth eclipses those who inherit rank from others."

I asked him one day why he had never written critically upon Shakespeare and assigned him his place upon the throne among the poets. He said that thoughts of doing so had arisen, but reflection always satisfied him that he was incompetent to write upon, much less to criticize, Shakespeare. He believed it could not be successfully done. Shakespeare was above all, could be measured by no rules of criticism; and much as he should have liked to dwell upon his transcendent genius, he had always recoiled from touching the subject. I said that I was prepared for this, after his tribute which stands to-day unequaled, and I recalled his own lines from his sonnet:

SHAKESPEARE

Others abide our question. Thou art free.
We ask and ask — Thou smilest and art still,
Out-topping knowledge. For the loftiest hill
Who to the stars uncrowns his majesty,

Planting his steadfast footsteps in the sea,
Making the heaven of heavens his dwelling-place,
Spares but the cloudy border of his base
To the foil'd searching of mortality;

And thou, who didst the stars and sunbeams know,
Self-school'd, self-scann'd, self-honour'd, self-secure,
Didst stand on earth unguess'd at — Better so!

All pains the immortal spirit must endure,
All weakness which impairs, all griefs which bow,
Find their sole voice in that victorious brow.

I knew Mr. Shaw (Josh Billings) and wished Mr. Arnold, the apostle of sweetness and light, to meet that rough diamond — rough, but still a diamond. Fortunately one morning Josh came to see me in the Windsor Hotel, where we were then living, and referred to our guest, expressing his admiration for him. I replied:

"You are going to dine with him to-night. The ladies are going out and Arnold and myself are to dine alone; you complete the trinity."

To this he demurred, being a modest man, but I was inexorable. No excuse would be taken; he must come to oblige me. He did. I sat between them at dinner and enjoyed this meeting of extremes. Mr. Arnold became deeply interested in Mr. Shaw's way of putting things and liked his Western anecdotes, laughing more heartily than I had ever seen him do before. One incident after another was told from the experience of the lecturer, for Mr. Shaw had lectured for fifteen years in every place of ten thousand inhabitants or more in the United States.

Mr. Arnold was desirous of hearing how the lecturer held his audiences.

"Well," he said, "you mustn't keep them laughing too long, or they will think you are laughing at them. After giving the audience amusement you must become earnest and play the serious role. For instance, 'There are two things in this life for which no man is ever prepared. Who will tell me what these are?' Finally some one cries out 'Death.' 'Well, who gives me the other?' Many respond — wealth, happiness, strength, marriage, taxes. At last Josh begins, solemnly: 'None of you has given the second. There are two things on earth for which no man is ever prepared, and them's twins,' and the house shakes." Mr. Arnold did also.

"Do you keep on inventing new stories?" was asked.

"Yes, always. You can't lecture year after year unless

you find new stories, and sometimes these fail to crack. I had one nut which I felt sure would crack and bring down the house, but try as I would it never did itself justice, all because I could not find the indispensable word, just one word. I was sitting before a roaring wood fire one night up in Michigan when the word came to me which I knew would crack like a whip. I tried it on the boys and it did. It lasted longer than any one word I used. I began: 'This is a highly critical age. People won't believe until they fully understand. Now there's Jonah and the whale. They want to know all about it, and it's my opinion that neither Jonah nor the whale fully understood it. And then they ask what Jonah was doing in the whale's — the whale's society.'"

Mr. Shaw was walking down Broadway one day when accosted by a real Westerner, who said:

"I think you are Josh Billings."

"Well, sometimes I am called that."

"I have five thousand dollars for you right here in my pocket-book."

"Here's Delmonico's, come in and tell me all about it."

After seating themselves, the stranger said he was part owner in a gold mine in California, and explained that there had been a dispute about its ownership and that the conference of partners broke up in quarreling. The stranger said he had left, threatening he would take the bull by the horns and begin legal proceedings. "The next morning I went to the meeting and told them I had turned over Josh Billing's almanac that morning and the lesson for the day was: 'When you take the bull by the horns, take him by the tail; you can get a better hold and let go when you've a mind to.' We laughed and laughed and felt that was good sense. We took your advice, settled, and parted good friends. Some one moved that five thousand dollars be given Josh, and as I was coming East they appointed me treasurer and I promised to hand it over. There it is."

The evening ended by Mr. Arnold saying:

"Well, Mr. Shaw, if ever you come to lecture in England, I shall be glad to welcome and introduce you to your first audience. Any foolish man called a lord could do you more good than I by introducing you, but I should so much like to do it."

Imagine Matthew Arnold, the apostle of sweetness and light, introducing Josh Billings, the foremost of jesters, to a select London audience.

In after years he never failed to ask after "our leonine friend, Mr. Shaw."

Meeting Josh at the Windsor one morning after the notable dinner I sat down with him in the rotunda and he pulled out a small memorandum book, saying as he did so:

"Where's Arnold? I wonder what he would say to this. The 'Century' gives me $100 a week, I agreeing to send them any trifle that occurs to me. I try to give it something. Here's this from Uncle Zekiel, my weekly budget: 'Of course the critic is a greater man than the author. Any fellow who can point out the mistakes another fellow has made is a darned sight smarter fellow than the fellow who made them.'"

I told Mr. Arnold a Chicago story, or rather a story about Chicago. A society lady of Boston visiting her schoolmate friend in Chicago, who was about to be married, was overwhelmed with attention. Asked by a noted citizen one evening what had charmed her most in Chicago, she graciously replied:

"What surprises me most isn't the bustle of business,

or your remarkable development materially, or your grand residences; it is the degree of culture and refinement I find here." The response promptly came:

"Oh, we are just dizzy on cult out here, you bet."

Mr. Arnold was not prepared to enjoy Chicago, which had impressed him as the headquarters of Philistinism. He was, however, surprised and gratified at meeting with so much "culture and refinement." Before he started he was curious to know what he should find most interesting. I laughingly said that he would probably first be taken to see the most wonderful sight there, which was said to be the slaughter houses, with new machines so perfected that the hog driven in at one end came out hams at the other before its squeal was out of one's ears. Then after a pause he asked reflectively:

"But why should one go to slaughter houses, why should one hear hogs squeal?" I could give no reason, so the matter rested.

Mr. Arnold's Old Testament favorite was certainly Isaiah: at least his frequent quotations from that great poet, as he called him, led one to this conclusion. I found in my tour around the world that the sacred books of other religions had been stripped of the dross that had necessarily accumulated around their legends. I remembered Mr. Arnold saying that the Scriptures should be so dealt with. The gems from Confucius and others which delight the world have been selected with much care and appear as "collects." The disciple has not the objectionable accretions of the ignorant past presented to him.

The more one thinks over the matter, the stronger one's opinion becomes that the Christian will have to follow the Eastern example and winnow the wheat from the chaff—worse than chaff, sometimes the positively pernicious and even poisonous refuse. Burns, in the

"Cotter's Saturday Night," pictures the good man taking down the big Bible for the evening service:

"He wales a portion with judicious care."

We should have those portions selected and use the selections only. In this, and much besides, the man whom I am so thankful for having known and am so favored as to call friend, has proved the true teacher in advance of his age, the greatest poetic teacher in the domain of "the future and its viewless things."

I took Arnold down from our summer home at Cresson in the Alleghanies to see black, smoky Pittsburgh. In the path from the Edgar Thomson Steel Works to the railway station there are two flights of steps to the bridge across the railway, the second rather steep. When we had ascended about three quarters of it he suddenly stopped to gain breath. Leaning upon the rail and putting his hand upon his heart, he said to me:

"Ah, this will some day do for me, as it did for my father."

I did not know then of the weakness of his heart, but I never forgot this incident, and when not long after the sad news came of his sudden death, after exertion in England endeavoring to evade an obstacle, it came back to me with a great pang that our friend had foretold his fate. Our loss was great. To no man I have known could Burns's epitaph upon Tam Samson be more appropriately applied:

> "Tam Samson's weel-worn clay here lies:
> Ye canting zealots, spare him!
> If honest worth in heaven rise,
> Ye'll mend or ye win near him."

The name of a dear man comes to me just here, Dr. Oliver Wendell Holmes, of Boston, everybody's doctor, whose only ailment toward the end was being eighty years of age. He was a boy to the last. When Matthew Arnold died a few friends could not resist taking steps toward a suitable memorial to his memory. These friends quietly provided the necessary sum, as no public appeal could be thought of. No one could be permitted to contribute to such a fund except such as had a right to the privilege, for privilege it was felt to be. Double, triple the sum could readily have been obtained. I had the great satisfaction of being permitted to join the select few and to give the matter a little attention upon our side of the Atlantic. Of course I never thought of mentioning the matter to dear Dr. Holmes — not that he was not one of the elect, but that no author or professional man should be asked to contribute money to funds which, with rare exceptions, are best employed when used for themselves. One morning, however, I received a note from the doctor, saying that it had been whispered to him that there was such a movement on foot, and that I had been mentioned in connection with it, and if he were judged worthy to have his name upon the roll of honor, he would be gratified. Since he had heard of it he could not rest without writing to me, and he should like to hear in reply. That he was thought worthy goes without saying.

This is the kind of memorial any man might wish. I venture to say that there was not one who contributed to it who was not grateful to the kind fates for giving him the opportunity.

CHAPTER XXIII
British Political Leaders

IN London, Lord Rosebery, then in Gladstone's Cabinet and a rising statesman, was good enough to invite me to dine with him to meet Mr. Gladstone, and I am indebted to him for meeting the world's first citizen. This was, I think, in 1885, for my "Triumphant Democracy"[1] appeared in 1886, and I remember giving Mr. Gladstone, upon that occasion, some startling figures which I had prepared for it.

I never did what I thought right in a social matter with greater self-denial, than when later the first invitation came from Mr. Gladstone to dine with him. I was engaged to dine elsewhere and sorely tempted to plead that an invitation from the real ruler of Great Britain should be considered as much of a command as that of the ornamental dignitary. But I kept my engagement and missed the man I most wished to meet. The privilege came later, fortunately, when subsequent visits to him at Hawarden were made.

Lord Rosebery opened the first library I ever gave, that of Dunfermline, and he has recently (1905) opened the latest given by me — one away over in Stornoway.

When he last visited New York I drove him along the Riverside Drive, and he declared that no city in the world possessed such an attraction. He was a man of brilliant parts, but his resolutions were:

"Sicklied o'er with the pale cast of thought."

[1] *Triumphant Democracy, or Fifty Years' March of the Republic.* London and New York, 1886.

Had he been born to labor and entered the House of Commons in youth, instead of being dropped without effort into the gilded upper chamber, he might have acquired in the rough-and-tumble of life the tougher skin, for he was highly sensitive and lacked tenacity of purpose essential to command in political life. He was a charming speaker — a eulogist with the lightest touch and the most graceful style upon certain themes of any speaker of his day. [Since these lines were written he has become, perhaps, the foremost eulogist of our race. He has achieved a high place. All honor to him!]

One morning I called by appointment upon him. After greetings he took up an envelope which I saw as I entered had been carefully laid on his desk, and handed it to me, saying:

"I wish you to dismiss your secretary." "That is a big order, Your Lordship. He is indispensable, and a Scotsman," I replied. "What is the matter with him?"

"This isn't your handwriting; it is his. What do you think of a man who spells Rosebery with two *r's*?"

I said if I were sensitive on that point life would not be endurable for me. "I receive many letters daily when at home and I am sure that twenty to thirty per cent of them mis-spell my name, ranging from 'Karnaghie' to 'Carnagay.'"

But he was in earnest. Just such little matters gave him great annoyance. Men of action should learn to laugh at and enjoy these small things, or they themselves may become "small." A charming personality withal, but shy, sensitive, capricious, and reserved, qualities which a few years in the Commons would probably have modified.

When he was, as a Liberal, surprising the House of

Lords and creating some stir, I ventured to let off a little of my own democracy upon him.

"Stand for Parliament boldly. Throw off your hereditary rank, declaring you scorn to accept a privilege which is not the right of every citizen. Thus make yourself the real leader of the people, which you never can be while a peer. You are young, brilliant, captivating, with the gift of charming speech. No question of your being Prime Minister if you take the plunge."

To my surprise, although apparently interested, he said very quietly:

"But the House of Commons couldn't admit me as a peer."

"That's what I should hope. If I were in your place, and rejected, I would stand again for the next vacancy and force the issue. Insist that one having renounced his hereditary privileges becomes elevated to citizenship and is eligible for any position to which he is elected. Victory is certain. That's playing the part of a Cromwell. Democracy worships a precedent-breaker or a precedent-maker."

We dropped the subject. Telling Morley of this afterward, I shall never forget his comment:

"My friend, Cromwell doesn't reside at Number 38 Berkeley Square." Slowly, solemnly spoken, but conclusive.

Fine fellow, Rosebery, only he was handicapped by being born a peer. On the other hand, Morley, rising from the ranks, his father a surgeon hard-pressed to keep his son at college, is still "Honest John," unaffected in the slightest degree by the so-called elevation to the peerage and the Legion of Honor, both given for merit. The same with "Bob" Reid, M.P., who became Earl Loreburn and Lord High Chancellor, Lord Haldane, his successor as Chancellor; Asquith, Prime Minister, Lloyd George, and others. Not even the rulers of our Republic to-day are more democratic or more thorough men of the people.

When the world's foremost citizen passed away, the question was, Who is to succeed Gladstone; who can succeed him? The younger members of the Cabinet agreed to leave the decision to Morley. Harcourt or Campbell-Bannerman? There was only one impediment in the path of the former, but that was fatal — inability to control his temper. The issue had unfortunately aroused him to such outbursts as really unfitted him for leadership, and so the man of calm, sober, unclouded judgment was considered indispensable.

I was warmly attached to Harcourt, who in turn was a devoted admirer of our Republic, as became the husband of Motley's daughter. Our census and our printed reports, which I took care that he should receive, interested him deeply. Of course, the elevation of the representative of my native town of Dunfermline (Campbell-Bannerman)[1] gave me unalloyed pleasure, the more so since in returning thanks from the Town House to the people assembled he used these words:

"I owe my election to my Chairman, Bailie Morrison."

The Bailie, Dunfermline's leading radical, was my uncle. We were radical families in those days and are so still, both Carnegies and Morrisons, and intense admirers of the Great Republic, like that one who extolled Washington and his colleagues as "men who knew and dared proclaim the royalty of man" — a proclamation worth while. There is nothing more certain than that the English-speaking race in orderly, lawful develop-

---

[1] Campbell-Bannerman was chosen leader of the Liberal Party in December, 1898.

ment will soon establish the golden rule of citizenship through evolution, never revolution:

> "The rank is but the guinea's stamp,
> The man's the gowd for a' that."

This feeling already prevails in all the British colonies. The dear old Motherland hen has ducks for chickens which give her much anxiety breasting the waves, while she, alarmed, screams wildly from the shore; but she will learn to swim also by and by.

In the autumn of 1905 Mrs. Carnegie and I attended the ceremony of giving the Freedom of Dunfermline to our friend, Dr. John Ross, chairman of the Carnegie Dunfermline Trust, foremost and most zealous worker for the good of the town. Provost Macbeth in his speech informed the audience that the honor was seldom conferred, that there were only three living burgesses — one their member of Parliament, H. Campbell-Bannerman, then Prime Minister; the Earl of Elgin of Dunfermline, ex-Viceroy of India, then Colonial Secretary; and the third myself. This seemed great company for me, so entirely out of the running was I as regards official station.

The Earl of Elgin is the descendant of The Bruce. Their family vault is in Dunfermline Abbey, where his great ancestor lies under the Abbey bell. It has been noted how Secretary Stanton selected General Grant as the one man in the party who could not possibly be the commander. One would be very apt to make a similar mistake about the Earl. When the Scottish Universities were to be reformed the Earl was second on the committee. When the Conservative Government formed its Committee upon the Boer War, the Earl, a Liberal, was appointed chairman. When the decision of the House of Lords brought dire confusion upon the United Free Church of Scotland, Lord Elgin was called upon as the Chairman of Committee to settle the matter. Parliament embodied his report in a bill, and again he was placed at the head to apply it. When trustees for the Universities of Scotland Fund were to be selected, I told Prime Minister Balfour I thought the Earl of Elgin as a Dunfermline magnate could be induced to take the chairmanship. He said I could not get a better man in Great Britain. So it has proved. John Morley said to me one day afterwards, but before he had, as a member of the Dunfermline Trust, experience of the chairman:

"I used to think Elgin about the most problematical public man in high position I had ever met, but I now know him one of the ablest. Deeds, not words; judgment, not talk."

Such the descendant of The Bruce to-day, the embodiment of modest worth and wisdom combined.

Once started upon a Freedom-getting career, there seemed no end to these honors.[1] With headquarters in London in 1906, I received six Freedoms in six consecutive days, and two the week following, going out by morning train and returning in the evening. It might be thought that the ceremony would become monotonous, but this was not so, the conditions being different in each case. I met remarkable men in the mayors and provosts and the leading citizens connected with municipal affairs, and each community had its own individual stamp and its problems, successes, and failures. There was generally one greatly desired improvement overshadowing all other questions engrossing the attention

---

[1] Mr. Carnegie had received no less than fifty-four Freedoms of cities in Great Britain and Ireland. This was a record — Mr. Gladstone coming second with seventeen.

of the people. Each was a little world in itself. The City Council is a Cabinet in miniature and the Mayor the Prime Minister. Domestic politics keep the people agog. Foreign relations are not wanting. There are inter-city questions with neighboring communities, joint water or gas or electrical undertakings of mighty import, conferences deciding for or against alliances or separations.

In no department is the contrast greater between the old world and the new than in municipal government. In the former the families reside for generations in the place of birth with increasing devotion to the town and all its surroundings. A father achieving the mayorship stimulates the son to aspire to it. That invaluable asset, city pride, is created, culminating in romantic attachment to native places. Councilorships are sought that each in his day and generation may be of some service to the town. To the best citizens this is a creditable object of ambition. Few, indeed, look beyond it — membership in Parliament being practically reserved for men of fortune, involving as it does residence in London without compensation. This latter, however, is soon to be changed and Britain follow the universal practice of paying legislators for service rendered. [In 1908; since realized; four hundred pounds is now paid.]

After this she will probably follow the rest of the world by having Parliament meet in the daytime, its members fresh and ready for the day's work, instead of giving all day to professional work and then with exhausted brains undertaking the work of governing the country after dinner. Cavendish, the authority on whist, being asked if a man could possibly finesse a knave, second round, third player, replied, after reflecting, "Yes, he might *after dinner.*"

The best people are on the councils of British towns, incorruptible, public-spirited men, proud of and devoted to their homes. In the United States progress is being made in this direction, but we are here still far behind Britain. Nevertheless, people tend to settle permanently in places as the country becomes thickly populated. We shall develop the local patriot who is anxious to leave the place of his birth a little better than he found it. It is only one generation since the provostship of Scotch towns was generally reserved for one of the local landlords belonging to the upper classes. That "the Briton dearly loves a lord" is still true, but the love is rapidly disappearing.

In Eastbourne, King's Lynn, Salisbury, Ilkeston, and many other ancient towns, I found the mayor had risen from the ranks, and had generally worked with his hands. The majority of the council were also of this type. All gave their time gratuitously. It was a source of much pleasure to me to know the provosts and leaders in council of so many towns in Scotland and England, not forgetting Ireland where my Freedom tour was equally attractive. Nothing could excel the reception accorded me in Cork, Waterford, and Limerick. It was surprising to see the welcome on flags expressed in the same Gaelic words, *Cead mille failthe* (meaning "a hundred thousand welcomes") as used by the tenants of Skibo.

Nothing could have given me such insight into local public life and patriotism in Britain as Freedom-taking, which otherwise might have become irksome. I felt myself so much at home among the city chiefs that the embarrassment of flags and crowds and people at the windows along our route was easily met as part of the duty of the day, and even the address of the chief magistrate usually furnished new phases of life upon which

I could dwell. The lady mayoresses were delightful in all their pride and glory.

My conclusion is that the United Kingdom is better served by the leading citizens of her municipalities, elected by popular vote, than any other country far and away can possibly be; and that all is sound to the core in that important branch of government. Parliament itself could readily be constituted of a delegation of members from the town councils without impairing its efficiency. Perhaps when the sufficient payment of members is established, many of these will be found at Westminster and that to the advantage of the Kingdom.

CHAPTER XXIV

Gladstone and Morley

MR. GLADSTONE paid my "American Four-in-Hand in Britain" quite a compliment when Mrs. Carnegie and I were his guests at Hawarden in April, 1892. He suggested one day that I should spend the morning with him in his new library, while he arranged his books (which no one except himself was ever allowed to touch), and we could converse. In prowling about the shelves I found a unique volume and called out to my host, then on top of a library ladder far from me handling heavy volumes:

"Mr. Gladstone, I find here a book 'Dunfermline Worthies,' by a friend of my father's. I knew some of the worthies when a child."

"Yes," he replied, "and if you will pass your hand three or four books to the left I think you will find another book by a Dunfermline man."

I did so and saw my book "An American Four-in-Hand in Britain." Ere I had done so, however, I heard that organ voice orating in full swing from the top of the ladder:

"What Mecca is to the Mohammedan, Benares to the Hindoo, Jerusalem to the Christian, all that Dunfermline is to me."

My ears heard the voice some moments before my brain realized that these were my own words called forth by the first glimpse caught of Dunfermline as we approached it from the south.[1]

---

[1] The whole paragraph is as follows: "How beautiful is Dunfermline seen from the Ferry Hills, its grand old Abbey towering over all, seeming to hallow the city, and to lend a charm and dignity to the lowliest tenement! Nor

"How on earth did you come to get this book?" I asked. "I had not the honor of knowing you when it was written and could not have sent you a copy."

"No!" he replied, "I had not then the pleasure of your acquaintance, but some one, I think Rosebery, told me of the book and I sent for it and read it with delight. That tribute to Dunfermline struck me as so extraordinary it lingered with me. I could never forget it."

This incident occurred eight years after the "American Four-in-Hand" was written, and adds another to the many proofs of Mr. Gladstone's wonderful memory. Perhaps as a vain author I may be pardoned for confessing my grateful appreciation of his no less wonderful judgment.

The politician who figures publicly as "reader of the lesson" on Sundays, is apt to be regarded suspiciously. I confess that until I had known Mr. Gladstone well, I had found the thought arising now and then that the wary old gentleman might feel at least that these appearances cost him no votes. But all this vanished as I learned his true character. He was devout and sincere if ever man was. Yes, even when he records in his diary (referred to by Morley in his "Life of Gladstone") that, while addressing the House of Commons on the budget for several hours with great acceptance, he was "conscious of being sustained by the Divine Power above." Try as one may, who can deny that to one of such abounding faith this belief in the support of the Unknown Power must really have proved a sustaining

is there in all broad Scotland, nor in many places elsewhere that I know of, a more varied and delightful view than that obtained from the Park upon a fine day. What Benares is to the Hindoo, Mecca to the Mohammedan, Jerusalem to the Christian, all that Dunfermline is to me." (*An American Four-in-Hand in Britain*, p. 282.)

influence, although it may shock others to think that any mortal being could be so bold as to imagine that the Creator of the Universe would concern himself about Mr. Gladstone's budget, prepared for a little speck of this little speck of earth? It seems almost sacrilegious, yet to Mr. Gladstone we know it was the reverse — a religious belief such as has no direct agents of God and doing His Work.

On the night of the Queen's Jubilee in June, 1887, Mr. Blaine and I were to dine at Lord Wolverton's in Piccadilly, to meet Mr. and Mrs. Gladstone — Mr. Blaine's first introduction to him. We started in a cab from the Metropole Hotel in good time, but the crowds were so dense that the cab had to be abandoned in the middle of St. James's Street. Reaching the pavement, Mr. Blaine following, I found a policeman and explained to him who my companion was, where we were going, and asked him if he could not undertake to get us there. He did so, pushing his way through the masses with all the authority of his office and we followed. But it was nine o'clock before we reached Lord Wolverton's. We separated after eleven.

Mr. Gladstone explained that he and Mrs. Gladstone had been able to reach the house by coming through Hyde Park and around the back way. They expected to get back to their residence, then in Carlton Terrace, in the same way. Mr. Blaine and I thought we should enjoy the streets and take our chances of getting back to the hotel by pushing through the crowds. We were doing this successfully and were moving slowly with the current past the Reform Club when I heard a word or two spoken by a voice close to the building on my right. I said to Mr. Blaine:

"That is Mr. Gladstone's voice."

He said: "It is impossible. We have just left him returning to his residence."

"I don't care; I recognize voices better than faces, and I am sure that is Gladstone's."

Finally I prevailed upon him to return a few steps. We got close to the side of the house and moved back. I came to a muffled figure and whispered:

"What does 'Gravity' out of its bed at midnight?"

Mr. Gladstone was discovered. I told him I recognized his voice whispering to his companion.

"And so," I said, "the real ruler comes out to see the illuminations prepared for the nominal ruler!"

He replied: "Young man, I think it is time you were in bed."

We remained a few minutes with him, he being careful not to remove from his head and face the cloak that covered them. It was then past midnight and he was eighty, but, boylike, after he got Mrs. Gladstone safely home he had determined to see the show.

The conversation at the dinner between Mr. Gladstone and Mr. Blaine turned upon the differences in Parliamentary procedure between Britain and America. During the evening Mr. Gladstone cross-examined Mr. Blaine very thoroughly upon the mode of procedure of the House of Representatives of which Mr. Blaine had been the Speaker. I saw the "previous question," and summary rules with us for restricting needless debate made a deep impression upon Mr. Gladstone. At intervals the conversation took a wider range.

Mr. Gladstone was interested in more subjects than perhaps any other man in Britain. When I was last with him in Scotland, at Mr. Armistead's, his mind was as clear and vigorous as ever, his interest in affairs equally strong. The topic which then interested him most, and about which he plied me with questions, was the tall steel buildings in our country, of which he had been reading. What puzzled him was how it could be that the masonry of a fifth floor or sixth story was often finished before the third or fourth. This I explained, much to his satisfaction. In getting to the bottom of things he was indefatigable.

Mr. Morley (although a lord he still remains as an author plain John Morley) became one of our British friends quite early as editor of the "Fortnightly Review," which published my first contribution to a British periodical.[1] The friendship has widened and deepened in our old age until we mutually confess we are very close friends to each other.[2] We usually exchange short notes (sometimes long ones) on Sunday afternoons as the spirit moves us. We are not alike; far from it. We are drawn together because opposites are mutually beneficial to each other. I am optimistic; all my ducks being swans. He is pessimistic, looking out soberly, even darkly, upon the real dangers ahead, and sometimes imagining vain things. He is inclined to see "an

[1] *An American Four-in-Hand in Britain.*

[2] "Mr. Carnegie had proved his originality, fullness of mind, and bold strength of character, as much or more in the distribution of wealth as he had shown skill and foresight in its acquisition. We had become known to one another more than twenty years before through Matthew Arnold. His extraordinary freshness of spirit easily carried Arnold, Herbert Spencer, myself, and afterwards many others, high over an occasional crudity or haste in judgment such as befalls the best of us in ardent hours. People with a genius for picking up pins made as much as they liked of this: it was wiser to do justice to his spacious feel for the great objects of the world — for knowledge and its spread, invention, light, improvement of social relations, equal chances to the talents, the passion for peace. These are glorious things; a touch of exaggeration in expression is easy to set right.... A man of high and wide and well-earned mark in his generation." (John, Viscount Morley, in *Recollections*, vol. II, pp. 110, 112. New York, 1919.)

officer in every bush." The world seems bright to me, and earth is often a real heaven — so happy I am and so thankful to the kind fates. Morley is seldom if ever wild about anything; his judgment is always deliberate and his eyes are ever seeing the spots on the sun.

I told him the story of the pessimist whom nothing ever pleased, and the optimist whom nothing ever displeased, being congratulated by the angels upon their having obtained entrance to heaven. The pessimist replied:

"Yes, very good place, but somehow or other this halo don't fit my head exactly."

The optimist retorted by telling the story of a man being carried down to purgatory and the Devil laying his victim up against a bank while he got a drink at a spring — temperature very high. An old friend accosted him:

"Well, Jim, how's this? No remedy possible; you're a gone coon sure."

The reply came: "Hush, it might be worse."

"How's that, when you are being carried down to the bottomless pit?"

"Hush" — pointing to his Satanic Majesty — "he might take a notion to make me carry him."

Morley, like myself, was very fond of music and reveled in the morning hour during which the organ was being played at Skibo. He was attracted by the oratorios as also Arthur Balfour. I remember they got tickets together for an oratorio at the Crystal Palace. Both are sane but philosophic, and not very far apart as philosophers, I understand; but some recent productions of Balfour send him far afield speculatively — a field which Morley never attempts. He keeps his foot on the firm ground and only treads where the way is cleared. No danger of his being "lost in the woods" while searching for the path.

Morley's most astonishing announcement of recent days was in his address to the editors of the world, assembled in London. He informed them in effect that a few lines from Burns had done more to form and maintain the present improved political and social conditions of the people than all the millions of editorials ever written. This followed a remark that there were now and then a few written or spoken words which were in themselves events; they accomplished what they described. Tom Paine's "Rights of Man" was mentioned as such.

Upon his arrival at Skibo after this address we talked it over. I referred to his tribute to Burns and his six lines, and he replied that he didn't need to tell me what lines these were.

"No," I said, "I know them by heart."

In a subsequent address, unveiling a statue of Burns in the park at Montrose, I repeated the lines I supposed he referred to, and he approved them. He and I, strange to say, had received the Freedom of Montrose together years before, so we are fellow-freemen.

At last I induced Morley to visit us in America, and he made a tour through a great part of our country in 1904. We tried to have him meet distinguished men like himself. One day Senator Elihu Root called at my request and Morley had a long interview with him. After the Senator left Morley remarked to me that he had enjoyed his companion greatly, as being the most satisfactory American statesman he had yet met. He was not mistaken. For sound judgment and wide knowledge of our public affairs, Elihu Root has no superior.

Morley left us to pay a visit to President Roosevelt at the White House, and spent several fruitful days in company with that extraordinary man. Later, Morley's remark was:

"Well, I've seen two wonders in America, Roosevelt and Niagara."

That was clever and true to life — a great pair of roaring, tumbling, dashing and splashing wonders, knowing no rest, but both doing their appointed work, such as it is.

Morley was the best person to have the Acton library, and my gift of it to him came about in this way: When Mr. Gladstone told me the position Lord Acton was in, I agreed, at his suggestion, to buy Acton's library and allow it to remain for his use during life. Unfortunately, he did not live long to enjoy it — only a few years — and then I had the library upon my hands. I decided that Morley could make the best use of it for himself and would certainly leave it eventually to the proper institution. I began to tell him that I owned it when he interrupted me, saying:

"Well, I must tell you I have known this from the day you bought it. Mr. Gladstone couldn't keep the secret, being so overjoyed that Lord Acton had it secure for life."

Here were he and I in close intimacy, and yet never had one mentioned the situation to the other; but it was a surprise to me that Morley was not surprised. This incident proved the closeness of the bond between Gladstone and Morley — the only man he could not resist sharing his happiness with regarding earthly affairs. Yet on theological subjects they were far apart where Acton and Gladstone were akin.

The year after I gave the fund for the Scottish universities Morley went to Balmoral as minister in attendance upon His Majesty, and wired that he must see me before we sailed. We met and he informed me His Majesty was deeply impressed with the gift to the universities and the others I had made to my native land, and wished him to ascertain whether there was anything in his power to bestow which I would appreciate.

I asked: "What did you say?"

Morley replied: "I do not think so."

I said: "You are quite right, except that if His Majesty would write me a note expressing his satisfaction with what I had done, as he has to you, this would be deeply appreciated and handed down to my descendants as something they would all be proud of."

This was done. The King's autograph note I have already transcribed elsewhere in these pages.

That Skibo has proved the best of all health resorts for Morley is indeed fortunate, for he comes to us several times each summer and is one of the family, Lady Morley accompanying him. He is as fond of the yacht as I am myself, and, fortunately again, it is the best medicine for both of us. Morley is, and must always remain, "Honest John." No prevarication with him, no nonsense, firm as a rock upon all questions and in all emergencies; yet always looking around, fore and aft, right and left, with a big heart not often revealed in all its tenderness, but at rare intervals and upon fit occasion leaving no doubt of its presence and power. And after that, silence.

Chamberlain and Morley were fast friends as advanced radicals, and I often met and conferred with them when in Britain. When the Home Rule issue was raised, much interest was aroused in Britain over our American Federal system. I was appealed to freely and delivered public addresses in several cities, explaining and extolling our union, many in one, the freest government of the parts producing the strongest government of the whole. I sent Mr. Chamberlain Miss Anna L. Dawes's "How We Are Governed," at his request for information, and had conversations with Morley, Gladstone, and many others upon the subject.

I had to write Mr. Morley that I did not approve of the first Home Rule Bill for reasons which I gave. When I met Mr. Gladstone he expressed his regret at this and a full talk ensued. I objected to the exclusion of the Irish members from Parliament as being a practical separation. I said we should never have allowed the Southern States to cease sending representatives to Washington.

"What would you have done if they refused?" he asked.

"Employed all the resources of civilization — first, stopped the mails," I replied.

He paused and repeated:

"Stop the mails." He felt the paralysis this involved and was silent, and changed the subject.

In answer to questions as to what I should do, I always pointed out that America had many legislatures, but only one Congress. Britain should follow her example, one Parliament and local legislatures (not parliaments) for Ireland, Scotland, and Wales. These should be made states like New York and Virginia. But as Britain has no Supreme Court, as we have, to decide upon laws passed, not only by state legislatures but by Congress, the judicial being the final authority and not the political, Britain should have Parliament as the one national final authority over Irish measures. Therefore, the acts of the local legislature of Ireland should lie for three months' continuous session upon the table of the House of Commons, subject to adverse action of the House, but becoming operative unless disapproved. The provision would be a dead letter unless improper legislation were enacted, but if there were improper legislation, then it would be salutary. The clause, I said, was needed to assure timid people that no secession could arise.

Urging this view upon Mr. Morley afterwards, he told me this had been proposed to Parnell, but rejected. Mr. Gladstone might then have said: "Very well, this provision is not needed for myself and others who think with me, but it is needed to enable us to carry Britain with us. I am now unable to take up the question. The responsibility is yours."

One morning at Hawarden Mrs. Gladstone said:

"William tells me he has such extraordinary conversations with you."

These he had, no doubt. He had not often, if ever, heard the breezy talk of a genuine republican and did not understand my inability to conceive of different hereditary ranks. It seemed strange to me that men should deliberately abandon the name given them by their parents, and that name the parents' name. Especially amusing were the new titles which required the old hereditary nobles much effort to refrain from smiling at as they greeted the newly made peer who had perhaps bought his title for ten thousand pounds, more or less, given to the party fund.

Mr. Blaine was with us in London and I told Mr. Gladstone he had expressed to me his wonder and pain at seeing him in his old age hat in hand, cold day as it was, at a garden party doing homage to titled nobodies. Union of Church and State was touched upon, and also my "Look Ahead," which foretells the reunion of our race owing to the inability of the British Islands to expand. I had held that the disestablishment of the English Church was inevitable, because among other reasons it was an anomaly. No other part of the race had it. All religions were fostered, none favored, in every other English-speaking state. Mr. Gladstone asked:

"How long do you give our Established Church to live?"

My reply was I could not fix a date, he had had more experience than I in disestablishing churches. He nodded and smiled.

When I had enlarged upon a certain relative decrease of population in Britain that must come as compared with other countries of larger area, he asked:

"What future do you forecast for her?"

I referred to Greece among ancient nations and said that it was, perhaps, not accident that Chaucer, Shakespeare, Spenser, Milton, Burns, Scott, Stevenson, Bacon, Cromwell, Wallace, Bruce, Hume, Watt, Spencer, Darwin, and other celebrities had arisen here. Genius did not depend upon material resources. Long after Britain could not figure prominently as an industrial nation, not by her decline, but through the greater growth of others, she might in my opinion become the modern Greece and achieve among nations moral ascendancy.

He caught at the words, repeating them musingly:

"Moral ascendancy, moral ascendancy, I like that, I like that."

I had never before so thoroughly enjoyed a conference with a man. I visited him again at Hawarden, but my last visit to him was at Lord Randall's at Cannes the winter of 1897 when he was suffering keenly. He had still the old charm and was especially attentive to my sister-in-law, Lucy, who saw him then for the first time and was deeply impressed. As we drove off, she murmured, "A sick eagle! A sick eagle!" Nothing could better describe this wan and worn leader of men as he appeared to me that day. He was not only a great, but a truly good man, stirred by the purest impulses, a high, imperious soul always looking upward. He had, indeed, earned the title: "Foremost Citizen of the World."

In Britain, in 1881, I had entered into business relations with Samuel Storey, M.P., a very able man, a stern radical, and a genuine republican. We purchased several British newspapers and began a campaign of political progress upon radical lines. Passmore Edwards and some others joined us, but the result was not encouraging. Harmony did not prevail among my British friends and finally I decided to withdraw, which I was fortunately able to do without loss.[1]

My third literary venture, "Triumphant Democracy,"[2] had its origin in realizing how little the best-informed foreigner, or even Briton, knew of America, and how distorted that little was. It was prodigious what these eminent Englishmen did not then know about the Republic. My first talk with Mr. Gladstone in 1882 can never be forgotten. When I had occasion to say that the majority of the English-speaking race was now republican and it was a minority of monarchists who were upon the defensive, he said:

---

[1] Mr. Carnegie acquired no less than eighteen British newspapers with the idea of promoting radical views. The political results were disappointing, but with his genius for making money the pecuniary results were more than satisfactory.

[2] *Triumphant Democracy or Fifty Years' March of the Republic.* London, 1886; New York, 1888.

"Why, how is that?"

"Well, Mr. Gladstone," I said, "the Republic holds sway over a larger number of English-speaking people than the population of Great Britain and all her colonies even if the English-speaking colonies were numbered twice over."

"Ah! how is that? What is your population?"

"Sixty-six millions, and yours is not much more than half."

"Ah, yes, surprising!"

With regard to the wealth of the nations, it was equally surprising for him to learn that the census of 1880 proved the hundred-year-old Republic could purchase Great Britain and Ireland and all their realized capital and investments and then pay off Britain's debt, and yet not exhaust her fortune. But the most startling statement of all was that which I was able to make when the question of Free Trade was touched upon. I pointed out that America was now the greatest manufacturing nation in the world. [At a later date I remember Lord Chancellor Haldane fell into the same error, calling Britain the greatest manufacturing country in the world, and thanked me for putting him right.] I quoted Mulhall's figures: British manufactures in 1880, eight hundred and sixteen millions sterling; American manufactures eleven hundred and twenty-six millions sterling.[1] His one word was:

"Incredible!"

Other startling statements followed and he asked:

"Why does not some writer take up this subject and present the facts in a simple and direct form to the world?"

[1] The estimated value of manufactures in Great Britain in 1900 was five billions of dollars as compared to thirteen billions for the United States. In 1914 the United States had gone to over twenty-four billions.

I was then, as a matter of fact, gathering material for "Triumphant Democracy," in which I intended to perform the very service which he indicated, as I informed him.

"Round the World" and the "American Four-in-Hand" gave me not the slightest effort, but the preparation of "Triumphant Democracy," which I began in 1882, was altogether another matter. It required steady, laborious work. Figures had to be examined and arranged, but as I went forward the study became fascinating. For some months I seemed to have my head filled with statistics. The hours passed away unheeded. It was evening when I supposed it was midday. The second serious illness of my life dates from the strain brought upon me by this work, for I had to attend to business as well. I shall think twice before I trust myself again with anything so fascinating as figures.

CHAPTER XXV
Herbert Spencer and His Disciple

HERBERT SPENCER, with his friend Mr. Lott and myself, were fellow travelers on the Servia from Liverpool to New York in 1882. I bore a note of introduction to him from Mr. Morley, but I had met the philosopher in London before that. I was one of his disciples. As an older traveler, I took Mr. Lott and him in charge. We sat at the same table during the voyage.

One day the conversation fell upon the impression made upon us by great men at first meeting. Did they, or did they not, prove to be as we had imagined them? Each gave his experience. Mine was that nothing could be more different than the being imagined and that being beheld in the flesh.

"Oh!" said Mr. Spencer, "in my case, for instance, was this so?"

"Yes," I replied, "you more than any I had imagined my teacher, the great calm philosopher brooding, Buddha-like, over all things, unmoved; never did I dream of seeing him excited over the question of Cheshire or Cheddar cheese." The day before he had peevishly pushed away the former when presented by the steward, exclaiming "Cheddar, Cheddar, not Cheshire; I said *Cheddar*." There was a roar in which none joined more heartily than the sage himself. He refers to this incident of the voyage in his Autobiography.[1]

Spencer liked stories and was a good laugher. American stories seemed to please him more than others, and

[1] *An Autobiography,* by Herbert Spencer, vol. I, p. 424. New York, 1904.

of those I was able to tell him not a few, which were usually followed by explosive laughter. He was anxious to learn about our Western Territories, which were then attracting attention in Europe, and a story I told him about Texas struck him as amusing. When a returning disappointed emigrant from that State was asked about the then barren country, he said:

"Stranger, all that I have to say about Texas is that if I owned Texas and h — l, I would sell Texas."

What a change from those early days! Texas has now over four millions of population and is said to have the soil to produce more cotton than the whole world did in 1882.

The walk up to the house, when I had the philosopher out at Pittsburgh, reminded me of another American story of the visitor who started to come up the garden walk. When he opened the gate a big dog from the house rushed down upon him. He retreated and closed the garden gate just in time, the host calling out:

"He won't touch you, you know barking dogs never bite."

"Yes," exclaimed the visitor, tremblingly, "I know that and you know it, but does the dog know it?"

One day my eldest nephew was seen to open the door quietly and peep in where we were seated. His mother afterwards asked him why he had done so and the boy of eleven replied:

"Mamma, I wanted to see the man who wrote in a book that there was no use studying grammar."

Spencer was greatly pleased when he heard the story and often referred to it. He had faith in that nephew.

Speaking to him one day about his having signed a remonstrance against a tunnel between Calais and Dover as having surprised me, he explained that for

himself he was as anxious to have the tunnel as anyone and that he did not believe in any of the objections
raised against it, but signed the remonstrance because
he knew his countrymen were such fools that the military and naval element in Britain could stampede the
masses, frighten them, and stimulate militarism. An
increased army and navy would then be demanded. He
referred to a scare which had once arisen and involved
the outlay of many millions in fortifications which had
proved useless.

One day we were sitting in our rooms in the Grand Hotel looking out over Trafalgar Square. The Life Guards
passed and the following took place:

"Mr. Spencer, I never see men dressed up like Merry
Andrews without being saddened and indignant that
in the nineteenth century the most civilized race, as we
consider ourselves, still finds men willing to adopt as a
profession — until lately the only profession for gentlemen — the study of the surest means of killing other men."

Mr. Spencer said: "I feel just so myself, but I will tell
you how I curb my indignation. Whenever I feel it rising I am calmed by this story of Emerson's: He had been
hooted and hustled from the platform in Faneuil Hall
for daring to speak against slavery. He describes himself walking home in violent anger, until opening his
garden gate and looking up through the branches of
the tall elms that grew between the gate and his modest home, he saw the stars shining through. They said
to him: 'What, so hot, my little sir?'" I laughed and he
laughed, and I thanked him for that story. Not seldom
I have to repeat to myself, "What, so hot, my little sir?"
and it suffices.

Mr. Spencer's visit to America had its climax in the

banquet given for him at Delmonico's. I drove him to it and saw the great man there in a funk. He could think of nothing but the address he was to deliver.[1] I believe he had rarely before spoken in public. His great fear was that he should be unable to say anything that would be of advantage to the American people, who had been the first to appreciate his works. He may have attended many banquets, but never one comprised of more distinguished people than this one. It was a remarkable gathering. The tributes paid Spencer by the ablest men were unique. The climax was reached when Henry Ward Beecher, concluding his address, turned round and addressed Mr. Spencer in these words:

"To my father and my mother I owe my physical being; to you, sir, I owe my intellectual being. At a critical moment you provided the safe paths through the bogs and morasses; you were my teacher."

These words were spoken in slow, solemn tones. I do not remember ever having noticed more depth of feeling; evidently they came from a grateful debtor. Mr. Spencer was touched by the words. They gave rise to considerable remark, and shortly afterwards Mr. Beecher preached a course of sermons, giving his views upon

---

[1] "An occasion, on which more, perhaps, than any other in my life, I ought to have been in good condition, bodily and mentally, came when I was in a condition worse than I had been for six and twenty years. 'Wretched night; no sleep at all; kept in my room all day' says my diary, and I entertained 'great fear I should collapse.' When the hour came for making my appearance at Delmonico's, where the dinner was given, I got my friends to secrete me in an anteroom until the last moment, so that I might avoid all excitements of introductions and congratulations; and as Mr. Evarts, who presided, handed me on the dais, I begged him to limit his conversation with me as much as possible, and to expect very meagre responses. The event proved that, trying though the tax was, there did not result the disaster I feared; and when Mr. Evarts had duly uttered the compliments of the occasion, I was able to get through my prepared speech without difficulty, though not with much effect." (Spencer's *Autobiography*, vol. II, p. 478.)

Evolution. The conclusion of the series was anxiously looked for, because his acknowledgment of debt to Spencer as his teacher had created alarm in church circles. In the concluding article, as in his speech, if I remember rightly, Mr. Beecher said that, although he believed in evolution (Darwinism) up to a certain point, yet when man had reached his highest human level his Creator then invested him (and man alone of all living things) with the Holy Spirit, thereby bringing him into the circle of the godlike. Thus he answered his critics.

Mr. Spencer took intense interest in mechanical devices. When he visited our works with me the new appliances impressed him, and in after years he sometimes referred to these and said his estimate of American invention and push had been fully realized. He was naturally pleased with the deference and attention paid him in America.

I seldom if ever visited England without going to see him, even after he had removed to Brighton that he might live looking out upon the sea, which appealed to and soothed him. I never met a man who seemed to weigh so carefully every action, every word — even the pettiest — and so completely to find guidance through his own conscience. He was no scoffer in religious matters. In the domain of theology, however, he had little regard for decorum. It was to him a very faulty system hindering true growth, and the idea of rewards and punishments struck him as an appeal to very low natures indeed. Still he never went to such lengths as Tennyson did upon an occasion when some of the old ideas were under discussion. Knowles[1] told me that Tennyson lost control of himself. Knowles said he was greatly dis-

---

[1] James Knowles, founder of the *Nineteenth Century*.

appointed with the son's life of the poet as giving no true picture of his father in his revolt against stern theology.

Spencer was always the calm philosopher. I believe that from childhood to old age — when the race was run — he never was guilty of an immoral act or did an injustice to any human being. He was certainly one of the most conscientious men in all his doings that ever was born. Few men have wished to know another man more strongly than I to know Herbert Spencer, for seldom has one been more deeply indebted than I to him and to Darwin.

Reaction against the theology of past days comes to many who have been surrounded in youth by church people entirely satisfied that the truth and faith indispensable to future happiness were derived only through strictest Calvinistic creeds. The thoughtful youth is naturally carried along and disposed to concur in this. He cannot but think, up to a certain period of development, that what is believed by the best and the highest educated around him — those to whom he looks for example and instruction — must be true. He resists doubt as inspired by the Evil One seeking his soul, and sure to get it unless faith comes to the rescue. Unfortunately he soon finds that faith is not exactly at his beck and call. Original sin he thinks must be at the root of this inability to see as he wishes to see, to believe as he wishes to believe. It seems clear to him that already he is little better than one of the lost. Of the elect he surely cannot be, for these must be ministers, elders, and strictly orthodox men.

The young man is soon in chronic rebellion, trying to assume godliness with the others, acquiescing outwardly in the creed and all its teachings, and yet at heart totally unable to reconcile his outward accordance with his inward doubt. If there be intellect and virtue in the man but one result is possible; that is, Carlyle's position after his terrible struggle when after weeks of torment he came forth: "If it be incredible, in God's name, then, let it be discredited." With that the load of doubt and fear fell from him forever.

When I, along with three or four of my boon companions, was in this stage of doubt about theology, including the supernatural element, and indeed the whole scheme of salvation through vicarious atonement and all the fabric built upon it, I came fortunately upon Darwin's and Spencer's works: "The Data of Ethics," "First Principles," "Social Statics," "The Descent of Man." Reaching the pages which explain how man has absorbed such mental foods as were favorable to him, retaining what was salutary, rejecting what was deleterious, I remember that light came as in a flood and all was clear. Not only had I got rid of theology and the supernatural, but I had found the truth of evolution. "All is well since all grows better" became my motto, my true source of comfort. Man was not created with an instinct for his own degradation, but from the lower he had risen to the higher forms. Nor is there any conceivable end to his march to perfection. His face is turned to the light; he stands in the sun and looks upward.

Humanity is an organism, inherently rejecting all that is deleterious, that is, wrong, and absorbing after trial what is beneficial, that is, right. If so disposed, the Architect of the Universe, we must assume, might have made the world and man perfect, free from evil and from pain, as angels in heaven are thought to be; but although this was not done, man has been given the power of advancement rather than of retrogression. The Old and New Testaments remain, like other sacred writings of other lands, of value as records of the past and for such good lessons as they inculcate. Like the ancient writers of the Bible our thoughts should rest upon this life and our duties here. "To perform the duties of this world well, troubling not about another, is the prime wisdom," says Confucius, great sage and teacher. The next world and its duties we shall consider when we are placed in it.

I am as a speck of dust in the sun, and not even so much, in this solemn, mysterious, unknowable universe. I shrink back. One truth I see. Franklin was right. "The highest worship of God is service to Man." All this, however, does not prevent everlasting hope of immortality. It would be no greater miracle to be born to a future life than to have been born to live in this present life. The one has been created, why not the other? Therefore there is reason to hope for immortality. Let us hope.[1]

---

[1] "A. C. is really a tremendous personality — dramatic, wilful, generous, whimsical, at times almost cruel in pressing his own conviction upon others, and then again tender, affectionate, emotional, always imaginative, unusual and wide-visioned in his views. He is well worth Boswellizing, but I am urging him to be 'his own Boswell.' ... He is inconsistent in many ways, but with a passion for lofty views; the brotherhood of man, peace among nations, religious purity — I mean the purification of religion from gross superstition — the substitution for a Westminster-Catechism God, of a Righteous, a Just God." (*Letters of Richard Watson Gilder*, p. 375.)

CHAPTER XXVI
Blaine and Harrison

WHILE one is known by the company he keeps, it is equally true that one is known by the stories he tells. Mr. Blaine was one of the best story-tellers I ever met. His was a bright sunny nature with a witty, pointed story for every occasion.

Mr. Blaine's address at Yorktown (I had accompanied him there) was greatly admired. It directed special attention to the cordial friendship which had grown up between the two branches of the English-speaking race, and ended with the hope that the prevailing peace and good-will between the two nations would exist for many centuries to come. When he read this to me, I remember that the word "many" jarred, and I said:

"Mr. Secretary, might I suggest the change of one word? I don't like 'many'; why not 'all' the centuries to come?"

"Good, that is perfect!"

And so it was given in the address: "for *all* the centuries to come."

We had a beautiful night returning from Yorktown, and, sitting in the stern of the ship in the moonlight, the military band playing forward, we spoke of the effect of music. Mr. Blaine said that his favorite just then was the "Sweet By and By," which he had heard played last by the same band at President Garfield's funeral, and he thought upon that occasion he was more deeply moved by sweet sounds than he had ever been in his life. He requested that it should be the last piece played that night. Both he and Gladstone were fond of simple music. They could enjoy Beethoven and the classic masters, but Wagner was as yet a sealed book to them.

In answer to my inquiry as to the most successful speech he ever heard in Congress, he replied it was that of the German, ex-Governor Ritter of Pennsylvania. The first bill appropriating money for inland *fresh* waters was under consideration. The House was divided. Strict constructionists held this to be unconstitutional; only harbors upon the salt sea were under the Federal Government. The contest was keen and the result doubtful, when to the astonishment of the House, Governor Ritter slowly arose for the first time. Silence at once reigned. What was the old German ex-Governor going to say—he who had never said anything at all? Only this:

"Mr. Speaker, I don't know much particulars about de constitution, but I know dis: I wouldn't gif a d—d cent for a constitution dat didn't wash in fresh water as well as in salt." The House burst into an uproar of uncontrollable laughter, and the bill passed.

So came about this new departure and one of the most beneficent ways of spending government money, and of employing army and navy engineers. Little of the money spent by the Government yields so great a return. So expands our flexible constitution to meet the new wants of an expanding population. Let who will make the constitution if we of to-day are permitted to interpret it.

Mr. Blaine's best story, if one can be selected from so many that were excellent, I think was the following:

In the days of slavery and the underground railroads, there lived on the banks of the Ohio River near Gallipolis, a noted Democrat named Judge French, who said to some anti-slavery friends that he should like them to bring to his office the first runaway negro that crossed the river, bound northward by the underground. He couldn't understand why they wished to run away. This was done, and the following conversation took place:

Judge: "So you have run away from Kentucky. Bad master, I suppose?"

Slave: "Oh, no, Judge; very good, kind massa."

Judge: "He worked you too hard?"

Slave: "No, sah, never overworked myself all my life."

Judge, hesitatingly: "He did not give you enough to eat?"

Slave: "Not enough to eat down in Kaintuck? Oh, Lor', plenty to eat."

Judge: "He did not clothe you well?"

Slave: "Good enough clothes for me, Judge."

Judge: "You hadn't a comfortable home?"

Slave: "Oh, Lor', makes me cry to think of my pretty little cabin down dar in old Kaintuck."

Judge, after a pause: "You had a good, kind master, you were not overworked, plenty to eat, good clothes, fine home. I don't see why the devil you wished to run away."

Slave: "Well, Judge, I lef de situation down dar open. You kin go rite down and git it."

The Judge had seen a great light.

> "Freedom has a thousand charms to show,
>   That slaves, howe'er contented, never know."

That the colored people in such numbers risked all for liberty is the best possible proof that they will steadily approach and finally reach the full stature of citizenship in the Republic.

I never saw Mr. Blaine so happy as while with us at Cluny. He was a boy again and we were a rollicking party together. He had never fished with a fly. I took him out on Loch Laggan and he began awkwardly, as all do, but he soon caught the swing. I shall never forget his first capture:

"My friend, you have taught me a new pleasure in life. There are a hundred fishing lochs in Maine, and I'll spend my holidays in future upon them trout-fishing."

At Cluny there is no night in June and we danced on the lawn in the bright twilight until late. Mrs. Blaine, Miss Dodge, Mr. Blaine, and other guests, were trying to do the Scotch reel, and "whooping" like Highlanders. We were gay revelers during those two weeks. One night afterwards, at a dinner in our home in New York, chiefly made up of our Cluny visitors, Mr. Blaine told the company that he had discovered at Cluny what a real holiday was. "It is when the merest trifles become the most serious events of life."

President Harrison's nomination for the presidency in 1888 came to Mr. Blaine while on a coaching trip with us. Mr. and Mrs. Blaine, Miss Margaret Blaine, Senator and Mrs. Hale, Miss Dodge, and Walter Damrosch were on the coach with us from London to Cluny Castle. In approaching Linlithgow from Edinburgh, we found the provost and magistrates in their gorgeous robes at the hotel to receive us. I was with them when Mr. Blaine came into the room with a cablegram in his hand which he showed to me, asking what it meant. It read: "Use cipher." It was from Senator Elkins at the Chicago Convention. Mr. Blaine had cabled the previous day, declining to accept the nomination for the presidency unless Secretary Sherman of Ohio agreed, and Senator Elkins no doubt wished to be certain that he was in correspondence with Mr. Blaine and not with some interloper.

I said to Mr. Blaine that the Senator had called to see me before sailing, and suggested we should have cipher words for the prominent candidates. I gave him a few and kept a copy upon a slip, which I put in my pocketbook. I looked and fortunately found it. Blaine was "Victor"; Harrison, "Trump"; Phelps of New Jersey, "Star"; and so on. I wired "Trump" and "Star."[1] This was in the evening.

We retired for the night, and next day the whole party was paraded by the city authorities in their robes up the main street to the palace grounds which were finely decorated with flags. Speeches of welcome were made and replied to. Mr. Blaine was called upon by the people, and responded in a short address. Just then a cablegram was handed to him: "Harrison and Morton nominated." Phelps had declined. So passed forever Mr. Blaine's chance of holding the highest of all political offices — the elected of the majority of the English-speaking race. But he was once fairly elected to the presidency and done out of New York State, as was at last clearly proven, the perpetrators having been punished for an attempted repetition of the same fraud at a subsequent election.

Mr. Blaine, as Secretary of State in Harrison's Cabinet, was a decided success and the Pan-American Congress his most brilliant triumph. My only political ap-

[1] "A code had been agreed upon between his friends in the United States and himself, and when a deadlock or a long contest seemed inevitable, the following dispatch was sent from Mr. Carnegie's estate in Scotland, where Blaine was staying, to a prominent Republican leader:

"'June 25. Too late victor immovable take trump and star.' WHIP. Interpreted, it reads: 'Too late. Blaine immovable, Take Harrison and Phelps. CARNEGIE.'" (*James G. Blaine*, by Edward Stanwood, p. 308. Boston, 1905.)

pointment came at this time and was that of a United States delegate to the Congress. It gave me a most interesting view of the South American Republics and their various problems. We sat down together, representatives of all the republics but Brazil. One morning the announcement was made that a new constitution had been ratified. Brazil had become a member of the sisterhood, making seventeen republics in all — now twenty-one. There was great applause and cordial greeting of the representatives of Brazil thus suddenly elevated. I found the South American representatives rather suspicious of their big brother's intentions. A sensitive spirit of independence was manifest, which it became our duty to recognize. In this I think we succeeded, but it will behoove subsequent governments to scrupulously respect the national feeling of our Southern neighbors. It is not control, but friendly cooperation upon terms of perfect equality we should seek.

I sat next to Manuel Quintana who afterwards became President of Argentina. He took a deep interest in the proceedings, and one day became rather critical upon a trifling issue, which led to an excited colloquy between him and Chairman Blaine. I believe it had its origin in a false translation from one language to another. I rose, slipped behind the chairman on the platform, whispering to him as I passed that if an adjournment was moved I was certain the differences could be adjusted. He nodded assent. I returned to my seat and moved adjournment, and during the interval all was satisfactorily arranged. Passing the delegates, as we were about to leave the hall, an incident occurred which comes back to me as I write. A delegate threw one arm around me and with the other hand patting me on the breast, exclaimed: "Mr. Carnegie, you have more here

than here" — pointing to his pocket. Our Southern brethren are so lovingly demonstrative. Warm climes and
warm hearts.

In 1891 President Harrison went with me from Washington to Pittsburgh, as I have already stated, to open the
Carnegie Hall and Library, which I had presented to Allegheny City. We traveled over the Baltimore and Ohio
Railroad by daylight, and enjoyed the trip, the President
being especially pleased with the scenery. Reaching Pittsburgh at dark, the flaming coke ovens and dense pillars of
smoke and fire amazed him. The well-known description
of Pittsburgh, seen from the hilltops, as "H —l with the
lid off," seemed to him most appropriate. He was the first
President who ever visited Pittsburgh. President Harrison,
his grandfather, had, however, passed from steamboat to
canal-boat there, on his way to Washington after election.

The opening ceremony was largely attended owing to
the presence of the President and all passed off well. Next
morning the President wished to see our steel works, and
he was escorted there, receiving a cordial welcome from
the workmen. I called up each successive manager of department as we passed and presented him. Finally, when
Mr. Schwab was presented, the President turned to me
and said,

"How is this, Mr. Carnegie? You present only boys to
me."

"Yes, Mr. President, but do you notice what kind of
boys they are?"

"Yes, hustlers, every one of them," was his comment.

He was right. No such young men could have been
found for such work elsewhere in this world. They had
been promoted to partnership without cost or risk. If
the profits did not pay for their shares, no responsibility

remained upon the young men. A giving thus to "partners" is very different from paying wages to "employees" in corporations.

The President's visit, not to Pittsburgh, but to Allegheny over the river, had one beneficial result. Members of the City Council of Pittsburgh reminded me that I had first offered Pittsburgh money for a library and hall, which it declined, and that then Allegheny City had asked if I would give them to her, which I did. The President visiting Allegheny to open the library and hall there, and the ignoring of Pittsburgh, was too much. Her authorities came to me again the morning after the Allegheny City opening, asking if I would renew my offer to Pittsburgh. If so, the city would accept and agree to expend upon maintenance a larger percentage than I had previously asked. I was only too happy to do this and, instead of two hundred and fifty thousand, I offered a million dollars. My ideas had expanded. Thus was started the Carnegie Institute.

Pittsburgh's leading citizens are spending freely upon artistic things. This center of manufacturing has had its permanent orchestra for some years — Boston and Chicago being the only other cities in America that can boast of one. A naturalist club and a school of painting have sprung up. The success of Library, Art Gallery, Museum, and Music Hall — a noble quartet in an immense building — is one of the chief satisfactions of my life. This is my monument, because here I lived my early life and made my start, and I am to-day in heart a devoted son of dear old smoky Pittsburgh.

Herbert Spencer heard, while with us in Pittsburgh, some account of the rejection of my first offer of a library to Pittsburgh. When the second offer was made, he wrote me that he did not understand how I could renew it; he never could have done so; they did not deserve it. I wrote the philosopher that if I had made the first offer to Pittsburgh that I might receive her thanks and gratitude, I deserved the personal arrows shot at me and the accusations made that only my own glorification and a monument to my memory were sought. I should then probably have felt as he did. But, as it was the good of the people of Pittsburgh I had in view, among whom I had made my fortune, the unfounded suspicions of some natures only quickened my desire to work their good by planting in their midst a potent influence for higher things: This the Institute, thank the kind fates, has done. Pittsburgh has played her part nobly.

CHAPTER XXVII
Washington Diplomacy

PRESIDENT HARRISON had been a soldier and as President was a little disposed to fight. His attitude gave some of his friends concern. He was opposed to arbitrating the Behring Sea question when Lord Salisbury, at the dictation of Canada, had to repudiate the Blaine agreement for its settlement, and was disposed to proceed to extreme measures. But calmer counsels prevailed. He was determined also to uphold the Force Bill against the South.

When the quarrel arose with Chile, there was a time when it seemed almost impossible to keep the President from taking action which would have resulted in war. He had great personal provocation because the Chilean authorities had been most indiscreet in their statements in regard to his action. I went to Washington to see whether I could not do something toward reconciling the belligerents, because, having been a member of the first Pan-American Conference, I had become acquainted with the representatives from our southern sister-republics and was on good terms with them.

As luck would have it, I was just entering the Shoreham Hotel when I saw Senator Henderson of Missouri, who had been my fellow-delegate to the Conference. He stopped and greeted me, and looking across the street he said:

"There's the President beckoning to you." I crossed the street.

"Hello, Carnegie, when did you arrive?"

"Just arrived, Mr. President; I was entering the hotel."

"What are you here for?"

"To have a talk with you."

"Well, come along and talk as we walk."

The President took my arm and we promenaded the streets of Washington in the dusk for more than an hour, during which time the discussion was lively. I told him that he had appointed me a delegate to the Pan-American Conference, that he had assured the South-American delegates when they parted that he had given a military review in their honor to show them, not that we had an army, but rather that we had none and needed none, that we were the big brother in the family of republics, and that all disputes, if any arose, would be settled by peaceful arbitration. I was therefore surprised and grieved to find that he was now apparently taking a different course, threatening to resort to war in a paltry dispute with little Chile.

"You're a New Yorker and think of nothing but business and dollars. That is the way with New Yorkers; they care nothing for the dignity and honor of the Republic," said his Excellency.

"Mr. President, I am one of the men in the United States who would profit most by war; it might throw millions into my pockets as the largest manufacturer of steel."

"Well, that is probably true in your case; I had forgotten."

"Mr. President, if I were going to fight, I would take some one of my size."

"Well, would you let any nation insult and dishonor you because of its size?"

"Mr. President, no man can dishonor me except myself. Honor wounds must be self-inflicted."

"You see our sailors were attacked on shore and two of them killed, and you would stand that?" he asked.

"Mr. President, I do not think the United States dishonored every time a row among drunken sailors takes place; besides, these were not American sailors at all; they were foreigners, as you see by their names. I would be disposed to cashier the captain of that ship for allowing the sailors to go on shore when there was rioting in the town and the public peace had been already disturbed."

The discussion continued until we had finally reached the door of the White House in the dark. The President told me he had an engagement to dine out that night, but invited me to dine with him the next evening, when, as he said, there would be only the family and we could talk.

"I am greatly honored and shall be with you to-morrow evening," I said. And so we parted.

The next morning I went over to see Mr. Blaine, then Secretary of State. He rose from his seat and held out both hands.

"Oh, why weren't you dining with us last night? When the President told Mrs. Blaine that you were in town, she said: 'Just think, Mr. Carnegie is in town and I had a vacant seat here he could have occupied.'"

"Well, Mr. Blaine, I think it is rather fortunate that I have not seen you," I replied; and I then told him what had occurred with the President.

"Yes," he said, "it really was fortunate. The President might have thought you and I were in collusion."

Senator Elkins, of West Virginia, a bosom friend of Mr. Blaine, and also a very good friend of the President, happened to come in, and he said he had seen the President, who told him that he had had a talk with me upon the Chilean affair last evening and that I had come down hot upon the subject.

"Well, Mr. President," said Senator Elkins, "it is not probable that Mr. Carnegie would speak as plainly to you as he would to me. He feels very keenly, but he would naturally be somewhat reserved in talking to you."

The President replied: "I didn't see the slightest indication of reserve, I assure you."

The matter was adjusted, thanks to the peace policy characteristic of Mr. Blaine. More than once he kept the United States out of foreign trouble as I personally knew. The reputation that he had of being an aggressive American really enabled that great man to make concessions which, made by another, might not have been readily accepted by the people.

I had a long and friendly talk with the President that evening at dinner, but he was not looking at all well. I ventured to say to him he needed a rest. By all means he should get away. He said he had intended going off on a revenue cutter for a few days, but Judge Bradley of the Supreme Court had died and he must find a worthy successor. I said there was one I could not recommend because we had fished together and were such intimate friends that we could not judge each other disinterestedly, but he might inquire about him — Mr. Shiras, of Pittsburgh. He did so and appointed him. Mr. Shiras received the strong support of the best elements everywhere. Neither my recommendation, nor that of any one else, would have weighed with President Harrison one particle in making the appointment if he had not found Mr. Shiras the very man he wanted.

In the Behring Sea dispute the President was incensed at Lord Salisbury's repudiation of the stipulations for settling the question which had been agreed to. The President had determined to reject the counter-proposition to submit it to arbitration. Mr. Blaine was with the President in this and naturally indignant that his plan, which Salisbury had extolled through his Ambassador, had been discarded. I found both of them in no compromising mood. The President was much the more excited of the two, however. Talking it over with Mr. Blaine alone, I explained to him that Salisbury was powerless. Against Canada's protest he could not force acceptance of the stipulations to which he had hastily agreed. There was another element. He had a dispute with Newfoundland on hand, which the latter was insisting must be settled to her advantage. No Government in Britain could add Canadian dissatisfaction to that of Newfoundland. Salisbury had done the best he could. After a while Blaine was convinced of this and succeeded in bringing the President into line.

The Behring Sea troubles brought about some rather amusing situations. One day Sir John Macdonald, Canadian Premier, and his party reached Washington and asked Mr. Blaine to arrange an interview with the President upon this subject. Mr. Blaine replied that he would see the President and inform Sir John the next morning.

"Of course," said Mr. Blaine, telling me the story in Washington just after the incident occurred, "I knew very well that the President could not meet Sir John and his friends officially, and when they called I told them so." Sir John said that Canada was independent, "as sovereign as the State of New York was in the Union." Mr. Blaine replied he was afraid that if he ever obtained an interview as Premier of Canada with the State authorities of New York he would soon hear something on the subject from Washington; and so would the New York State authorities.

It was because the President and Mr. Blaine were convinced that the British Government at home could not fulfill the stipulations agreed upon that they accepted Salisbury's proposal for arbitration, believing he had done his best. That was a very sore disappointment to Mr. Blaine. He had suggested that Britain and America should each place two small vessels on Behring Sea with equal rights to board or arrest fishing vessels under either flag — in fact, a joint police force. To give Salisbury due credit, he cabled the British Ambassador, Sir Julian Pauncefote, to congratulate Mr. Blaine upon this "brilliant suggestion." It would have given equal rights to each and under either or both flag for the first time in history — a just and brotherly compact. Sir Julian had shown this cable to Mr. Blaine. I mention this here to suggest that able and willing statesmen, anxious to cooperate, are sometimes unable to do so.

Mr. Blaine was indeed a great statesman, a man of wide views, sound judgment, and always for peace. Upon war with Chile, upon the Force Bill, and the Behring Sea question, he was calm, wise, and peace-pursuing. Especially was he favorable to drawing closer and closer to our own English-speaking race. For France he had gratitude unbounded for the part she had played in our Revolutionary War, but this did not cause him to lose his head.

One night at dinner in London Mr. Blaine was at close quarters for a moment. The Clayton-Bulwer Treaty came up. A leading statesman present said that the impression they had was that Mr. Blaine had always been inimical to the Mother country. Mr. Blaine disclaimed this, and justly so, as far as I knew his sentiments. His correspondence upon the Clayton-Bulwer Treaty was instanced. Mr. Blaine replied:

"When I became Secretary of State and had to take up that subject I was surprised to find that your Secretary for Foreign Affairs was always informing us what Her Majesty 'expected,' while our Secretary of State was telling you what our President 'ventured to hope.' When I received a dispatch telling us what Her Majesty expected, I replied, telling you what our President 'expected.'"

"Well, you admit you changed the character of the correspondence?" was shot at him.

Quick as a flash came the response: "Not more than conditions had changed. The United States had passed the stage of 'venturing to hope' with any power that 'expects.' I only followed your example, and should ever Her Majesty 'venture to hope,' the President will always be found doing the same. I am afraid that as long as you 'expect' the United States will also 'expect' in return."

One night there was a dinner, where Mr. Joseph Chamberlain and Sir Charles Tennant, President of the Scotland Steel Company, were guests. During the evening the former said that his friend Carnegie was a good fellow and they all delighted to see him succeeding, but he didn't know why the United States should give him protection worth a million sterling per year or more, for condescending to manufacture steel rails.

"Well," said Mr. Blaine, "we don't look at it in that light. I am interested in railroads, and we formerly used to pay you for steel rails ninety dollars per ton for every ton we got—nothing less. Now, just before I sailed from home our people made a large contract with our friend Carnegie at thirty dollars per ton. I am somewhat under the impression that if Carnegie and others had not risked their capital in developing their manufacture on our side of the Atlantic, we would still be paying you ninety dollars per ton to-day."

Here Sir Charles broke in: "You may be sure you would. Ninety dollars was our agreed-upon price for you foreigners."

Mr. Blaine smilingly remarked: "Mr. Chamberlain, I don't think you have made a very good case against our friend Carnegie."

"No," he replied; "how could I, with Sir Charles giving me away like that?" — and there was general laughter.

Blaine was a rare raconteur and his talk had this great merit: never did I hear him tell a story or speak a word unsuitable for any, even the most fastidious company to hear. He was as quick as a steel trap, a delightful companion, and he would have made an excellent and yet safe President. I found him truly conservative, and strong for peace upon all international questions.

CHAPTER XXVIII
Hay and McKinley

JOHN HAY was our frequent guest in England and Scotland, and was on the eve of coming to us at Skibo in 1898 when called home by President McKinley to become Secretary of State. Few have made such a record in that office. He inspired men with absolute confidence in his sincerity, and his aspirations were always high. War he detested, and meant what he said when he pronounced it "the most ferocious and yet the most futile folly of man."

The Philippines annexation was a burning question when I met him and Henry White (Secretary of Legation and later Ambassador to France) in London, on my way to New York. It gratified me to find our views were similar upon that proposed serious departure from our traditional policy of avoiding distant and disconnected possessions and keeping our empire within the continent, especially keeping it out of the vortex of militarism. Hay, White, and I clasped hands together in Hay's office in London, and agreed upon this. Before that he had written me the following note:

London, August 22, 1898

MY DEAR CARNEGIE:

I thank you for the Skibo grouse and also for your kind letter. It is a solemn and absorbing thing to hear so many kind and unmerited words as I have heard and read this last week. It seems to me another man they are talking about, while I am expected to do the work. I wish a little of the kindness could be saved till I leave office finally.

I have read with the keenest interest your article in the

"North American."[1] I am not allowed to say in my present fix how much I agree with you. The only question on my mind is how far it is now *possible* for us to withdraw from the Philippines. I am rather thankful it is not given to me to solve that momentous question.[2]

It was a strange fate that placed upon him the very task he had congratulated himself was never to be his.

He stood alone at first as friendly to China in the Boxer troubles and succeeded in securing for her fair terms of peace. His regard for Britain, as part of our own race, was deep, and here the President was thoroughly with him, and grateful beyond measure to Britain for standing against other European powers disposed to favor Spain in the Cuban War.

The Hay-Pauncefote Treaty concerning the Panama Canal seemed to many of us unsatisfactory. Senator Elkins told me my objections, given in the "New York Tribune" reached him the day he was to speak upon it, and were useful. Visiting Washington soon after the article appeared, I went with Senator Hanna to the White House early in the morning and found the President much exercised over the Senate's amendment to the treaty. I had no doubt of Britain's prompt acquiescence in the Senate's requirements, and said so. Anything in reason she would give, since it was we who had to furnish the funds for the work from which she would be, next to ourselves, the greatest gainer.

Senator Hanna asked if I had seen "John," as he and President McKinley always called Mr. Hay. I said I had not. Then he asked me to go over and cheer him up,

---

[1] The reference is to an article by Mr. Carnegie in the *North American Review*, August, 1898, entitled: "Distant Possessions — The Parting of the Ways."

[2] Published in Thayer, *Life and Letters of John Hay*, vol. II, p. 175. Boston and New York, 1915.

for he was disconsolate about the amendments. I did so. I pointed out to Mr. Hay that the Clayton-Bulwer Treaty had been amended by the Senate and scarcely anyone knew this now and no one cared. The Hay-Pauncefote Treaty would be executed as amended and no one would care a fig whether it was in its original form or not. He doubted this and thought Britain would be indisposed to recede. A short time after this, dining with him, he said I had proved a true prophet and all was well.

Of course it was. Britain had practically told us she wished the canal built and would act in any way desired. The canal is now as it should be — that is, all American, with no international complications possible. It was perhaps not worth building at that time, but it was better to spend three or four hundred millions upon it than in building sea monsters of destruction to fight imaginary foes. One may be a loss and there an end; the other might be a source of war, for

> "Oft the sight of means to do ill deeds
> Make deeds ill done."

Mr. Hay's *bête noire* was the Senate. Upon this, and this only, was he disregardful of the proprieties. When it presumed to alter one word, substituting "treaty" for "agreement," which occurred in one place only in the proposed Arbitration Treaty of 1905, he became unduly excited. I believe this was owing in great degree to poor health, for it was clear by that time to intimate friends that his health was seriously impaired.

The last time I saw him was at lunch at his house, when the Arbitration Treaty, as amended by the Senate, was under the consideration of President Roosevelt. The arbitrationists, headed by ex-Secretary of State Foster, urged the President's acceptance of the amended treaty. We thought he was favorable to this, but from my subsequent talk with Secretary Hay, I saw that the President's agreeing would be keenly felt. I should not be surprised if Roosevelt's rejection of the treaty was resolved upon chiefly to soothe his dear friend John Hay in his illness. I am sure I felt that I could be brought to do, only with the greatest difficulty, anything that would annoy that noble soul. But upon this point Hay was obdurate; no surrender to the Senate. Leaving his house I said to Mrs. Carnegie that I doubted if ever we should meet our friend again. We never did.

The Carnegie Institution of Washington, of which Hay was the chairman and a trustee from the start, received his endorsement and close attention, and much were we indebted to him for wise counsel. As a statesman he made his reputation in shorter time and with a surer touch than anyone I know of. And it may be doubted if any public man ever had more deeply attached friends. One of his notes I have long kept. It would have been the most flattering of any to my literary vanity but for my knowledge of his most lovable nature and undue warmth for his friends. The world is poorer to me to-day as I write, since he has left it.

The Spanish War was the result of a wave of passion started by the reports of the horrors of the Cuban Revolution. President McKinley tried hard to avoid it. When the Spanish Minister left Washington, the French Ambassador became Spain's agent, and peaceful negotiations were continued. Spain offered autonomy for Cuba. The President replied that he did not know exactly what "autonomy" meant. What he wished for Cuba was the rights that Canada possessed. He understood these. A cable was shown to the President by the French Minister stating that Spain granted this and he, dear man, supposed all was settled. So it was, apparently.

Speaker Reed usually came to see me Sunday mornings when in New York, and it was immediately after my return from Europe that year that he called and said he had never lost control of the House before. For one moment he thought of leaving the chair and going on the floor to address the House and try to quiet it. In vain it was explained that the President had received from Spain the guarantee of self-government for Cuba. Alas! it was too late, too late!

"What is Spain doing over here, anyhow?" was the imperious inquiry of Congress. A sufficient number of Republicans had agreed to vote with the Democrats in Congress for war. A whirlwind of passion swept over the House, intensified, no doubt, by the unfortunate explosion of the warship Maine in Havana Harbor, supposed by some to be Spanish work. The supposition gave Spain far too much credit for skill and activity.

War was declared — the Senate being shocked by Senator Proctor's statement of the concentration camps he had seen in Cuba. The country responded to the cry, "What is Spain doing over here anyhow?" President McKinley and his peace policy were left high and dry, and nothing remained for him but to go with the country. The Government then announced that war was not undertaken for territorial aggrandizement, and Cuba was promised independence — a promise faithfully kept. We should not fail to remember this, for it is the one cheering feature of the war.

The possession of the Philippines left a stain. They were not only territorial acquisition; they were dragged from reluctant Spain and twenty million dollars paid for them. The Filipinos had been our allies in fighting

Spain. The Cabinet, under the lead of the President, had agreed that only a coaling station in the Philippines should be asked for, and it is said such were the instructions given by cable at first to the Peace Commissioners at Paris. President McKinley then made a tour through the West and, of course, was cheered when he spoke of the flag and Dewey's victory. He returned, impressed with the idea that withdrawal would be unpopular, and reversed his former policy. I was told by one of his Cabinet that every member was opposed to the reversal. A senator told me Judge Day, one of the Peace Commissioners, wrote a remonstrance from Paris, which if ever published, would rank next to Washington's Farewell Address, so fine was it.

At this stage an important member of the Cabinet, my friend Cornelius N. Bliss, called and asked me to visit Washington and see the President on the subject. He said:

"You have influence with him. None of us have been able to move him since he returned from the West."

I went to Washington and had an interview with him. But he was obdurate. Withdrawal would create a revolution at home, he said. Finally, by persuading his secretaries that he had to bend to the blast, and always holding that it would be only a temporary occupation and that a way out would be found, the Cabinet yielded.

He sent for President Schurman, of Cornell University, who had opposed annexation and made him chairman of the committee to visit the Filipinos; and later for Judge Taft, who had been prominent against such a violation of American policy, to go as Governor. When the Judge stated that it seemed strange to send for one who had publicly denounced annexation, the President said that was the very reason why he wished him for the place. This was all very well, but to refrain from annexing and to relinquish territory once purchased are different propositions. This was soon seen.

Mr. Bryan had it in his power at one time to defeat in the Senate this feature of the Treaty of Peace with Spain. I went to Washington to try to effect this, and remained there until the vote was taken. I was told that when Mr. Bryan was in Washington he had advised his friends that it would be good party policy to allow the treaty to pass. This would discredit the Republican Party before the people; that "paying twenty millions for a revolution" would defeat any party. There were seven staunch Bryan men anxious to vote against Philippine annexation.

Mr. Bryan had called to see me in New York upon the subject, because my opposition to the purchase had been so pronounced, and I now wired him at Omaha explaining the situation and begging him to wire me that his friends could use their own judgment. His reply was what I have stated — better have the Republicans pass it and let it then go before the people. I thought it unworthy of him to subordinate such an issue, fraught with deplorable consequences, to mere party politics. It required the casting vote of the Speaker to carry the measure. One word from Mr. Bryan would have saved the country from the disaster. I could not be cordial to him for years afterwards. He had seemed to me a man who was willing to sacrifice his country and his personal convictions for party advantage.

When I called upon President McKinley immediately after the vote, I condoled with him upon being dependent for support upon his leading opponent. I explained just how his victory had been won and suggested that he should send his grateful acknowledgments to Mr.

Bryan. A Colonial possession thousands of miles away was a novel problem to President McKinley, and indeed to all American statesmen. Nothing did they know of the troubles and dangers it would involve. Here the Republic made its first grievous international mistake — a mistake which dragged it into the vortex of international militarism and a great navy. What a change has come over statesmen since!

At supper with President Roosevelt at the White House a few weeks ago (1907), he said:

"If you wish to see the two men in the United States who are the most anxious to get out of the Philippines, here they are," pointing to Secretary Taft and himself.

"Then why don't you?" I responded. "The American people would be glad indeed."

But both the President and Judge Taft believed our duty required us to prepare the Islands for self-government first. This is the policy of "Don't go into the water until you learn to swim." But the plunge has to be and will be taken some day.

It was urged that if we did not occupy the Philippines, Germany would. It never occurred to the urgers that this would mean Britain agreeing that Germany should establish a naval base at Macao, a short sail from Britain's naval base in the East. Britain would as soon permit her to establish a base at Kingston, Ireland, eighty miles from Liverpool. I was surprised to hear men — men like Judge Taft, although he was opposed at first to the annexation — give this reason when we were discussing the question after the fatal step had been taken. But we know little of foreign relations. We have hitherto been a consolidated country. It will be a sad day if we ever become anything otherwise.

CHAPTER XXIX
Meeting the German Emperor

MY first Rectorial Address to the students of St. Andrews University attracted the attention of the German Emperor, who sent word to me in New York by Herr Ballin that he had read every word of it. He also sent me by him a copy of his address upon his eldest son's consecration. Invitations to meet him followed; but it was not until June, 1907, that I could leave, owing to other engagements. Mrs. Carnegie and I went to Kiel. Mr. Tower, our American Ambassador to Germany, and Mrs. Tower met us there and were very kind in their attentions. Through them we met many of the distinguished public men during our three days' stay there.

The first morning, Mr. Tower took me to register on the Emperor's yacht. I had no expectation of seeing the Emperor, but he happened to come on deck, and seeing Mr. Tower he asked what had brought him on the yacht so early. Mr. Tower explained he had brought me over to register, and that Mr. Carnegie was on board. He asked:

"Why not present him now? I wish to see him."

I was talking to the admirals who were assembling for a conference, and did not see Mr. Tower and the Emperor approaching from behind. A touch on my shoulder and I turned around.

"Mr. Carnegie, the Emperor."

It was a moment before I realized that the Emperor was before me. I raised both hands and exclaimed:

"This has happened just as I could have wished,

with no ceremony, and the Man of Destiny dropped from the clouds."

Then I continued: "Your Majesty, I have traveled two nights to accept your generous invitation, and never did so before to meet a crowned head."

Then the Emperor, smiling — and such a captivating smile:

"Oh! yes, yes, I have read your books. You do not like kings."

"No, Your Majesty, I do not like kings, but I do like a man behind a king when I find him."

"Ah! there is one king you like, I know, a Scottish king, Robert the Bruce. He was my hero in my youth. I was brought up on him."

"Yes, Your Majesty, so was I, and he lies buried in Dunfermline Abbey, in my native town. When a boy, I used to walk often around the towering square monument on the Abbey — one word on each block in big stone letters 'King Robert the Bruce' — with all the fervor of a Catholic counting his beads. But Bruce was much more than a king, Your Majesty, he was the leader of his people. And not the first; Wallace the man of the people comes first. Your Majesty, I now own King Malcolm's tower in Dunfermline[1] — he from whom you derive your precious heritage of Scottish blood. Perhaps you know the fine old ballad, 'Sir Patrick Spens.'

> "'The King sits in Dunfermline tower
> Drinking the bluid red wine.'

I should like to escort you some day to the tower of

[1] In the deed of trust conveying Pittencrieff Park and Glen to Dunfermline an unspecified reservation of property was made. The "with certain exceptions" related to King Malcolm's Tower. For reasons best known to himself Mr. Carnegie retained the ownership of this relic of the past.

your Scottish ancestor, that you may do homage to his memory." He exclaimed:

"That would be very fine. The Scotch are much quicker and cleverer than the Germans. The Germans are too slow."

"Your Majesty, where anything Scotch is concerned, I must decline to accept you as an impartial judge."

He laughed and waved adieu, calling out:

"You are to dine with me this evening" — and excusing himself went to greet the arriving admirals.

About sixty were present at the dinner and we had a pleasant time, indeed. His Majesty, opposite whom I sat, was good enough to raise his glass and invite me to drink with him. After he had done so with Mr. Tower, our Ambassador, who sat at his right, he asked across the table — heard by those near — whether I had told Prince von Bülow, next whom I sat, that his (the Emperor's) hero, Bruce, rested in my native town of Dunfermline, and his ancestor's tower in Pittencrieff Glen, was in my possession.

"No," I replied; "with Your Majesty I am led into such frivolities, but my intercourse with your Lord High Chancellor, I assure you, will always be of a serious import."

We dined with Mrs. Goelet upon her yacht, one evening, and His Majesty being present, I told him President Roosevelt had said recently to me that he wished custom permitted him to leave the country so he could run over and see him (the Emperor). He thought a substantial talk would result in something good being accomplished. I believed that also. The Emperor agreed and said he wished greatly to see him and hoped he would some day come to Germany. I suggested that he (the Emperor) was free from constitutional barriers and could sail over and see the President.

"Ah, but my country needs me here! How can I leave?"

I replied:

"Before leaving home one year, when I went to our mills to bid the officials good-bye and expressed regret at leaving them all hard at work, sweltering in the hot sun, but that I found I had now every year to rest and yet no matter how tired I might be one half-hour on the bow of the steamer, cutting the Atlantic waves, gave me perfect relief, my clever manager, Captain Jones, retorted: 'And, oh, Lord I think of the relief we all get.' It might be the same with your people, Your Majesty."

He laughed heartily over and over again. It opened a new train of thought. He repeated his desire to meet President Roosevelt, and I said:

"Well, Your Majesty, when you two do get together, I think I shall have to be with you. You and he, I fear, might get into mischief."

He laughed and said:

"Oh, I see! You wish to drive us together. Well, I agree if you make Roosevelt first horse, I shall follow."

"Ah, no, Your Majesty, I know horse-flesh better than to attempt to drive two such gay colts tandem. You never get proper purchase on the first horse. I must yoke you both in the shafts, neck and neck, so I can hold you in."

I never met a man who enjoyed stories more keenly than the Emperor. He is fine company, and I believe an earnest man, anxious for the peace and progress of the world. Suffice it to say he insists that he is, and always has been, for peace. [1907.] He cherishes the fact that he has reigned for twenty-four years and has never shed human blood. He considers that the German navy is too small to affect the British and was never intended to be a rival. Nevertheless, it is in my opinion very unwise, because unnecessary, to enlarge it. Prince von Bülow holds these sentiments and I believe the peace of the world has little to fear from Germany. Her interests are all favorable to peace, industrial development being her aim; and in this desirable field she is certainly making great strides.

I sent the Emperor by his Ambassador, Baron von Sternberg, the book, "The Roosevelt Policy,"[1] to which I had written an introduction that pleased the President, and I rejoice in having received from him a fine bronze of himself with a valued letter. He is not only an Emperor, but something much higher — a man anxious to improve existing conditions, untiring in his efforts to promote temperance, prevent dueling, and, I believe, to secure International Peace.

I have for some time been haunted with the feeling that the Emperor was indeed a Man of Destiny. My interviews with him have strengthened that feeling. I have great hopes of him in the future doing something really great and good. He may yet have a part to play that will give him a place among the immortals. He has ruled Germany in peace for twenty-seven years, but something beyond even this record is due from one who has the power to establish peace among civilized nations through positive action. Maintaining peace in his own land is not sufficient from one whose invitation to other leading civilized nations to combine and establish arbitration of all international disputes would be gladly responded to. Whether he is to pass into history as only

[1] *The Roosevelt Policy: Speeches, Letters and State Papers relating to Corporate Wealth and closely Allied Topics.* New York, 1908.

the preserver of internal peace at home or is to rise to his appointed mission as the Apostle of Peace among leading civilized nations, the future has still to reveal.

The year before last (1912) I stood before him in the grand palace in Berlin and presented the American address of congratulation upon his peaceful reign of twenty-five years, his hand unstained by human blood. As I approached to hand to him the casket containing the address, he recognized me with outstretched arms, exclaimed:

"Carnegie, twenty-five years of peace, and we hope for many more."

I could not help responding:

"And in this noblest of all missions you are our chief ally."

He had hitherto sat silent and motionless, taking the successive addresses from one officer and handing them to another to be placed upon the table. The chief subject under discussion had been World Peace, which he could have, and in my opinion, would have secured, had he not been surrounded by the military caste which inevitably gathers about one born to the throne — a caste which usually becomes as permanent as the potentate himself, and which has so far in Germany proved its power of control whenever the war issue has been presented. Until militarism is subordinated, there can be no World Peace.

.   .   .   .

As I read this to-day [1914], what a change! The world convulsed by war as never before! Men slaying each other like wild beasts! I dare not relinquish all hope. In recent days I see another ruler coming forward upon the world stage, who may prove himself the immortal one. The man who vindicated his country's honor in the Panama Canal toll dispute is now President. He has the indomitable will of genius, and true hope which we are told,

"Kings it makes gods, and meaner creatures kings."

Nothing is impossible to genius! Watch President Wilson! He has Scotch blood in his veins.

[Here the manuscript ends abruptly.]

BIBLIOGRAPHY AND INDEX

BIBLIOGRAPHY

MR. CARNEGIE'S chief publications are as follows:
An American Four-in-Hand in Britain. New York, 1884.
Round the World. New York, 1884.
Triumphant Democracy, or Fifty Years' March of the Republic. New York, 1886.
The Gospel of Wealth and Other Timely Essays. New York, 1900.
The Empire of Business. New York, 1903.
James Watt. New York, 1905.
Problems of To-day. Wealth — Labor — Socialism. New York, 1908.

He was a contributor to English and American magazines and newspapers, and many of the articles as well as many of his speeches have been published in pamphlet form. Among the latter are the addresses on Edwin M. Stanton, Ezra Cornell, William Chambers, his pleas for international peace, his numerous dedicatory and founders day addresses. A fuller list of these publications is given in Margaret Barclay Wilson's *A Carnegie Anthology,* privately printed in New York, 1915.

A great many articles have been written about Mr. Carnegie, but the chief sources of information are:
ALDERSON (BERNARD). *Andrew Carnegie. The Man and His Work.* New York, 1905.
BERGLUND (ABRAHAM). *The United States Steel Corporation.* New York, 1907.
CARNEGIE (ANDREW). *How I Served My Apprenticeship as a Business Man.* Reprint from Youth's Companion. April 23, 1896.
COTTER (ARUNDEL). *Authentic History of the United States Steel Corporation.* New York, 1916.
HUBBARD (ELBERT). *Andrew Carnegie.* New York, 1909. (Amusing, but inaccurate.)
MACKIE (J. B.). *Andrew Carnegie. His Dunfermline Ties and Benefactions.* Dunfermline, n. d.
Manual of the Public Benefactions of Andrew Carnegie. Published by the Carnegie Endowment for International Peace. Washington, 1919.

Memorial Addresses on the Life and Work of Andrew Carnegie. New York, 1920.

Memorial Service in Honor of Andrew Carnegie on His Birthday, Tuesday, November 25, 1919. Carnegie Music Hall, Pittsburgh, Pennsylvania.

Pittencrieff Glen: Its Antiquities, History and Legends. Dunfermline, 1903.

POYNTON (JOHN A.). *A Millionaire's Mail Bag.* New York, 1915. (Mr. Poynton was Mr. Carnegie's secretary.)

PRITCHETT (HENRY S.). *Andrew Carnegie.* Anniversary Address before Carnegie Institute, November 24, 1915.

SCHWAB (CHARLES M.). *Andrew Carnegie. His Methods with His Men.* Address at Memorial Service, Carnegie Music Hall, Pittsburgh, November 25, 1919.

WILSON (MARGARET BARCLAY). *A Carnegie Anthology.* Privately printed. New York, 1915.

INDEX

God, each stage of civilization creates its own, 75.

Gorman, Senator Arthur P., and the tariff, 147–148.

Gospel of Wealth, The, published, 255.

Gould, Jay, 152.

Grant, Gen. U.S., and Secretary Stanton, 106; some characteristics of, 107; unjustly suspected, 108.

Greeley, Horace, 68, 81.

Grey, Earl, trustee of Carnegie United Kingdom Trust, 290 and *n*.

Hague Conference, 283–284.

Haldane, Lord Chancellor, error as to British manufactures, 331.

Hale, Eugene, visits Mr. Carnegie, 216.

Hale, Prof. George E., of the Mount Wilson Observatory, 261.

Halkett, Sir Arthur, killed at Braddock's defeat, 187, 188.

Hamilton College, Elihu Root Foundation at, 275.

Hampton Institute, 276.

Hanna, Senator Mark, 233–234, 359; Chair in Western Reserve University named for, 275.

Harcourt, Sir William Vernon, 312.

Harris, Joel Chandler, 295.

Harrison, President Benjamin, opens Carnegie Hall at Allegheny City, 259, 347; his nomination, 344, 345; dispute with Chile, 350–353; the Behring Sea question, 350, 353–355.

Hartman Steel Works, 226.

Hawk, Mr., of the Windsor Hotel, New York, 150.

Hay, Secretary John, comment on Lincoln, 101–102; visits Mr. Carnegie, 216 *n.*; chairman of directors of Carnegie Institution, 260; Library, at Brown University, 275; as Secretary of State, 358; the Hay-Pauncefote Treaty, 359; the Senate his *bête noire*, 360–361.

Hay, John, of Allegheny City, 34–37.

Head-ication versus Hand-ication, 4.

Henderson, Ebenezer, 5.

Henderson, Ella Ferguson, 25, 55.

Hero Fund, 262–266.

Hewitt, Abram S., 260.

Higginson, Maj. F. L., 260.

Higginson, Col. Thomas Wentworth, 150.

Hill, David Jayne, on the German Hero Fund, 263–264.

Hogan, Maria, 70.

Hogan, Uncle, 36, 77.

Holls, G. F. W., and the Hague Conference, 284.

Holmes, Oliver Wendell, and the Matthew Arnold memorial, 307–308.

Homestead Steel Mills, consolidated with Carnegie Brothers & Co., 225, 226; strike at, 228–239; address of workmen to Mr. Carnegie, 257.

Hughes, Courtney, 58.

Huntington, Collis P., 205.

Ignorance, the main root of industrial trouble, 240.

In the Time of Peace, by Richard Watson Gilder, 262–263.

Ingersoll, Col. Robert G., 210, 300.

Integrity, importance of, in business, 172.

Ireland, Mr. Carnegie's freedom tour in, 314 *n.*, 316.

Irish Home Rule, 326–327.

Irwin, Agnes, receives doctor's degree from St. Andrews University, 272–273.

Isle of Wight, 215.

Jackson, Andrew, and Simon Cameron, 104–105.

Jewett, Thomas L., President of the Panhandle Railroad, 117.

Jones, Henry ("Cavendish"), anecdote of, 315.

Jones, Mr. ("The Captain"), 202–204, 241–242, 369; prefers large salary to partnership, 203.

Just by the Way, poem on Mr. Carnegie, 238.

Kaiser Wilhelm, and Mr. Carnegie, 366–371.

Katte, Walter, 123.

Keble, Bishop, godfather of Matthew Arnold, 298.

Kelly, Mr., chairman of blast-furnaces committee, 241–243.

Kennedy, Julian, 220.

Kenyon College, gift to, 106 *n.*; Stanton Chair of Economics, 275.

Keokuk, Iowa, 154.

Keystone Bridge Works, 116, 122–128, 176.

Keystone Iron Works, 130.

Kilgraston, Scotland, 215, 216.

Kind action never lost, 85–86.

King Edward VII, letter from, 264–265, 326.

Kloman, Andrew, partner with Mr. Carnegie, 130, 178, 179; a great mechanic, 131, 134; in bankruptcy, 194–196.

Printed in the USA
CPSIA information can be obtained
at www.ICGtesting.com
LVHW051927021223
764870LV00001B/2